The Congressman Who Got Away with Murder

The Congressman
Who Got Away with Murder

NAT BRANDT

SYRACUSE UNIVERSITY PRESS

First Edition 1991
91 92 93 94 95 96 97 98 99   6 5 4 3 2 1

The paper used in this publication meets the minimum requirements of American National Standard for information Sciences—
Permanence of Paper for Printed Library Materials, ANSI Z39.48-1984. ∞™

Library of Congress Cataloging-in-Publication Data

Brandt, Nat.
    The congressman who got away with murder / by Nat Brandt.—
1st ed.
        p.   cm.
    Includes bibliographical references and index.
    ISBN 0-8156-0251-0
    1. Sickles, Daniel Edgar, 1825-1914.   2. United States. Congress.
House—Biography.   3. Legislators—United States—Biography.
4. Murder—Washington (D.C.)   I. Title.
E664.S597B73   1991
328.73'092—dc20
[B]   90-26831
                                                                      CIP

Manufactured in the United States of America

It was a dirty room in a rundown house in a squalid section of the city. Its windows were closed tight against the February cold and its shutters barred the feeble winter sunlight. A fire burned in the small hearth. Some pieces of wood for it lay nearby. The furnishings were sparse: a simple bureau, a rumpled bedstead, and a basin with a pitcher. Soiled towels were strewn about the room. Through the connecting door, scattered about an adjoining room, were a comb, a pair of gloves, some cigarettes in a package on the mantel, a man's winter shawl. The bed and bedding there were wrinkled, too, as though no one had bothered to make it up for a week or so.

She undressed—taking off her black velvet cloak trimmed with lace, the black velvet shawl trimmed with fringe, the plaid silk dress, her undergarments—and now lay naked in the bed, waiting for him to appear. Her dark hair was undone and draped across the pillow.

He entered the room. What was that remark he had made about what he liked? "French intrigue and romance, with a good spice of danger in it!" He started to take off his clothes. And what was that boast of his? "He only asked thirty-six hours with any woman to make her do what he pleased."

He lay down next to her and they embraced. Then they kissed and "did what is usual for a wicked woman to do."[1]

Again, and as ever, to my wife, Yanna

A journalist by profession, NAT BRANDT has been a newswriter for CBS News, a reporter on a number of newspapers, an editor on *The New York Times*, managing editor of *American Heritage*, and editor-in-chief of *Publishers Weekly*. Since 1980, Mr. Brandt has been a free-lance writer, chiefly in the area of American history. He is the author of *The Man Who Tried to Burn New York*, which won the 1987 Douglas Southall Freeman History Award; *The Town That Started the Civil War*, a Book-of-the-Month Club and History Book Club selection; and with John Sexton, *How Free Are We? What the Constitution Says We Can and Cannot Do*.

Contents

Illustrations

Preface

How do you describe a man who almost singlehandedly made possible the creation of Central Park in New York City, a man who was a congressman and confidant of the nation's fifteenth president, a Civil War hero who lost his leg leading his troops in the crucial phase of the Battle of Gettysburg, who served as American minister to Spain, a man whom House Speaker Champ Clark called "one of the kindest men I ever knew and . . . [who] demonstrates the truth of the poet's dictum 'the bravest are the gentlest'"?[1]

And how do you describe a man who was a lawyer who lived on the cusp of legal scandals, who was a Tammany brawler, a man who was a philanderer censured by his fellow lawmakers for bringing his mistress into the halls of the state legislature, a man who killed a friend and whom a newspaper headlined as a "Rowdy, Confidence-Man . . . Satrap, Politician, &c . . . [and] Scoundrel"?[2]

Both men were one man: Daniel Edgar Sickles.

In many ways, Dan Sickles embodied both the best and worst of the American character of the nineteenth century—public-spirited but opportunistic, bold yet also rash, ambitious and self-serving, too. This is the story of but one episode in his long career, a story that has a fair share of mysteries and represents a landmark case in legal history. It is also a story that tells as much about Sickles as it does about our then swiftly growing nation and the double standard of sexual behavior that existed at the time.

The story begins in the city in which the vices, the virtues, and the violence of American society in the mid-nineteenth century were best mirrored: Washington, the nation's capital.

Acknowledgments

FOR ASSISTANCE in doing research on this book, I wish to thank in particular Margaret N. Burri, Curator of Collections, the Historical Society of Washington, D.C. Also Sarah Shaffer of the Decatur House on Lafayette Square, Washington, and Concepta Sciarra of St. Patrick's Old Cathedral, Mulberry Street, New York. I am grateful for the help provided by the staff of the New-York Historical Society and staff members of the following divisions of the Library of Congress: Manuscript, Geography and Map, Local History and Genealogy, and Rare Book and Special Collections.

I am, as usual, indebted to my dear friend, Prof. Bernard A. Weisberger, for his helpful suggestions and wise counsel. Any errors or misconceptions are, however, mine.

Nat Brandt

New York City
January 1991

The Congressman Who Got Away with Murder

ONE

New Year's Day, 1859

To that gay Capital where congregate
The worst and wisest of this mighty State;
Where patriot politicians yearly wend,
The Nation's fortunes, and their own, to mend;
Where snobbish scribblers eke the scanty dole
By telegraphing lies from pole to pole;
Where bad Hotels impose their onerous tax;
And countless Jehus sport untiring hacks . . .[1]

> (From "A Metrical Glance at the Fancy
> Ball" by Major John De Haviland, com-
> memorating the masquerade ball given by
> Senator and Mrs. William McK. Gwin on
> April 8, 1858)

THE YEAR BEGAN on a glorious note. The pelting rain driven by a northerly wind that soaked Washington the night before was spent and "the pitchy gloom" that accompanied it gave way to clearing skies on the morning of Saturday, January 1.[1] Families in a hundred homes were preparing to "throw open their doors with a wide hospitality"—a custom, said an Ohio-born lawyer who practiced in the capital, "that exists nowhere else."[2] The streets were still muddy and the roads into the capital so impassable that produce merchants had little fresh merchandise to offer. But nearly half the stores and business offices were shuttered anyway, because New Year's Day was fast becoming a general holiday. As usual, all the federal departments were closed, because this day, like the Fourth of July, was a special day, when federal officials, among others, paid congratulatory calls on the President.

I

The euphoric mood was a welcome change after the melancholy that had settled on the White House during the tenancy of the previous president, Franklin Pierce; the death of Pierce's eleven-year-old son in a train accident on the eve of his inauguration had cast a gloom over his entire four years in office. But that pall was now gone. Instead, Washington now reveled in such merriment that people said the city hadn't seen its equal since the presidency of John Quincy Adams thirty years before. Many people, in fact, spoke of the current administration as the "gayest" the nation had yet experienced.[3] The result was a curious paradox that permeated Washington. A bitter controversy over whether to admit a Kansas already torn with bloodshed as a free or a slave state was being fought in Congress at the same time that the most resplendent parties, receptions, and balls were being given in the capital's homes and hotels. "While a life-and-death struggle raged between political parties, and oratorical battles of ominous import were fought daily in Senate Chamber and House," observed Virginia Tunstall Clay, the acknowledged leader of Washington society, "a very reckless gaiety was everywhere apparent in social circles."[4]

The wife of Alabama Senator Clement C. Clay, Jr., Virginia Clay said an evening at home was "a rare luxury."[5] Hostesses, she complained, were so "mad with rivalry and vanity"[6] that a hundred of them "vied with each other in evolving novel social relaxations."[7] The entertainments they arranged, said her friend, Sara Agnes Pryor, included "morning receptions, evening receptions, dinners, musicales, children's parties, old-fashioned evening parties with music and supper, and splendid balls. So many of these were crowded into a season that we often attended three balls in one evening."[8] The money spent on such entertaining was staggering. "It is said," Virginia Clay declared, "that Gwin is spending money at the rate of $75,000 a year, and Brown and Thompson quite the same." Even the wife of Georgia Senator Robert Toombs—"who is sober, and has but one [marriagable] daughter," she noted—"says *they* spend $1,800 a month, or $21,000 per annum."[9]

The festive atmosphere was nowhere more evident than at the Executive Mansion on Pennsylvania Avenue. By eleven o'clock on New Year's Day, lines of carriages and hacks, and thousands of persons on foot, were outside its entrance when the front doors were thrust open. By protocol, members of the cabinet were the first to enter the White House, followed by foreign diplomats, then officers of the Army and Navy. James Buchanan, the nation's fifteenth chief executive, waited to receive them in the Blue Room, while off in another small parlor the Marine Band played such popular tunes as "Hail to the Chief," "Hail, Columbia," "The Star-Spangled Banner" and other airs. The sixty-seven-year-old president was a methodical man, up early, in his office every morning after breakfast, working at his desk well before the day's official agenda started. He liked to take lone walks, and most days after five o'clock in the afternoon he could be seen striding down Pennsylvania Avenue, or in Lafayette Square. He was a commanding figure—tall, white-haired, clean-shaven. He always wore a high-collar white shirt, which hid a neck scar. An eye defect prompted him to lean slightly forward, tilting his head to one side in such a way that any person talking to him thought he was being attentive to what was being said. Most persons found him "excedingly [sic] amiable and courteous," "genial and delightful" with "a keen sense of humor," and "often agreeable and instructive in conversation."[10]

But for all his social graces, Buchanan was a man not suited to the exigencies of the time. "He was not deficient in talent or culture," a White House neighbor said, "but lacked judgment and firmness."[11] Even worse, at a time when the nation needed a strong leader, Buchanan was out of tune with the times. Take the cabinet ministers whose hands he was now shaking as each wished him well. Buchanan had tried to achieve a "sacred balance" between slave and nonslaveholding states in his cabinet appointments, but most of his department heads and advisers were southerners, or prosouthern in their sympathies—men such as Postmaster General Aaron V. Brown of Tennessee, and his secretaries of the treasury, of war, and of the interior—Howell Cobb of Georgia, John B.

Floyd of Virginia and Jacob Thompson of Mississippi. Brown would die before the year was three months old, but the others would all serve the Confederacy—Cobb and Floyd as generals, Thompson as a secret agent of the Richmond government. Even Buchanan's secretary of the navy, Isaac Toucey, a former governor of Connecticut, was a southern sympathizer. He would be accused of dispersing American naval forces to aid the South before war broke out, and his portrait would be forcibly removed from a gallery of ex-governors in the Hartford statehouse. Both of Buchanan's other two cabinet officials—Secretary of State Lewis Cass of Michigan and a fellow Pennsylvanian, Attorney General Jeremiah S. Black—were strong advocates of compromise with secessionists. Buchanan himself personally preferred southerners as friends, counted Jefferson Davis of Mississippi among the best of them and believed the current political hostilities dividing the nation were the fault of abolitionists. "I am disappointed," wrote Benjamin Brown French, one-time Clerk of the House of Representatives who chronicled Washington during the more than forty years between the presidencies of Andrew Jackson and Ulysses S. Grant. Buchanan's "course in regard to Kansas has been vacillating and weak, & unbecoming a President of the U.S.," French declared. "Even some of his warmest friends and supporters have deserted him."[12] French, who was originally from New Hampshire, would come to believe that Buchanan's name "*must* go down to posterity associated with shame, infamy, & I fear with *Treason!*"[13]

The Washington these men worked in mirrored the nation's split personality. Novelist Mary Clemmer Ames, who lived in the city for a decade, likened Washington to "a third-rate Southern city,"[14] a perhaps overcritical comparison, though there was no doubt that the capital was indeed southern in its outlook, customs and manners, and its society was dominated by southern women—the "belles" of fact and fiction. For one thing, before the trafficking in slaves in the District of Columbia was prohibited as part of the hodgepodge Compromise of 1850, the District—which was tucked between two slave states, Virginia and Maryland—was the center of the domestic slave traffic in the United States. There were at least four slave pens in the city proper. One of them, a series of six thirty-foot-long arched cells with heavy iron doors and iron rings embedded on the walls, was in the basement of the St. Charles Hotel, on the northeast corner of Third Street and Pennsylvania Avenue; recessed grilles in the sidewalks of both the street and the avenue provided the cells with light and ventilation. Another pen had been built in the rear of the Decatur House on Lafayette Square by tavern keeper John Gadsby when he owned the home.

Even though trafficking in slaves was banned in 1850, owning slaves was perfectly legal. There were nearly one thousand slaveholders in the District in the 1850s; they were entitled to buy from, and to sell to, other local residents. It was not uncommon to see an advertisement in a Washington newspaper for such sales with the proviso added: "Not to be removed beyond the limits of the District of Columbia."[15] Manumission was rare, rarer even than in Maryland or Delaware.[16] Nevertheless, the number of slaves in Washington steadily declined after 1850. Still, of the nearly eleven thousand blacks who lived in Washington in the late 1850s, more than seventeen hundred were slaves. In all, blacks—free and enslaved—made up almost eighteen percent of the total population.[17] The more than nine thousand free blacks were relegated almost without exception to the most menial of jobs or worked as domestic servants—if men, as laborers, porters, barbers, well-diggers, carriage drivers, plasterers and whitewashers, waiters, and cooks; if women, as washerwomen, nurses, seamstresses, and maids. As was common even in northern communities, city directories carried the abbreviation "(col.)" after the name of the few free blacks that were listed.[18] And, although there was no such thing as segregated housing, free blacks generally lived in the most derelict of neighborhoods, which, in the Washington of the 1850s, could be but a block or two away from the most respectable of residences. One block—between Ninth and Tenth streets west and N and O streets north—was called Nigger Hill.[19] The National Theater on E Street admitted blacks, but they could only sit in the upper gallery. The city had a severe black code, first adopted in 1836, that compelled every free black who wanted to settle in it to post a bond and be sponsored by a white person. Moreover, neither free nor enslaved black could testify in court against a white person. Similar restrictions were not unknown in many northern states, but blacks in Washington were also forbidden to hold public gatherings unless they had the mayor's permission, secret meetings were banned altogether, and there was a 10:00 P.M. curfew for all blacks. Police brutality was common, and considering their proportion to the total population, blacks were arrested three times as frequently as whites were.[20]

It was just as well that members of Congress did not ordinarily attend these traditional New Year's Day receptions. The first session of the Thirty-fifth Congress the previous year had been an acrimonious one, torn by the controversy over Kansas. Buchanan's own Democratic Party had split over the issue, and the verbal clashes had led, portentiously, to a physical brawl on the House floor. Buchanan was so determined to keep the Union together that he often vacillated when he should have been assertive. As one local reporter put it, "With secession in sight, his one aim was to get out of the White House before the scrap began."[21]

That same reporter likened Buchanan to "an aristocrat," and found that he was not only susceptible to southern influence, but to "feminine influence" as well.[22] This was true although the president had experienced a painful crisis as a young man when his fiancée threw him over and then tragically died. A lifelong bachelor, he was the only president to remain single while occupying the White House. Yet, there was no doubt that he had an eye for the ladies—and that women enjoyed an unusual advantage with him. "After all," *The New-York Times* correspondent in Washington remarked, "it is but natural that where institutions do not favor the entrance of the best men into public life, the woman element, so brilliant everywhere, should utterly out-dazzle the other sex, and even the most unseemly woman appear an angel by the side of a tobacco-chewing deputy."[23] One of the most influential women in Buchanan's life was standing near him on the reception line. Harriet Lane, official hostess for her uncle, was a popular, cheerful, and tactful young lady. Other women eyed her carefully; the previous year, she had set a fashion trend by wearing "the most bewitching of bonnets" at the president's first New Year's Day reception.[24] It was "Miss Harriet," everyone agreed, who had revived the social magnificence that the White House now bathed in.

As the cabinet members filed past the president, they headed into the East Room, all but Secretary of State Cass. He stayed behind to introduce the next group of guests, members of the diplomatic corps assigned to the United States, resplendent in their court dress. The ministers included envoys from France, Russia, the Netherlands, Belgium, Austria, Brazil, and, everyone's favorite, the envoy extraordinary and minister plenipotentiary from England, the genial Lord Napier. Cass's role was perfunctory; Buchanan knew them all. The president, who had once served as American minister to Russia and later to the Court of St. James's, prided himself on his foreign policy. Indeed, above all else, he wanted to be remembered as an empire builder, and for years had made a special effort to wrest Cuba from Spain's domination either by purchasing the island or by annexing it outright. But he was frustrated by northern congressmen who viewed his Cuban policy as well as his efforts to establish a protectorate over northern Mexico as just schemes to permit the expansion of slavery.

Next in the reception line came members of the Supreme Court led by gaunt, eighty-one-year-old Roger Brooke Taney. Despite almost constant poor health, he had now served on the Court for more than twenty-two years. Of late, Taney, a Marylander, had become the target of savage criticism for his majority opinion in the Dred Scott case, which left blacks with no rights whatsoever under the Constitution. Northerners charged that five of the Court's justices, Taney included, were slaveholders themselves.[25]

Following behind the justices were high-ranking officers of the American Army and Navy. Many of them would face the dilemma of whether to be loyal to the United States or to their home state, but that decision was two years into the future; for today, they all proudly wore their full-dress uniforms. They greeted the president with smart salutes, bowed courteously to his niece, and strode into the East Room, which was now quite crowded with promenaders. Cabinet ministers, diplomats, justices, generals and admirals, colonels and commodores, their wives, and sometimes children, provided a colorful scene, chatting and laughing as the Marine Band continued to play, off in the distance. Those who wished to leave—to attend to other New Year's Day social calls—exited through one of the large windows on the north side of the room. A wooden ramp was set up so that visitors could step over the sill.

At precisely noon, Colonel William Selden, marshal of the District of Columbia, signaled his police contingent to let the general public enter the building. For the next two hours, thousands of ordinary citizens—minor federal officials and employees, local residents, lobbyists, strangers—had the opportunity to shake hands with the president, perhaps say a few words or plead a special cause, and pass on. "Every citizen of the United States who visits Washington," a recent visitor wrote, "considers that he has a claim to visit the Chief Magistrate of the Union; and he is accordingly presented to him, and, after *shaking hands* and conversing for a moment, retires, delighted with the suavity of the President, and elevated in his own estimation. It is easier to gain an interview with the President of the United States than with the most insignificant, petty noble in a monarchy."[26] The number of visitors to the nation's capital, especially the "great influx of bridal pairs," always surprised Mary Clemmer Ames: "Whence they all come no mortal can tell; but they do come, and can never be mistaken."[27] They came from virtually every one of what were now the nation's thirty-two states and seven territories, for the United States of 1859 was bursting with energy, growth, and opportunity. The country was in the midst of both the Industrial Revolution and expansion westward. Factories and farms were being tied together by an increasing network of railroads. Amazingly, the center of the nation's population was already poised to leap across the Ohio River from western Virginia into southern Ohio.[28]

Selden kept close tabs on the visitors. Unpleasant incidents were not uncommon. The unruliness of the crowd the previous year, when many women had been "jostled and discommoded,"[29] had prompted the marshal to reinforce the police detachment, and he had his men form a gauntlet from the front door to where the president stood and posted other officers throughout the premises and grounds. But even more serious than unruliness was the fact that there was no law against carrying firearms. In fact, guns were accepted as a way of life, vital for the hunting of game or protection from Indians if you lived on the frontier, and just as important as a security measure against thieves if you were a city dweller. There were no restrictions on the purchase of weapons. Many persons like Selden could remember when, twenty-four years earlier, a deranged housepainter fired two pistols point-blank at President Andrew Jackson as he left the Capitol Building after attending a congressman's funeral. Jackson, no stranger to brawls and the participant in several duels, escaped unharmed when both pistols misfired. And only two years earlier, in 1857, at the final levee in the White House itself given by Franklin Pierce, a city councilman seized a merchant from Alexandria, Virginia, by the collar and accused him of picking his pocket. The next morning, the merchant sought out the councilman to explain that he was mistaken, but the councilman was adamant and, in the argument that ensued, the merchant struck the councilman with a stick and was in return shot dead by the councilman, who then fled to Virginia "to avoid unpleasant consequences."[30]

The unseemly behavior experienced at the New Year's Day reception the previous year and the presence of so many policemen now apparently discouraged many people from attending this year's reception; still, the Washington *Evening Star* estimated that "five or six thousand persons, of both sexes and all ages . . . paid their respects to the occupant of the Executive Mansion."[31]

At two o'clock, the last of the guests were ushered from the East Room, the gates of the White House were closed, and the reception was officially over—to the relief, one can imagine, of the president, whose hand must have been sore if not swollen. One nineteenth-century observer was sure that such "species of torture" had hastened William Henry Harrison's death after only one month in office.[32] Leaving the grounds, the throng broke into myriad groups, to call upon friends or to drop by the open houses. It was also customary to exchange gifts, or to reward a subordinate with a present on New Year's Day.

One gift-giver was Washington's district attorney, Philip Barton Key. He stopped by City Hall to give a court clerk a gold pen. It would figure in the most sensational murder case in the city's history, a case that involved not only Key, but also one of the president's closest friends and advisers, Congressman Daniel Edgar Sickles, and Sickles's wife, Teresa.

TWO

Barton, Dan, and Teresa

But mark attentively yon gathering crowd!
There cluster those of whom the country's proud;
Historic names and words of present power,
Who rule the fortunes of the passing hour . . .

THE FRIENDSHIP between Philip Barton Key and Daniel Edgar Sickles—between Barton and Dan, as their friends called them—was cemented at an all-male whist party in early March of 1857, shortly after Buchanan's inauguration. Their host was Jonah D. Hoover, then marshal of the District of Columbia, who lived on G Street east of the White House.[1] Sickles was the new representative from New York's Third Congressional District. He and his young wife Teresa were guests in Hoover's home, staying there during the round of festivities connected with Buchanan's inauguration. Sickles would make Hoover's home his own until he found quarters for his family in the fall.[2] The first session of the Thirty-fifth Congress to which Sickles had been elected would not open for another nine months. Hoover had met Sickles four years earlier, when Sickles visited Washington for the inauguration of Franklin Pierce. Hoover knew Key even longer, at least ten years, worked closely with him at the district court and considered Key his "most intimate and cherished friend."[3]

A friend of Sickles's, Representative John B. Haskin of Westchester County, was also at the card party. He remembered that it was Sickles who brought up the question of Key's future. Key was an appointee of Pierce. What did he expect would happen under Buchanan? Although a Democrat, Key was uncertain whether the new president would rename him as district attorney for the District of Columbia. Sickles, who knew the new president well, was supportive and reassuring. He said he would urge that Key be kept in office, that "he believed the President would reappoint him." Key said he hoped Sickles would "persist in urging his claims" and thanked him for his "intercession."[4]

In some ways, the two men were alike—both debonair, ingratiating, wise to the way of politics, egocentric and rebellious, arrogant and quick to take affront, yet sociable. Both were dissemblers—Barton, for one thing, about his health, Dan about politics and religion. And both were womanizers. They even looked a little bit alike, though that was probably because they both sported moustaches, a fad that spread through Washington in the mid-1850s.[5] There were, however, many differences between the two men, especially when it came to the question of their family backgrounds. Few names in Maryland—or, for that matter, in Washington and the rest of the nation—were more illustrious than Key's. The first Key—Barton's great, great grandfather Philip Key—emigrated to Maryland in 1720 from England, where he had been a sheriff, delegate, and councilor. His second wife, Theodosia Barton, was so kind to her stepchildren that her maiden name was passed along by them to their descendants. Two Key brothers fought during the American Revolution, but on opposite sides. One, Barton's grandfather, John Ross Key, served with a rifle battalion of Maryland troops. The other, Barton's namesake, great-uncle Philip Barton Key, joined British forces in Philadelphia and became a captain in a regiment of Maryland Loyalists. After the war, he went to England, became a lawyer, then returned to Maryland in 1785 and started a law practice. In 1794, Philip Barton Key was elected to the Maryland House of Delegates, became a Federalist, was appointed a federal circuit court judge, and, in 1806, after resigning his British half-pay and despite criticism for having served in the British army, was nevertheless elected to the first of three terms in Congress.

Though Philip Barton brought renown to the family, the surname became a household name because of Barton's father, Francis Scott Key. He was born on Pipe Creek in the Valley of the Monocacy in what was then part of Frederick County, Maryland.[6] He studied law at St. John's College in Annapolis, where he met a fellow student who was to marry his sister Anne, Roger Brooke Taney. Francis Scott's own marriage to Mary Tayloe Lloyd produced eleven children, all born in a house on Bridge Street in Georgetown, to which Francis Scott had moved in order to go into law practice with his Uncle Philip, who lived on an estate, Woodley, bordering Rock Creek. There was a poetic streak in Francis Scott—an impulse to translate his feelings into words that one genealogist traced back to 1641 and England's first poet laureate, John Key, and that would, in the twentieth century, lead to a distant descendant, Francis Scott Key Fitzgerald (F. Scott Fitzgerald).[7] As a hobby, Francis Scott wrote verses and composed hymns and religious verses.[8] Asked to arrange the release of a prominent Maryland physician seized by the British during the War of 1812, Key was aboard an American vessel, in sight of Baltimore, when the British bombarded Fort McHenry during the night of September 13–14, 1814. Intensely excited on seeing the American flag still flying above the fort at sunrise, he hastened to express his emotions in a poem, "The Star-Spangled Banner." The verse, widely circulated and sung to the English tune "To Anacreon in Heaven," quickly became one of the most popular of songs in young America.

Each time a child was born to Francis Scott and Mary Key the father had a small circular bed of plants that spelled the name of the baby laid out in their garden. On April 5, 1818, a new planting was prepared for the birth of their eighth child, the fifth of their sons. He was named for Uncle Philip, but was called by his middle name, Barton. While Barton was still a teenager, Francis Scott decided that the recently completed Chesapeake and Ohio Canal nearby created too much noise and boisterousness to raise a family in Georgetown, and he moved his family into Washington. Their new home, on C Street between 3d and 4 1/2 streets, was near Judiciary Square, a block from City Hall, in a neighborhood known as Senatorial Row because of all the senators that resided on the street.

Barton grew up to be, like his father, tall, good-looking, a lover of horseflesh and a lawyer. Francis Scott Key had served as district attorney of the District of Columbia from 1833 to 1841—had, indeed, been the prosecutor at the trial of the mad housepainter who had tried to assassinate Andrew Jackson (and who was still, in 1859, committed in the Government Hospital for the Insane). Barton was appointed to the same post in 1853. But there the resemblances in appearance, character, and career ended. Francis Scott was a well-read, religious man who had once considered entering the Episcopal clergy. He had freed his slaves and was one of the founders of the American Colonization Society.[9] Son Barton evinced no religious inclinations whatsoever, was a friend to some of Washington's most avid secessionists, and, instead of being one of the pillars of the community, was known as a popular society figure about whom a constant whirl of gossip flowed. He was, for one thing, known as a "lady's man."[10] It was said that he narrowly escaped having to duel an army colonel who believed that Barton had robbed him of the affections of the woman who became Barton's wife, Ellen Swan of Baltimore.[11] The couple were married in 1845, two years after Francis Scott's death,[12] and had four children—three daughters and a son—before Ellen herself died in the mid-1850s.[13]

His wife's death shattered Barton, at least that is what many people believed. Most people were aware that he worried about his health, took a trip to Cuba to try to recover, but still suffered from bouts of weakness. His appearance took on "a sickly hue," one newspaper account reported, "and he had been for some time suffering from heart-disease, or imagined he was, which gave him a soured and discontented look."[14] Another newspaper said "his nerves were shattered" not only by the loss of his wife but also "doubtless almost together by his dissipated habits," though he had given up drinking.[15] His friends insisted he was not a "libertine,"[16] but those who knew him acknowledged that "he had become peevish, discontented, and fretful."[17] Still, it is doubtful that his behavior was due to ill health—unless it was psychosomatic—because despite what he claimed, his heart was healthy, and his social life, far from being impeded, flourished.[18] Ill health, however, made for a ready excuse to be away from his office. Barton had "never studied very hard," relying instead on his "natural talents" as an attorney.[19] His library contained more than five hundred books, at least half of which were law books, but, judging by the publication dates, most of the works seemed to have been inherited from his father.[20] Barton's attentiveness to his duties was, in fact, being increasingly questioned, especially after he failed to prosecute successfully Representative Philemon T. Herbert of California, who was indicted for murder in 1856. Herbert, who had been drinking at Willard's Hotel, got into a furious argument with a waiter named Keating, pulled out a pistol and shot Keating dead in front of a number of witnesses. The congressman was acquitted, chiefly, many people thought, because Barton had not pressed the case well enough.

Instead of avidly pursuing his position as district attorney, after his wife's death Barton returned to "his ancient prestige" as a lady's man, and his time seems to have been spent more on matters social rather than official.[21] Washington hostess Virginia Clay said that he not only ranked among the foremost of the popular men of the capital, but that he was also "the handsomest man in all Washington society. In appearance an Apollo, he was a prominent figure at all the principal fashionable functions; a graceful dancer, he was a favourite with every hostess of the day. Clever at repartee, a generous and pleasing man."[22] Barton's "tall figure, his white riding-cap, well trimmed moustache, and iron-grey horse" became a familiar sight along Washington streets,[23] and he earned a reputation for being "what some may call a 'first-rate fellow;' [sic] ready at a joke or a frolic," a wonderful story-teller. Barton was "lavish" with money[24] and, despite the fact that he was a widower with four growing children, paid no attention to

The womanizer: Washington's most sought-after man–about–town, widower Philip Barton Key. *Courtesy New-York Historical Society.*

amassing any property to leave to them.[25] He held the rank of captain as leader of Washington's militia unit, the Montgomery Guards, and, mounted on his favorite horse Lucifer, liked to lead the troops in his green and gold uniform.[26] When not in uniform on parade, however, "he affected eccentricity in manner and costume; was uncouth in speech and rough in address purposely. He would come to dinner with a riding whip under his arm, and was sometimes seen in the street wearing top-boots and leather leggings." In other words, Barton was "a young man of fashion, who dared to be unconventional."[27]

He gained a particular notoriety for being "most assiduous in his attentions to such ladies as pleased him,"[28] and "no man in Washington was more popular with the ladies, or more redoubted as a rival."[29] He was "well known as a man of gallantry, and took but little pains to disguise the fact"[30]—"tall, slender, with rather a sad yet handsome face, he was just the man to win a woman's heart," said one social commentator.[31]

Thanks to Dan Sickles's "intercession," Key was reappointed district attorney. In the months ahead, Sickles also recommended him to a friend from Albany who needed legal services handled in Washington, and Sickles himself asked Key to handle some minor difficulty he had with the lease on a house he rented for his family that fall. They soon shared the same social connections and considered each other "mutual friends,"[32] though they made an odd pair. For all their similarities in temperament, their backgrounds could not have been more dissimilar. Where Barton had been nurtured in a stable, community-conscious family, Dan was the product of a bizarre childhood and young manhood with a wide diversity of experience. Moreover, for all his life, Dan enjoyed a good fortune that shielded him from the most frightful consequences of his behavior.

Dan could trace his ancestry to Zachariah Sickles of Vienna, who worked for the Dutch West India Company and settled in the New Amsterdam area in 1656. Dan was born in New York on October 20, 1819, the only child of Susan Marsh and George Garrett Sickles.[33] His father was a real-estate speculator who made and lost fortunes as regularly as economic booms and busts occurred. When Dan was a young boy the Sickles were able to afford to send him to a private school in Glens Falls, New York. But one thing Dan did not tolerate was corporal punishment, so when the preceptor whipped him severely for some infraction, the boy bolted the school. He found work in the office of the local newspaper, learning the printing trade over the year and a half he was there. His parents eventually visited him, bringing with them Lorenzo L. Da Ponte, a professor of belles lettres from the recently founded

University of the City of New York (later renamed New York University). A warmhearted man in his mid-thirties, Da Ponte apparently helped to persuade Dan to return to New York to help out his father, who had suffered one of his reversals of fortune. By the mid-1830s, however, George Sickles was flush once again; he owned so much property that he opened an office on Wall Street and purchased a farm in New Jersey, where Dan was sent in the hope of interesting him in agriculture. After a year on the farm, Dan "begged, coaxed, and demanded" to return to New York to continue his education, and when the father refused to let him do so, he simply bolted again, tying up "a change of linen in a handkerchief, and, on a calm morning before daybreak," walked away "with a few shillings in his pocket." He started out for Philadelphia, but on reaching Princeton, he got work in the local newspaper office, resuming the printer's trade, and tried to enroll in Princeton College. Unable to pay the tuition, he again took to the road, this time reaching Philadelphia and going to work for a magazine. A family friend recognized him, and soon Dan received a note that urged him to return home "for his mother's sake." All would be forgiven, and he would get the education he wanted.[34]

Dan agreed to return if one condition—a fateful one in his life as it turned out to be—was met: that he be allowed to study and live with Da Ponte to prepare for college. His parents acceded. So Dan joined what was one of the most exotic domiciles imaginable. The household was headed by Da Ponte's father, eighty-nine-year-old Lorenzo Da Ponte, librettist for three of Mozart's great operas—Le Nozze di Figaro, Cosi Fan Tutti, and Don Giovanni. The elder Da Ponte was a Venetian-born Jew whose incredible life and career began with his converting to Catholicism, becoming a priest, and then being banned from Venice for committing adultery. A volatile character as well as a rake, Da Ponte had antagonized theatrical circles in Europe and London. He arrived in America in 1805 with his mistress and their children, tried his hand at running a grocery shop, then became a teacher of Italian language and literature. The Da Ponte residence at 91 Spring

Street was a strange mixture of bohemian types, all of whom seemed to speak a different language—Italian, of course, but also Spanish and French—all of which were often spoken at once, and loudly. For some unexplained reason, the elder Da Ponte in 1833 adopted Maria Cooke, a fourteen-year-old girl from Croton Falls in Westchester who had an obscure background. She shortly thereafter married one of his visitors from Europe, Antonio Bagioli. A native of Bologna, Bagioli had been *gran maestro* of the Montressor Opera Company, the first Italian opera troupe to appear in America when it came to New York in 1832. The *maestro* chose to remain in New York when the opera company continued on to Havana. He became a well-known singing teacher and before long was being hailed as being "largely instrumental in making Italian music popular" in America. Da Ponte's "Hymn to America," first performed in 1833 and with which he opened concerts and closed seasons, was set to music by Bagioli.[35] The Bagiolis had only one child—a daughter, Teresa, sometimes called Terese, born about 1836. The three of them continued to live at 91 Spring Street even after the death in 1838 of the elder Da Ponte, who, like Mozart, was buried in an unmarked grave, in a Catholic cemetery on Second Avenue near Eleventh Street.[36]

Approaching his twentieth birthday, Dan had finally found a home and relationships that his parents could not provide. He became close to the Bagiolis, played with their infant daughter, and was particularly attached to his mentor, Lorenzo L. The younger Da Ponte had been a lawyer, but followed his father in becoming a teacher of classics. He wrote a history of Florence under the Medicis and, although most people credited his father, was the translator of American editions of his father's librettos. Lorenzo L., "a slow-moving, absent-minded fellow," was "greatly beloved for his droll ways and words."[37] A devoted student, Dan became Lorenzo L.'s protégé and, after he helped him out with tests during a faculty dispute, was allowed to take some courses at the university without paying any tuition.

Dan was so attached to him that when Lorenzo L., who

suffered from intestinal tuberculosis, caught pneumonia and died in 1840, he broke down uncontrollably at his funeral, a scene that became indelibly etched in the memory of a fellow student, C. H. A. Bulkley. As Da Ponte's body was being lowered into the ground, a "spasm of grief" overcame Dan. Bulkley rushed to his side with several other mourners. Dan was frantic. "He raved, and tore up and down the graveyard shrieking and I might even say yelling," Bulkley recalled, "so much so that it was impossible for us who were his friends to mollify him in any measure by words." Dan's histrionics were "so excessive" that he was "aggravating the grief of the mourners" and Bulkley feared he might do "some further violence to himself, and that his mind would entirely give way." Bulkley and the others took hold of Dan "and by friendly force" were able to restrain him and lead him from the cemetery. Bulkley, who later became a minister and officiated at many funeral services, said the outburst, which lasted almost ten minutes, was "the most remarkable one I ever saw." Bulkley was similarly amazed when he met Dan a few days later. Dan was "rather lighter-headed, and apparently too much so under the circumstances." He displayed a "light-heartedness" that Bulkley found "unnatural in contrast with the grief he had exhibited two days before." Dan, he realized, "was subject to very sudden emotions."[38] Dan's contrasting behavior at the cemetery and two days afterwards would be chillingly repeated nearly twenty years later.

Dan dropped out of school after Lorenzo L.'s death. Instead, he decided to become a lawyer, and since at the time it was not necessary to attend a school to do so, he entered the offices of Benjamin F. Butler to study law. At one time, Butler, a leading Democrat, had been a law partner of Martin Van Buren, had served as attorney general in Andrew Jackson's administration and also briefly as secretary of war. Butler's connections—it was said that he could have had any post he wanted to when Van Buren became president—added a dimension to Dan's education that opened yet another avenue for him to pursue: politics.

After a brief period of study, and even before he was admitted to the bar, Dan in late 1841 opened his own law offices on Nassau Street.[39] In unusual fashion, in September of the following year, his father began the study of law with him.[40] Dan's office was in the Kent Building, 79 Nassau Street, which the elder Sickles later owned.[41] Dan finally passed his bar examination in 1843. George Sickles spent two years studying with his son, and a further year with a law firm before being admitted to the bar in 1845. Although father studied with son, they lived apart. In late 1843, Dan was boarding at a home on lower Broadway overlooking Bowling Green on the tip of Manhattan, while George was on Cliff Street, east of City Hall Park. The next year, Dan took rooms farther up Broadway, only about a block and a half from 422 Broome Street, to which the Bagiolis had moved after Lorenzo L. Da Ponte's death.

By this time, Dan had already developed a reputation for sharp practices. As early as 1837, he and another man were indicted for obtaining money under false pretenses. A few years later, the Court of General Sessions ordered him to show cause why he should not be prosecuted for appropriating funds that belonged to a man named Moore. He also was accused of pocketing and then spending "at a fashionable watering place" some $1,000 raised to issue a political pamphlet.[42] He avoided prosecution each time, but was fast gaining a notoriety that would one day prompt New York diarist George Templeton Strong to comment: "One might as well try to spoil a rotten egg as to damage Dan's character."[43]

He was also getting heavily involved in politics. He was, he bragged, "a tough Democrat; a fighting one; a Tammany Hall Democrat."[44] Immersing himself in the internecine battles for power within Tammany, Dan was, successively, a member of a faction known as the Hunkers (as opposed to the Barnburners); the Hard Shells, which were an offshoot of the Hunkers, and the Half Shells (as opposed to the Soft Shells). Stephen Fiske, who got to know Dan during a local election campaign, said that he was "guilty of Talleyrand's unpardon-

The cuckold: The always-dapper congressman and Tammany Hall politician, Daniel Edgar Sickles. *Courtesy New-York Historical Society.*

able fault—too much zeal."[45] Dan was linked to stories about both tampering with and stealing ballot boxes, brawls—he was bodily thrown down a stairway at a rally—and deceptive political manipulations. "He worked hard for the Democratic party and for himself," said Fiske. "He made money and friends."[46]

The friends Dan made ran the gauntlet between rich and ruffian, reliable and rambunctious, rebel and raconteur. They were men like August Belmont, agent for the Rothschilds in

America and on his way to becoming one of the city's leading financiers; Isaiah Rynders, commander of the dreaded Dead Rabbits gang who controlled the Irish immigrant vote in the notorious Five Points section near City Hall; Emanuel B. Hart, a surveyor and party stalwart who became especially attached to Dan; John L. Graham, a "hard-drinking lawyer" who horsewhipped newspaper editor James Gordon Bennett in broad daylight on Broadway, oblivious to the screams of Bennett's wife[47]; Thomas F. Meagher, a tempestuous Irish revolutionary who had escaped imprisonment in a British penal colony and worked both as a lawyer and as the editor of the *Irish News*; and Henry Wikoff, the "Chevalier," a worldly, refined busybody who spent his time traveling between America and Europe, where he was welcome in "the most exclusive and interesting circles."[48] Interestingly, at a time when discrimination was rampant, Dan's choice of friends not only crossed social lines, but religious ones, too. A High Episcopal—his mother was a parishioner of Trinity Church—he counted Jews and Catholics as well as Protestants among his friends. A favorite hangout for them was the lobby restaurant of the grande dame of all New York hotels, the Astor House, on Broadway across from City Hall Park, where, as one political observer noted, "the leading characters of the period" congregated to discuss "politics and poetry, science and art, steam-ships and railroads, candidates and creeds."[49]

New York City at that time was basking in its new-found importance. The opening of the Erie Canal in 1825, which linked the ever-expanding West with seaboard New York, and the numerous rail connections that followed a generation later, sealed New York's future as the nation's preeminent city, the focus of the transshipment of goods south, west and abroad, and the financial center of the country. Between 1830 and 1840, its population doubled, and in the two decades after that its total population leaped from nearly 313,000 inhabitants to more than 813,000.[50] The city was "a great emporium of commerce," wrote English novelist Charles Dickens, who visited in 1842. "By the water side, where the bowsprits of ships stretch across the footway, and almost thrust themselves into the windows, lie the noble American vessels which have made their Packet Service the finest in the world."[51] By the time of the Civil War, American clipper ships, which "became supreme in the trade with China, in the California Gold Rush and on the Atlantic," would carry one-third of the world's total tonnage,[52] the greater part of which flowed through New York. "What Venice was once on the sluggish lagoons of the small Adriatic," predicted August Belmont, "New-York would ere long become to the two hemispheres, proudly resting on the bosom of the broad Atlantic."[53]

Because of its connections with British mercantile interests, New York became the center of the cotton trade, providing capital and loans for southern planters and, in turn, offering British manufacturers access to markets for the goods they made from the cotton. Its financial ties prompted one New York newspaper to proclaim that the city "belongs as much to the South as to the North."[54] A New Orleans editor declared that New York was "almost as dependent upon Southern slavery as Charleston itself" and that without slavery "ships would rot at her docks; grass would grow in Wall Street and Broadway, and the glory of New York, like that of Babylon and Rome, would be numbered with the things of the past."[55] Such connections with cotton planters gave the city a pro-southern outlook, and later New Yorkers would play with the idea of seceding from the Union and becoming an independent, free-trade city. Twice—just before and during the Civil War—New York's voters would reject Abraham Lincoln by two-to-one vote margins.

The vessels that hugged Manhattan's shores also carried the human cargo that was dramatically altering the city's personality. The ships, Dickens observed, "have brought hither the foreigners who abound in all the streets . . . they pervade the town."[56] Nine out of ten immigrants to America from Europe came through the Port of New York,[57] a fact that gave New York a special flavor and colored its politics. Most of them were either Irish or German, and they competed for work along the docks, in the factories, and in the shops. Politicians fed on these newcomers. The old-time mercantile families that had ruled the city's political and social life were swiftly being brushed aside by young men with an eye for power, many of whom, like Belmont, who was born in the Rhineland, were not native New Yorkers but were lured to the city by its potential for making money. Almost all of them were members of one faction or another within the Democratic Party. With both the city and nation expanding rapidly, men involved in shipping, railroads, and banking found that connections at City Hall and within the party gave them a leading edge in situations where land values would be affected, or when contracts were awarded, or in otherwise doing business with the municipal, state, or federal government. A special political plum was the Custom House. It controlled every vessel that reached the city, from the time the ship entered port to the time she left. Permits were required before a ship could unload her cargo, and customs officers could stymy the process by hauling away part of the cargo to test the ship's invoice. Expediters learned to avoid costly delays by bribing officials. The Collectorship of the port, a federal post, became the most sought-after patronage position in the nation.

Dan, Stephen Fiske said, "pushed his own fortunes by generously helping those of other people."[58] His political career began in earnest in 1844 when he wrote a campaign paper urging the election of James G. Polk as president. At the time, and until his own election to the New York Assembly in 1847, he "drunk to the dregs the cup of dissipation," as one magazine put it. "In plain language, he led the life of a very fast young man."[59] He was still having legal troubles, too. A man named Kemble said he lent Dan $800, receiving a mortgage from him as security. But Dan, he contended, asked for the mortgage back in order to record it, and then refused altogether to return either the money or the document. Dan won a directed verdict of acquittal because the mortgage was not properly made out.[60] He was still the rebel, too. For some years, Dan lived with, or spent a good deal of his free time with, a woman named Fanny White who ran a bordello on Mercer Street. After his election to the State Assembly, he brought her to Albany and audaciously escorted her on a tour of the Assembly chamber—to the chagrin and outrage of his fellow legislators, who promptly censured him.

On September 27, 1852, Dan shocked his parents, his friends and the Bagiolis by marrying the Bagiolis's daughter, Teresa. He was about a month shy of his thirty-third birthday, twice as old as Teresa, who was sixteen. They were married by Mayor Ambrose C. Kingsland in a private civil ceremony, but, as a newspaper shockingly reported—at a time when sex and pregnancy were taboo subjects of conversation—"The consequences of this secret wedding soon made concealment impossible."[61] Teresa was pregnant, but when had she conceived? The birth date of their daughter, Laura, is unknown. Laura would be described in February, 1859, as being six years old, which means that Teresa may well have conceived in the summer of 1852, before the civil ceremony. Did Dan marry her because he felt it his duty to do so? What is known for a fact is that both sets of parents objected to the marriage. Teresa, they believed, was too young to marry, and Dan was too old for her. After all, he had bounced her on his knees when she was a youngster, and not that long ago. She was still a student at a Catholic boarding school operated by the Society of the Sacred Heart in upper Manhattan.[62]

What had attracted Dan to Teresa? How had the intimacies of friendship they already shared turned carnal? Was she, as the researcher of one biographer reported, simply a "beautiful, voluptuous siren, without brains or shame" whose "damning effect was a lust for men"?[63] Or was it her beauty? Her innocence? She was "remarkable," one description of her said, "for something especially soft, lovely, and youthful in the type of her peculiar beauty. She is of Italian origin, and possesses all the Italian lustre and depth of eye, united with a singular candor and delicacy of feature."[64] Her Mediterranean ancestry prompted another writer to compare her to the Italian coloratura Maria Piccolomini, a pretty, coquettish soprano who

Seductress or naif? Teresa Bagioli Sickles, who married Dan when she was sixteen years old and pregnant. He was twice her age. *Courtesy New-York Historical Society.*

came to America on tour in the late 1850s; except for their size—Teresa was not as petite as Piccolomini—the two young women resembled one another "so closely that one might easily mistake them for each other."[65] Even later, as the mother of a six-year-old child in 1859, Teresa would be portrayed in a magazine as being "in her manner more like a school girl than a polished woman of the world, joyous in her disposition, with a fearlessness of character that seemed almost unfeminine, and with a hoydenish love of sport that made her ready at all

times for any kind of amusement."[66] Another observed that
there was "something inexpressably fascinating and delightful
about her fresh girlish face, and her sweet, amicable manner."[67]

The families were reconciled to the marriage after a second
ceremony was held on March 1, 1853, this one officiated by
Catholic Archbishop John Hughes. It was held in the bishop's
private residence at the corner of Madison Avenue and Thirty-
sixth Street[68] and recorded at St. Patrick's Cathedral on
Mulberry Street.[69] By then Teresa must have been noticeably
pregnant, and her parents, it can be imagined, undoubtedly
requested the religious rite. Whatever the circumstances, Dan
and Teresa went to live with the Bagiolis, who now resided in
a house at 92 Prince Street, on the southeast corner of Prince
and Mercer Streets.[70] Her mother and father obviously intended to be at Teresa's side when she went into labor.

Meanwhile, Dan's career was blossoming. He had been
named Corporation Counsel in January, a post that paid lucra-
tive fees for negotiating city contracts. He was also a leading
member of the ruling clique at Tammany Hall, and was on
speaking terms with President Franklin Pierce. He visited and
dined with Pierce in Washington, trying at the time to help
friend August Belmont win a diplomatic appointment over-
seas.[71] And then an incredible opportunity for a post abroad
presented itself through the person of John W. Forney, one-
time Clerk of the House of Representatives and editor of
Pierce's official party newspaper, the *Washington Union*. Forney, who first met Dan at a political convention in Baltimore,
bumped into him again in May 1853, at a Democratic gathering in New York. Pierce had just named James Buchanan to
be American minister in London, and Buchanan, Forney
knew, was looking for an assistant to accompany him there as
secretary to the legation. Forney broached the idea of the position to Dan, who immediately asked what the salary was. Informed it was $2,500 a year, Dan responded, "Why bless you,
my dear fellow, that would hardly pay for my wine and ci-
gars. My annual income is fifteen times more than that; I
could not think of such a sacrifice."[72] Though he rejected the

offer at first, the chance to visit England and Europe attracted Dan. He reconsidered the idea and asked Forney to arrange an interview with Buchanan. Forney did so, and Dan was introduced to Buchanan at his home, Wheatland, in Lancester, Pennsylvania. Buchanan "was most favorably impressed" with Dan, only complaining to Forney—as he would always complain about Dan—that he "writes as bad a hand as you do."[73] Despite the illegibility of Dan's penmanship, Buchanan informed Pierce that he was "very much pleased" with Dan: "I confess I think that his manners, appearance, & intelligence are all that could be desired."[74] Although separated by almost thirty years in age—Buchanan was sixty-two, Dan thirty-three —the two men "got on very well," Forney thought.[75] In time, Dan and Buchanan became, in Dan's word, "intimate,"[76] and *The New-York Times* would acknowledge that "Mr. SICKLES, perhaps better than any other . . . understands" Buchanan "and knows how to appeal to the few weak points in his character."[77]

The two men left New York by ship for London on Saturday, August 6, 1853. Buchanan met Teresa the night before sailing, when he spent an hour with her. "She is both handsome & agreeable," he wrote niece Harriet Lane.[78] For the moment, Teresa was staying behind, undoubtedly because Laura was too young to travel, but she was not happy with being left alone and did not wait too many months to follow Dan to London. "I think it will not be long before his lady follows him; & he is evidently very anxious for this result," Buchanan wrote his niece from London on September 30.[79] Teresa, as Buchanan predicted, arrived in the spring of 1854, apparently with her mother to help with the baby.[80] Until Harriet Lane herself reached England, Teresa proceeded to play hostess for Buchanan, was presented to the queen, and won the admiration of the English court. London newspapers later referred to Teresa, Harriet, and the wife of another of Buchanan's aides as "The Three American Graces."[81] Buchanan grew so fond of Teresa that he could not tolerate her being hurt. He demonstrated his attachment to her when John A. Thomas, a former army general from Tennessee, came to London as an assistant secretary of state on a special diplomatic mission. Thomas's wife asked to be presented at court, and when the day arrived, Buchanan told her to place herself under the charge of Teresa, who would accompany her to the palace. Mrs. Thomas refused, apparently because she felt that Teresa, who was then only about eighteen years old, was not a fitting escort. Buchanan was so upset by Mrs. Thomas's attitude that she was never presented at court, and when he became president, he dismissed her husband from his post.[82]

At the same time, Buchanan was growing closer to Dan. "But what shall I say about Sickles?" the ambassador wrote Forney. "I am warmly & strongly attached to him." True, his handwriting was "deficient," but "Sickles possesses qualifications both of mind & manners for a much higher place than that of Secretary of Legation."[83] Buchanan wrote those words despite an embarrassing incident Dan caused that, as Dan's luck would have it, endeared him to Irish voters back in New York City. George Peabody, an expatriate Bostonian who was a wealthy London financier, liked to encourage relations between England and the United States by giving dinners and inviting prominent Americans and Britons. He made a special event of the Fourth of July, ordinarily celebrating the American holiday with a banquet at the Crystal Palace. In 1854, however, he chose the Star and Garter Hotel at Richmond-on-the-Thames for the annual get-together. The idea that toasts would be drunk both to the president and the queen bothered Dan, who suggested that Peabody instead host a dinner for Americans only. Peabody made some minor changes in his plans for the festivities, but not in his guest list or the overall program. When Dan showed up, along with Buchanan and some 150 other guests, there on the wall near the head of the table were lifesize portraits of Queen Victoria and her prince consort, overshadowing a small portrait of George Washington that was hung between them. There was no portrait whatsoever of the American president, Franklin Pierce. Moreover, according to the printed schedule, an Englishman, Sir James

Tennant, was assigned to give the toast to Washington, which would follow the toast to the queen. And, ironically, considering what would occur five years later, certain uncomplimentary references to the British in "The Star-Spangled Banner" were removed—to wit, "the foe's haughty host," "their foul footsteps' pollution" and "the hireling and slave." It was all too much for Dan. When Peabody rose to give the welcoming speech and ended, with a flourish, raising his glass on high, "Gentlemen . . . the Queen!,", Dan, his face red as a beet, stayed glued to his chair while the rest of the banqueters jumped to their feet to salute the queen's portrait. And then he walked out.[84] Five months later, after Dan had returned home, Buchanan wrote him, "Your refusal to rise when the Queen's health was proposed is still mentioned in society, but," said Buchanan, who understood Dan's feelings about the matter, "I have always explained & defended you."[85]

Dan and Teresa returned that July to New York, but his stay at home was brief. It was so short that after a quick trip to Washington, Dan headed back to London aboard the same ship that had brought him to New York. Dan was bearing messages between Pierce and Buchanan and Pierre Soule, the American minister to Spain, having to do with shaping a policy for the acquisition of Cuba from Spain. Going further than instructed, Buchanan, Soule, and the American minister to France—John Y. Mason—that fall drew up a manifesto that was an international powder keg. Calling Cuba indispensable to the security of slavery, the manifesto said the United States should make every effort to buy the island from Spain, but, failing that, the United States would be justified in taking it by force. Pierce immediately repudiated it.

Because his role was that of a functionary, Dan was untouched by the brouhaha, and when he sailed back to New York for good on December 16 it was with Buchanan's "best wishes for his future welfare."[86] He and Teresa were now living with her mother and father on East Fifteenth Street in a neighborhood Bagioli probably chose because it was close to a number of music and piano stores on Union Square.[87] Both

Dan and his father had offices at 111 Nassau Street and they soon became embroiled in a lawsuit dealing with a patent for making artificial teeth and were charged with unethical practices. Nothing came of the lawsuit, and unblemished by the episode, Dan announced his intention to run in the fall for the New York State Senate, and was elected.

By now, Dan was chairman of the executive committee of Tammany Hall and, "as an adjunct," had organized a special "consulting committee of twenty-four gentlemen, prominent in our municipal social life, with whom I was in the habit of conferring upon all questions of importance." Prominent among them were Belmont, who was becoming noted for his taste in women and horses; James T. Brady, a brilliant criminal lawyer; John J. Cisco, a railroad investment entrepreneur; and Colonel Henry G. Stebbins, who had organized the luxuriously uniformed Twelfth Regiment of the New York National Guard in which Dan served as an officer. With their help, he now was able to complete a project that he started when he was corporation counsel but which was interrupted by his service abroad. For all his life, and for all he accomplished, Dan was proudest of his role in the creation of Central Park. As corporation counsel, he had been successful in consolidating all the advocates of a park, herding the sponsors of defeated bills around a dinner table to agree on one site, and maneuvering the governor, Horatio C. Seymour, into signing enabling legislation. His motives at first were mixed. Dan and several friends had organized a syndicate to purchase a thousand building lots near the park. Lots on Fifth Avenue and Bloomingdale Road, as uptown Broadway was then called, were going for from $100 to $250 each, and Dan "foresaw visions of fortune for myself and associates in the not far distant future." The syndicate was abandoned but, to Dan's credit, his enthusiasm in developing a park was not. While he was away in London, however, the proposal lay dormant and the land chosen as the site remained "one of the roughest and most forbidding spots on the face of the globe. It was a vast mass of rocks and boulders, variegated here and there by an irredeemable swamp. Not a tree was visible." On his return home, Dan picked up where he left off. He got friend John Graham's brother Charles, a surveyor, to make huge panoramas of the site, one showing its present topography, the other "as near the Garden of Eden" as Graham could "delineate." Dan had the panoramas hung on the walls of the anteroom of the state senate chamber—and won his point. "I was denounced by adversaries, sometimes as a fool, sometimes as a knave," he explained. "A fool, because no amount of money could ever transform the rocks and boulders covering the territory in a park;—a knave, because the whole scheme was extravagant, gotten up for political purposes, as a sop to the 'unwashed multitude', who would use the place in their own vulgar way, to the exclusion of the better element, who would never be seen in the so-called Park." Using "what is now concisely called a 'pull,'" Dan successfully steered the measure through the legislature, and soon "the rocks in Central Park [were] covered with soil drawn thither in carts; swamps filled with earth; great basins for lakes excavated; a comprehensive drainage system inaugurated; countless trees planted; many miles of macadamized road constructed; long bridle paths made; bridges of many graceful forms erected." Driving through "these charming pleasure grounds" and seeing "thousands enjoying them," he said a half-century later, "I sometimes feel a complacent pride in the recollection that I helped to create this park."[88]

It is ironic that Dan received little credit and is not remembered for the critical part he played in the establishment of Central Park; yet he received a great deal of publicity for a speech he made in which he unabashedly distorted the truth. His address, to the state legislature, was instrumental in defeating a bill to break up the multimillion-dollar real-estate holdings of Trinity Church and distribute its wealth to smaller, less well-off churches in the diocese.[89] Considering that he was not a religious person, his words illustrate how dissembling Dan could be; even one of his harshest critics, George Templeton Strong, a Trinity parishioner, could not fault him on the issue. "I was born and reared within the bosom of this church, and in this parish," Dan piously declared. "The graves of my humble ancestors lie within its sacred enclosures. The marriage sacrament—the baptismal blessings were pronounced by the side of its altars, upon those from whom I am descended. It is the only church possessing adequate revenues, that now remains within my district, to take care of its poor; to relieve their wants—to visit them when sick—to clothe them when naked—and to lead them to a good immortality."[90]

Spring of 1856 was a busy time for Dan. Buchanan returned from London, arriving in New York to a rousing welcome arranged by Dan, who also spearheaded the formation of Keystone Clubs to promote Buchanan's candidacy for the Democratic nomination for President. Then Dan announced that he himself was going to run for Congress. Campaigning would again mean his being away from home frequently. Teresa, who was unhappy when Dan first went off to London without her, never grew accustomed to his travels, whether for politics or business. She did not like to be left alone. Writing on May 5 to a close friend she referred to as "My own dear sister Florence," Teresa complained that "Dan is going to Washington this evening—from Washington to Richmond, Virginia, back to W. & then home. He will be gone for a week or ten days." Realizing how she felt about his being away, Dan had invited her to join him, "but I have too much to look after at home—what with dressmakers, seamstresses, shoemakers, etc. etc. I have my hands full." In addition, she and Dan were now in search of a house of their own—"on *this* side of the Hudson"—and if they did find one, settling into it would certainly make it difficult for them even to spend some time in the White Mountains in New Hampshire in the summer, as they planned to do, especially because "it is such a bother travelling with a young child." But aside from confiding to her friend, Teresa kept her thoughts to herself. "Please do not dear Florence read my notes to any one," she added to her letter. "I would rather you would destroy them."[91]

For his own part, Dan was campaigning for election to rep-
resent the Third Congressional District, although he did not
live in it. His office on Nassau Street, however, was within its
boundaries. The district was a fascinating composite of all that
New York symbolized. It covered most of the oldest section
of Manhattan, spreading like a fan from where the island at its
southern tip was but a few feet wide, up the East River to
Spruce Street on one side, and up the Hudson River to Houston Street on the other. Its northern boundary ended at St.
Thomas' (Episcopal) Church at the corner of Houston and
Broadway. There, the district swung south along Broadway
until the end of City Hall Park and then around the park until
it connected with Spruce Street. Encompassed within its borders were the city's financial center, the Custom House, the
Merchants Exchange, the busiest stretch of Broadway, ferry
slips linking Manhattan to New Jersey, Staten Island, and the
city of Brooklyn, and miles of wharves lined with ships from
all over the world. Its population was 94,062 residents, almost
half of whom were foreign-born, the Irish outnumbering the
Germans by more than a three-to-one margin.[92] It was, in no
uncertain terms, Tammany country.

Before the fall, the Sickleses—Dan, Teresa, and Laura—
moved into their own home, on the shore of the Hudson
River at Ninety-first Street in the village of Bloomingdale, a
tiny picturesque suburban hamlet composed of estates with
vast "emerald lawns" that sloped down to the water. They
had enough land to raise horses and keep hens, cows, and
pets. Their new home was some six miles from Dan's office
downtown, but could be reached by either Broadway or Sixth
Avenue streetcars that went to Thirty-second Street, from
which stages to Bloomingdale left, fare twelve cents.[93] When
Dan was around, there was the theater to go to, or events
such as the benefit fair at the Crystal Palace being held to fund
a hospital. Teresa visited the fair five times, but was again
complaining to Florence about feeling neglected. Dan had
gone to Wilmington and Philadelphia, leaving her alone to entertain herself. She "would like to go to Laura Keene's—they

say it is a beautiful house, and besides they are playing a comedy at it now." Her parents were minding Laura downtown in Manhattan, and though a friend had sent a pony, without Dan around Teresa said she "found it rather stupid riding on horseback every day alone." Again, she added, "Please do not let any one see" her letter.[94]

Dan was an attractive candidate—scrupulous about his appearance, "of good presence and graceful manners;" said one description, "form, not stout but well knit together, complexion fair, eyes blue and expressive, mouth firm, and his general bearing . . . thoroughly indicative of . . . unflinching determination." His service in Albany, it said, "was distinguished by an unusual coolness and self-possession, which gave him great advantages in debate."[95] The criticism Dan drew usually came from political rivals and was echoed in unfriendly local newspapers or by an old-line self-righteous New Yorker such as George Templeton Strong. The *Evening Post* said his "political ambition" got him into such "bad political and personal associations" that "he very soon betrayed the promise of his youth."[96] The *Post* was sure that Dan was "kept" by a steamship company based in New York.[97] Strong referred to him as belonging "to the filthy sediment of the [law] profession, and lying somewhere in its lower strata. Perhaps better to say that he's one of the bigger bubbles of the scum of the profession, swollen and windy, and puffed out with fetid gas."[98] One recurrent criticism was that Dan "was fond of gayety" and exhibited an "undue fondness for the female sex."[99] He was, said one critic, "somewhat of a 'lady-killer'."[100]

That November, Dan was elected to the House of Representatives by a wide margin, and Buchanan was elected president, carrying New York City with 53 percent of the vote, thanks to Dan and his Tammany friends. They would wield an unusual influence with Buchanan, who was beholden to them. The nation's capital now beckoned.

THREE

"The City of Magnificent Intentions"

Where Gamblers bland with Statesmen freely mix,
And seem sometimes to make exchange of tricks;
Where Impudence and Pertness takes the floor,
While modest Merit waits without the door;
Where Party decks the brawling Partisan
With wreaths and spoils,—no matter what the man . . .

IMAGINE, IF YOU WILL, going to Washington for the first time in the late 1850s. See it as Teresa must have seen it: a huge, sprawling, still maturing metropolis with broad avenues and wide streets, none of them paved and many of them unpopulated—a city so unlike the New York to which she was accustomed. The traffic jams of Broadway were unknown. Foreign accents were the oddity rather than the rule. The hectic business world was subordinated here to a daily round of leisurely morning and afternoon receptions, dinner parties, and balls. As Englishman Laurence Oliphant observed, "it is a town without a population, and exists only by virtue of its being the seat of Government."[1] Here, politics, not commerce, ruled daily life. "Every man, woman, and child in Washington is a politician," said another contemporary observer. "The people inhale politics with the air they breathe, and talk and think of but little else."[2]

Some visitors arrived by steamboat or stagecoach, but most, like Teresa, came by train. The rail trip from New York was an arduous one; even if you made the necessary connections with trains at Philadelphia and Baltimore—and that wasn't always possible—you had to start from New York

37

at eight o'clock in the morning in order to arrive in the capital shortly before seven at night, a journey of nearly eleven hours. Many passengers broke the trip up by making an overnight stop in Philadelphia. Surprisingly, considering the fact that the city symbolized the heart of the country's political life, Washington was a bit of a dead end. Only one railroad connected Washington with the north, and there was no through connection south. A traveler heading from, say, New York to Charleston had to disembark at the Baltimore & Ohio depot near Capitol Hill and take an omnibus down Maryland Avenue and over the Long Bridge to make the train connection south to Charleston at Alexandria on the other side of the Potomac. Until 1852, Congress had even refused to allow steam engines to enter the city limits, and horses had been used to draw trains to the depot. Congress recanted in 1854 and allowed the Alexandria & Washington Railroad to lay tracks across town—as long as the rails did not run on Pennsylvania Avenue. Despite an outburst of civic protest, the tracks were laid, but they soon grew rusty when the railroad company failed.

Washington, as Teresa undoubtedly quickly discovered, was also a difficult city to get to know, though on the surface its carefully designed layout belied that. Any visitor looking at a contemporary map of Washington would have been struck by the orderliness of Pierre L'Enfant's plan for the capital—in all, 1,170 blocks or squares bounded by twenty-one avenues and more than one hundred streets. Guide maps echoed L'Enfant's detailed design, which was described as "a chessboard overlaid with a wagon wheel."[3] But the neat patterns of boulevards, streets, squares, and circles were not reality yet. As one guidebook warned, "The map represents the City, not as it is, but as it is intended it shall be. Some streets and avenues are only partially opened."[4] For, despite the growth of what contemporaries called Washington City, not that much had changed since Charles Dickens's visit in 1842: "Spacious avenues, that begin nothing, and lead nowhere; streets, mile-long, that only want houses, roads, and inhabitants; public

buildings that need but a public to be complete; and orna-
ments of great thoroughfares, which only lack great thoroughfares to ornament, are its leading features."⁵ A numbering
scheme to help visitors was devised in 1854 so that Pennsylvania Avenue and all the lettered streets that ran east to
west were numbered consecutively starting at Rock Creek.
Streets running north to south were numbered consecutively
beginning at the city's northern limit, Boundary Street (later
renamed Florida Avenue), and moving southward to the Potomac River. The city was divided into four zones emanating
from the Capitol Building—east, west, north, and south—
and, to facilitate searches, street addresses were often provided
with the nearest cross street. (The modern numbering system,
with the street number coordinated with the avenue—thus,
1600 Pennsylvania Avenue for the White House, on Pennsylvania Avenue at Sixteenth Street—was not put into effect until the 1870s.) Even when provided with the cross street in the
late 1850s, the visitor sometimes found it difficult to find his
or her way. One longtime resident spoke of Washington as
"a city of streets without a curve and most of them without names."⁶ The Rev. Dr. Joseph T. Kelly, who grew up in
Washington and was about ten years old in the late 1850s,
remembered it as "nothing more than a great straggling
town."⁷ Cows passed his home on Fourth Street, near Judiciary Square, every evening on their way home for milking, as
did "long files of solemn geese," but "best of all were the pigs
which also made up the procession."⁸ Not too far from his
home was a marshy stretch of land at Eighth and L streets
known as "The Slashes," where "hunters shot reed birds and
frogs croaked."⁹ The city was, he said, "a place of wide, un-
built areas of land, oftentimes dreary commons, wide open
spaces, creeks and rills cutting across in unexpected places,
few buildings of any pretensions; not a sewer anywhere."¹⁰
Author Mary Clemmer Ames found that "even its mansions
were without modern improvements or conveniences, while
the mass of its buildings were low, small and shabby in the
extreme. The avenues, superb in length and breadth, in their

proportions afforded a painful contrast to the hovels and sheds which often lined them on either side for miles. Scarcely a public building was finished."[11] As Charles Dickens put it, Washington "is sometimes called the City of Magnificent Distances, but it might with greater propriety be termed the City of Magnificent Intentions."[12]

Everywhere, it seemed, construction was going on. Like the nation itself, Washington was expanding dramatically. The evidence of building—whether home, store, or public edifice—was all around. The Capitol, the most dominant structure of all, was itself covered with a web of scaffolding, and piles of huge granite blocks and construction debris lay scattered over Capitol Hill as work progressed on completing its new wings and replacing the building's dome.

Despite the awkward way the Capitol Building looked as it was being enlarged, there was still something majestic about it. Emerging from a long walk in the woods by the Potomac River, naturalist John Burroughs saw the building "soaring over the green swell of earth immediately in front . . . Of all the sights in Washington, that which will survive longest in my memory is the vision of the great dome thus rising cloud-like above the hills."[13]

Unfortunately, the view from the vantage point of Capitol Hill was the opposite. The Capitol Building overlooked the city's eyesore—worse, its major health menace—the Washington Canal. The canal was built in 1815 as part of L'Enfant's plan to bring vessels bearing produce from the countryside direct to the city's markets. The Potomac River then touched the southern grounds of the White House and cut close to where the Washington Monument was being erected. The canal ran from the river along the northern edge of the Mall— what became Constitution Avenue—then zigzagged by the base of Capitol Hill and continued southward, dividing into two arms leading to the Anacostia or Eastern Branch of the Potomac. Joseph Kelly recalled the canal's being "a filthy, sluggish stream . . . foul and noisome, especially under the hot sun." It cut off "the southern part of the city, which thus surrounded by water, went by the name of 'The Island,' much to the disgust and against the protests of its residents." The canal was spanned by seven bridges, and in walking over them, Kelly said, "you encountered all sights and smells that came from muddy flats, dead cats and dogs, and occasionally a human derelict who had stumbled to his death through drink."[14] What made matters worse was that one of the markets L'Enfant envisioned the canal servicing was the Fish Market, which backed onto it. Live fish were kept in wire baskets lowered into the canal, which also became the repository of "all the refuse and offal from the fish that were cleaned."[15]

Washington lay near the head of an estuary, below the Great Falls of the Potomac, where the river drops from the hard rocks of the piedmont plateau to the soft sand, gravel, and clay of the tidewater plain. This was the limit of navigation upstream; sailing ships from Europe arrived at adjacent Georgetown and Alexandria opposite to unload their cargoes. The river below the White House was a mile wide in 1792, but silt from poorly contoured farmlands and hillsides stripped of timber had created marshlands in the intervening years, and the old Maryland tobacco port of Bladensburgh, on the Potomac's Eastern Branch, was no longer open to oceangoing vessels. The extensive marshes and shoals harbored all sorts of birdlife—swallows, herons, rails, thrushes, meadowlarks, woodpeckers, hawks, owls and, in winter, ducks by the thousands. Many of the birds were hunted and sold as table fare in the city's markets, especially the bobolinks. The marshes also became the breeding grounds for mosquitoes that bedeviled the District's citizens.

The mosquitoes vied with the climate as the most popular topic of conversation for everyone who lived in or visited the city. A reporter for the anti-administration *New-York Times* suggested, "You can no more depend upon Washington weather than upon Mr. BUCHANAN's friendship."[16] The authors of *Avifauna Columbiana* were harsher: "the National Capital was a mud-puddle in winter, a dust-heap in summer, a cow-pen and pigsty all year round."[17] Sara Agnes Pryor, a

Virginian by birth, was dismayed by city's weather in general: "the cold, the ice-laden streets in winter; the whirlwinds of dust and driving rains of spring; the swift-coming fierceness of summer heat; the rapid atmospheric changes which would give us all these extremes in one week, or even one day, until it became the part of prudence never to sally forth on any expedition without 'a fan, an overcoat, and an umbrella.'"[18] Pryor's friend, Virginia Clay, called Pennsylvania Avenue "a perfect romping ground for the winds."[19] Similarly, a correspondent from *Harper's Weekly Magazine* complained one April day that "Cold blasts sweep down the valley from the Cumberland mountains, raising Sahara-like clouds of dust."[20]

Washington never seemed more southern than in the spring and the summer. Laurence Oliphant, a well-traveled twenty-four-year-old who served as secretary to Lord Elgin during negotiations in Washington in 1853 for a reciprocity treaty with British Canada, compared Washington's climate in springtime to that he found in Southeast Asia: "a most relaxing and depressing place, close muggy air—Kandy [Ceylon] temperature exactly—and streets silent and lifeless." Oliphant, a bachelor, said the city was "the last place in the world, notwithstanding the pretty girls, that I should choose as a residence."[21]

Oliphant left Washington before July, missing what was usually the city's "warmest month," when the mean temperature was about 77.[22] July also shared with August the time of year when the most deaths were registered. Those two months also registered the most rainfall. In all, it rained an average of about forty inches a year, and any sustained shower was particularly devastating because of the porous soil upon which the city rested. The "spongy nature of the ground in the vicinity of the Avenue," young Joseph Kelly recalled, was responsible in part for recurrent floods. The "most memorable" one completely covered Pennsylvania Avenue, "especially at 6th Street, where the water extended from C Street on the North, far down across the Mall, completely isolating the people on the Island. One Sunday we were amazed to find boats plying on the Avenue."[23] Mary Clemmer Ames said, "In spring and autumn the entire west end of the city was one vast slough of impassible [sic] mud. One would have to walk many blocks before he found it possible to cross a single street."[24] Mark Twain thought that if only the mud could be slightly diluted, the streets of Washington could serve as canals.[25] After heavy rains, Kelly remembered, the end of a coffin could be seen elevated six or eight feet above the sidewalk in the old burying ground of St. Patrick's Parish, near the corner of Ninth and F streets.[26] Kelly also recalled the time the Seventh Regiment of New York came to Washington to participate in a parade: striding from the B & O depot, the soldiers "left 700 pairs of rubbers in the heavy mud of Indiana Avenue."[27]

Despite all its faults, even the city's fiercest critics waxed poetic about the beauty of Washington's setting. "We rarely have spring in this latitude," wrote Mary Clemmer Ames. "Full panoplied, summer springs from under the mail of long lingering winter. . . . No long waiting and watching for slow budding blossoms here. Some night when we are all asleep there is a silent burst of bloom; and we wake to find the trees that we left here, when we shut our blinds on them the night before, all tremulous with new life, and the whole city set in glowing emerald."[28]

One March day, John Burroughs said, "I heard the song of the Canada sparrow, a soft, sweet note, almost running into a warble. Saw a small, black, velvety butterfly with a yellow border to its wings. Under a warm bank found two flowers of the houstonia in bloom. Saw frogs' spawn . . . and heard the hyla."[29]

For all her complaints about the weather, Sara Pryor nevertheless thought of Washington "only as a garden of delights, over which the spring trailed an early robe of green, thickly embroidered with gems of amethyst and ruby, pearl and sapphire. The crocuses, hyacinths, tulips, and snowdrops made haste to bloom before the snows had fairly melted. The trees donned their diaphanous veils of green earlier in the White House grounds, the lawn of the Smithsonian Institution, and the gentle slopes around the Capitol, than anywhere else in less distinguished localities. To walk through these incense-laden grounds, to traverse the avenue of blossoming crab-apples, was pleasure. The shaded avenues were delightful long lanes, where one was sure to meet friends, and where no law of etiquette forbade a pause in the public street for a few words of kindly inquiry, or a bit of gossip."[30]

The city's pride was Pennsylvania Avenue. Throughout its length—from Rock Creek to the Eastern Branch of the Potomac—"The Avenue," as Washingtonians called it, was 160 feet wide. It made "a downright misnomer" of Broadway in New York City, observed Virginia Tunstall Clay.[31] "Broadway," Mary Clemmer Ames insisted, "cannot compare with it in magnificent proportions. It is as wide as two Broadways."[32] Few streets in Washington were lit with gas lamps, but several hundred of the ornate fixtures—cast-iron standards with a grape-and-ivy design—graced both sides of the Avenue, and, instead of street signs at major intersections, the lamps' tapered square glass lanterns bore the names of the streets.

The most prestigious shops and businesses could be found on both sides of the mile-long stretch between the Capitol and the Treasury Building, giving the Avenue, Ames said, "with its double drive . . . its borders of bloom, its gay promenades and flashing turn-outs . . . a certain splendor of its own, of which no monopoly can wholly rob it."[33] Here were Taylor & Maury's Bookstore, Gilman's Drug Store and, occupying the three floors above Gilman's, Mathew Brady's National Photographic Art Gallery. There were, in all, forty-one confectioners in Washington, but not one could match Charles Gautier's on the Avenue. His "Saloon" not only sold "a rich and varied assortment of French Fancy Goods," but also contained a restaurant famed for its meals as well as "Elegant Suites of Parlor, Reception, and Dining Rooms" for private functions. Gautier's was prepared to cater the "largest dinners, balls, and parties at a few hours' notice . . . together with everything that is in any manner connected with the most fashionable entertainments."[34] Mrs. Gautier presided over the counter in the confectionary and, according to Sara Pryor, she sat ensconced "in an arm-chair" and told the visitor "the precise social status of every one of her customers." For the fashionable, there was also "the little corner shop" where Madame Delarue sold hats and gloves and where François—"the one and only hairdresser of note," Sara Pryor insisted—worked. He "had adjusted coronets on noble heads, and . . . could (if he so minded) talk of them agreeably in Parisian French."[35]

France set the pattern for fashion in both dress and dining. What could not be purchased on a buying trip to New York City was copied by local dressmakers. The "favourite mantua-maker" was a Mrs. Rich, Virginia Clay said, but if she was busy—and she always seemed to be—"a hasty journey" was made to Mlle. Rountree in Philadelphia.[36] Hair arrangements sometimes tended to be elaborate, necklines were low and jewels were "conspicuous even in men's dressing."[37]

Gautier advertised proudly that he had a "first-class French chef" who could be "sent to your house" to prepare dinner "at a small of charge of $2 for his services." A rival, restauranteur J. G. Weaver, boasted "French dinners, &c.—Mons. L. Cabantous, from Paris, having been taken in my employ this day, I shall be prepared to furnish dinners, and suppers, and parties of every description in the most approved style." And the dishes Mons. Cabantous could serve up included D'Entree Froid a la Gelee, Saute de Filet de Poulet au Supreme, Pate Chaud de Callis aux Gratin and Timbale de Maccaroni a la Parisien—"Day boarders $1 per day; weekly boarders $5 per week."[38] To go with those meals, vintners along the Avenue sold the French champagnes Moet & Chandon, Mumm's, and Piper & Co.'s Heidsick, assortments of hock and port wines, sherrys, clarets and sauternes as well as brandies and cordials.

Stretching back from Pennsylvania Avenue between Seventh and Ninth streets was the principal one of the city's four markets, Centre Market. Sara Pryor found it "abundantly supplied with the finest game and fish from the Eastern Shore of Maryland and Virginia, and the waters of the Potomac. Brant, ruddy duck, canvasback duck, sora [a type of marsh bird], oysters, and terrapin were within the reach of any housekeeper." (A housewife, she pointed out, could "plant" the oysters in her cellars, which "fed with salt water . . . were protected from invasion by the large terrapins kept there—a most efficient police force, crawling about with their out-stretched necks and wicked eyes.")[39] The market, however, had been organized around the turn of the century and additions over the years to the open, low-roofed structure had turned it into a collection of "long low sheds" that were "dirty and filthy." It was known as the "Marsh Market" because of the low ground on which it stood, and at its rear, on the edge of the Washington Canal, was the equally repugnant Fish Market.[40] Joseph Kelly was impressed by the "intimate and friendly relations existing between dealers and customers." In wintertime, "rich and poor alike" huddled by charcoal braziers at the market to warm their hands and feet before setting out for home.[41] Everyone in those days had to lug their purchases home on foot, unless they could find a hack or had their own carriages, because although cities such as New York, Baltimore, Boston, New Orleans, and Philadelphia had horse-drawn streetcars, Washington had resisted having a modern public transportation system.

Moreover, for all its attractions, Pennsylvania Avenue was not paved and, as Virginia Clay noted, "The greatest contrasts in architecture existed, hovels often all but touching the mansions of the rich."[42] At first the Avenue was originally lined with hundreds of Federal rowhouses, two to four stories high, but the symmetry of the skyline was lost as dozens of the rowhouses were combined and enlarged to form a number of large hotels, among them Willard's, or were destroyed altogether to make way for new hotels such as the National and Brown's.

◎   ◎   ◎

Teresa first visited Washington for James Buchanan's inauguration on March 7, 1857.[43] Together with Dan, she remained in Jonah Hoover's residence on G Street for several weeks before returning home. Dan stayed on, making Hoover's home his official residence for the time being when in Washington.[44] The first session of the Thirty-fifth Congress did not begin until December, and when he had time he busied himself trying to find a place for his family to live before the opening of Congress.

It can safely be presumed that like any newcomer to Washington, Teresa took in the sights. There was the White House, of course; she and Dan would be frequent guests of the president and Harriet Lane. There were the twice-a-week Marine Band concerts—on the grounds of Capitol Hill every Wednesday, or on the slope of the White House overlooking the Potomac River every Saturday afternoon, when, as one resident put it, "thither the whole world repaired, to walk, or to sit in open carriages, and talk of everything except politics."[45] The Capitol Building itself was a major attraction, also, though the wings containing the new House and Senate chambers weren't quite completed when Teresa first saw it.[46] Then, too, there was the aborted Washington Monument on the westernmost edge of the Mall, its construction stalled for the lack of funds; most every store had a little glass receptacle on its counter to collect coins to help pay for the monument. Two particular favorites of every visitor were the crenellated building that housed the Smithsonian Institution and the Patent Office with its displays of inventors' models. Even the Wisconsin Avenue Reservoir—an odd, circular domed brick building for storing water brought into the city from the Great Falls of the Potomac fourteen miles away—attracted sightseers. More unusual was the Aqueduct Bridge that connected adjoining Georgetown with Alexandria County, Virginia, across the Potomac. Its lower level carried vehicular traffic; its upper level, filled with water, carried barges between the Chesapeake and Ohio Canal and the Alexandria Canal.

Another of Washington's features, on the other, eastern end of the city, overlooking the Eastern Branch of the Potomac, was the Congressional Cemetery. Among the notables buried there were Elbridge Gerry, a signer of the Declaration of Independence, military officers who had fought in the War of 1812 and the Mexican War, and, of particular interest for some strange reason, the grave of Push-Ma-Ta-Ha, the Choctaw chief who had fought under Andrew Jackson and died of diphtheria while negotiating a treaty in Washington in 1825. The cemetery was originally known as the Washington Parish Burial Ground but it got its new name because senators and representatives who died in office were interred there, either permanently or until the bodies could be transported to their home states. It became a tradition to erect a monument to each member who did die in office, and row upon row of short, stubby look-alike cenotaphs dedicated to deceased congressmen already graced the top of the quiet hill.

The cemetery, far from the center of Washington and isolated, was an ideal if unusual place for a private moment. It became one of Teresa's favorite haunts.

FOUR

"Armed to the Teeth"

Where Murder boldly stalks, nor cares a straw
For useless Police, or unused Law;
Where shrieking Kansas whirls her frantic arms
To fright the country with her false alarms;. . .

WASHINGTON ORDINARILY CAME TO LIFE in the fall, as congressmen began to arrive for the annual term, mandated then by the Constitution, to assemble the first Monday in December. Many of the legislators brought their families, and their coming was also the signal for thousands of strangers to descend on the capital as well—government contractors, lobbyists, seekers of personal favors, gamblers, and prostitutes. "As the month of December approached," Dr. John B. Ellis noted, "the town began to fill up, hotels and boarding-houses lost their deserted aspect, and their proprietors' grum [*sic*] faces began to be wreathed with smiles."[1] Oddly, employees in federal departments worked from 8:00 A.M. to 3:00 P.M. in summertime, but from nine to three in the winter, even though the winter months were the busiest time of the year.[2] Shorter hours or not, Ellis said, "the Departments commenced to show signs of life and activity" as December neared. "Clerks and officials, who had dozed away the summer months, assumed energetic and important airs, and every body [*sic*] in any way connected with the Government seemed to undergo a marvellous transformation."[3]

In odd-numbered years every two years, Congress had to adjourn by March 3, because newly elected members took of-

49

fice the following day. In even-numbered years, Congress ordinarily continued in session into the summer, as it did in
1858, when the question of whether Kansas should be admitted to the Union as a slave or free state was fiercely debated. Neither the House nor the Senate finally adjourned that
year until June. Even then, a goodly number of senators and
representatives stayed in the city beyond adjournment to work
on committee reports and complete other business.

Although the number of fatalities increased dramatically in
the summer, especially among strangers unused to Washington's heat and humidity, one guidebook insisted that the city's
climate was not responsible. Instead, it said, the deaths could
be attributed to the "entire change of diet and mode of life, by
which the constitution is weakened and every lurking disease
strengthened, and too frequently the casting away of the moral
integrity of home, by which the same result is obtained.[4] A
special threat to morality, in John Ellis's opinion, were the
numerous "houses of ill fame" whose patrons included "men
high in public office, officers of the army and navy, Governors of States, lawyers, doctors, and the very best class of the
city population."[5]

John Ellis's judgments tended to be harsh, but that was because he was particularly biased against federal employees and
politicians; they were all in his mind corrupt, so used to suc-
cumbing to the enticements of lobbyists, he said, that "the
integrity of many men in public life is doubted." In fact, Ellis
wondered how many of them could afford to maintain their
life-style. "Few public men above the position of clerks, can
or do live upon their official salaries," he observed. "They
spend annually more than double the sum received from the
Government, and many of them have no other visible source
of income. It is said that most of this splendor is paid for by
the lobby, and that the majority of public men are always
open to bribes."[6]

What troubled one congressman, however, was the drinking habits of his colleagues. John Kelly of New York, who
served in both the Thirty-fourth and Thirty-fifth congresses,

was especially distraught that members could imbibe within the Capitol Building. There was a bar called the "Hole-in-the-Wall" outside the House chamber that, he said, "was the downward path to irretrievable ruin":

> While the Democrats and Republicans were in a deadly struggle on the floor of the House over questions involving the destinies of the Union, and the lives and fortunes of millions of human beings, the tipplers were in the bar-room drinking, or on the sofas of the lobby dozing in their cups. A vote is wanting to carry an imperiled measure to victory,—the inebriate is lifted into a sitting posture, dragged to the floor, and bid to vote aye, or no, provided he is there to mumble out the word. Too often he is absent, having been carried off to his lodgings in a state of drunken imbecility.[7]

Kelly was not alone in his concern. Representative Alexander H. Stephens of Georgia complained that Republicans prevailed on a key vote in 1858 on the Kansas question because some of the thirteen southern Democrats who were absent "were too drunk to be got into the House." Stephens despaired, "How shamefully the South is represented! . . . Have we any future but miserable petty squabbles, parties, factions, and fragments of organizations, led on by contemptible drunken demagogues?"[8]

Ellis said the problem was citywide. He described the "canterburies and concert halls" that abounded in Washington as "low and disgusting" and warned that "men are drugged by the confederates of the keepers of these places, robbed, and maltreated, and sometimes murdered."[9] Lawlessness in Washington —whether robbery, assault, arson, vandalism, or prostitution—was, in fact, a growing problem in the 1850s. Poverty increased concomitantly, and became so alarming that the city council set up a central board in 1859 to try to oversee relief efforts; nearly six percent of the municipal budget that year was set aside to care for the needy. A salaried police force, created in 1851, was too small to handle effectively the surge in crime over such a large, dispersed city. A detachment of Marines from the Navy Yard had to be summoned when members of the Know-Nothing Party tried to prevent "foreigners" and Catholics from voting at a city polling station on Mount Vernon Square in 1857. The Marines were able to wrest a cannon from the rioters and, when the mob refused to disperse, fired it, killing six of them and injuring twenty-one others. "Riot and bloodshed are of daily occurrence," a Senate committee reported in 1858. "Innocent and unoffending persons are shot, stabbed, and otherwise shamefully maltreated. . . . The increase in juvenile delinquency was especially distressing."[10]

To protect themselves, citizens went armed in the streets. Englishman Laurence Oliphant was amazed to discover that even "members have come to Congress every night armed to the teeth."[11] The favored weapon was the reliable and "deadly" single-shot derringer, so small that it fit easily into a vest pocket; politicians often carried a brace of them.[12] Dan Sickles, for one, possessed two derringers and also a five-shot revolver.

The crime that plagued Washington was not, however, unique to it alone; other cities were experiencing problems, too, caused in part by sudden and dramatic increases in population. Washington's population soared from almost exactly 40,000 inhabitants in 1850 to nearly 61,000 by 1860, an increase of more than fifty percent.[13] In addition, there was a vast transient population. Many of the people who flocked to the city for the sessions of Congress—"an average floating population" of "from ten to twenty-five thousand persons," John Ellis estimated[14]—came from states or territories where the border between urbane urban living and rustic rural frontier brushed close. In an effort to compensate for its lack of manpower, the city's police department adopted in 1859 a new "deadly weapon" for its night division—an "old-fashioned hickory sponton [short pike] with spear formed iron head."[15]

More ominous was the undercurrent of hostility in Congress. Emotions touched off by the growing animosity between southerners and northerners led to threats, unseemly fist fights and sometimes worse. As one South Carolina representative stood by to prevent anyone's interfering, another

South Carolina representative attacked Charles Sumner of
Massachusetts at his desk on the Senate floor in 1856 and so
seriously caned him that the senator did not return to his seat
for two years. One of those Carolinians, Laurence M. Keitt,
touched off a free-for-all on the House floor two years later
when he called a Pennsylvania congressman a "black Republican puppy." Somebody might have gotten seriously injured,
but the toupee of a Mississippi congressman came off in the
hand of the Wisconsin member who was grappling with him
and contagious laughter fortunately dispelled the rancor.

Some arguments in Congress led to duels, which were condoned, though not sanctioned. Congress in 1839 had made
dueling in the District punishable by ten years of hard labor in
the penitentiary, so aggrieved parties simply rode out to what
everybody knew about and called "The Duelling-Ground," a
sequestered clearing four miles outside the city in the small
village of Bladensburgh.

Politics spilled over from Capitol Hill into a number of
Washington's twenty-nine hotels. The grandest—it had been
enlarged twice and now occupied the entire block—was the
National at the corner of Pennsylvania Avenue and Sixth
Street, which one visitors' guide described as "the stamping
ground of politicians, and the grand centre of political intrigue." The National's "proximity to the Capitol, and excel-
lent management" made it "the most favored hotel in Washington."[16] A block away from it was the Indian Queen,
remodeled and renamed Brown's Marble Hotel. Its innovative
features included the city's first bridal chamber and first gas
kitchen. A chief rival to both of them was Willard's Hotel,
which went by its old name, the City Hotel, on some guide
maps. Despite animosities between northerners and southerners during the 1850s, Willard's, a local reporter noted, "became a kind of headquarters for the two political extremes."[17]
The hotel boasted two entrances, through Greek Revival por-
ticos on both Pennsylvania Avenue and Fourteenth Street.
None of the dining rooms in the city's hotels were especially
noted for their cuisine—in general, both hotels and boarding
houses "set but indifferent tables," opined John Ellis[18]—but

Willard's had the best reputation. Its kitchen, consisting of rows of large open fireplaces, was ninety-four feet long and had numerous doors leading to the vast dining chamber that ran parallel to it.

In the spring of 1857 Dan Sickles stayed at Willard's on one of his periodic trips to Washington before the opening of the Thirty-fifth Congress. At the time, Dan was lobbying to have his friend Charles K. Graham, the surveyor who helped him with his Central Park project, appointed to the post of civil engineer of the Brooklyn Navy Yard, a patronage position. But first Dan had to get the current holder of the job dismissed. The civil engineer then was a man named J. McLeod Murphy, who took offense at some "unjust imputations" that he attributed to Dan. Murphy sent Dan a note accusing him of "assailing his private character." When Dan responded that the note was "only a vague and unmeaning menace," Murphy sent a friend to confront Dan. Dan demanded to be told the name of Murphy's informant. Instead, the friend, on behalf of Murphy, challenged Dan to a duel. Dan denied defaming Murphy and said he could see no reason for Murphy's demand for an explanation or "a hostile meeting." Murphy, however, was not appeased. On the morning of Wednesday, May 6, while Dan was still in bed, Murphy was able to contrive his way into Dan's room at Willard's Hotel and started to whip him with a cowhide. Jolted awake by the blows, Dan fought back and the two men struggled fiercely. Dan was struck on the face, but he managed to wrest the cowhide from Murphy, who then fled.

The incident became "the staple of town talk."[19] As one newspaper wryly remarked, "Never was a place mad for scandal than Washington."[20] Another commented, "Gossip here swells every molehill to a mountain, and stamps a sinister meaning on every smile."[21]

For Dan, the scrap with Murphy was just another imbroglio in his long career that caught the public's attention. It was the first time that Dan set Washington's tongues wagging, but it was not the last.

FIVE

"The Domestic Sphere"

Turn where you may, and gaze where'er you will
The gorgeous combination changes still;
A rich kaleidoscope of dazzling forms
Enchants the eye, and the rapt senses warms . . .

TERESA RETURNED TO WASHINGTON, to set up her household, in late fall of 1857, and, as the wife of a congressman, was immediately thrust into the city's hectic social whirl. It was considered etiquette "as soon as you arrive," one local wit said, "to empty your trunk, and hire a hack to drive around and call on people." Some people even advertised in newspapers to "please ring the bell."[1] The wives of congressmen held morning or afternoon receptions weekly, and together with their husbands hosted late suppers one night a week as well.

Virgina Clay was so exhausted by the constant round of socializing that "in preparation for the evening's pleasure" her maid Emily "was wont to get out my 'shocking-box' (for so she termed the electrical apparatus upon which I often depended), and, to a full charge of magical current and a half-hour's nap before dinner, I was indebted for many a happy evening."[2] What surprised many people, including a Philadelphia reporter, was the way "North and South mingle in general harmony," particularly at receptions given by Senator Stephen A. Douglas and his young second wife, Adele, despite the bitter reaction engendered by the senator's position in the Kansas controversy.[3]

Teresa's receptions were held on Tuesday mornings, and together with Dan she hosted a dinner party every Thursday evening. Otherwise, virtually every day and night she was out, attending receptions, dinners, and parties. The pace was overwhelming. One night, Teresa attended a dinner party at one home and a party afterwards at Postmaster General Aaron V. Brown's residence. She didn't get home until three in the morning, she wrote her friend Florence, as a result of which, she moaned: "I awakened yesterday with a severe bilious & nervous headache, stiff neck, and feeling otherwise so much indisposed that I sent for the Dr." As it was, Teresa continued, "We had quite a wedding take place here (in W.) about a week ago, but I was too busy to go to it or the reception either." The Douglases, she reported, were planning a party— "a perfect crush—so many invitations are out. We were invited to dine at Gwin's . . . [and] on Thursday we have another large dinner party."[4]

Sara Pryor, whose husband was elected in 1859, wrote:

> Everybody in Washington dined early. Congress usually adjourned at four o'clock, and my little boys were wont to be on the roof of our house, to watch the falling of the flag over the House of Representatives, the signal that we might soon have dinner. The evening meal was late, usually handed. It was considered not 'stylish' to serve it at a table. A servant would enter the drawing-room about eight o'clock, with a tray holding plates and little doilies. Another would bring in buttered biscuits and chipped beef or ham, and a third tray held cups of tea and coffee. Some delicate sweet would follow. Little tables of Chinese lacquer were placed between two or more ladies, and lucky was the man who would be invited to share one of them. Otherwise he must improvise a rest for his plate on his trembling knees. . . . There would be punch and sandwiches at eleven.[5]

Washington hostesses, Sara Pryor contended, always gave a "*good* supper" though not necessarily a "fine supper." It was a good supper if "the old family receipt [*sic*] book had been consulted, especially if our hostess had come from Kentucky, Maryland, or Virginia."[6] Evening parties, she noted, "were arranged that pleasant people might meet distinguished strangers," and there purposely were "no blatant bands to make conversation impossible."[7] However, if a ballroom was attached to a host's salon, "dancing was expected; but the parlors were distant and people could talk!"[8]

As might be expected, there was a great deal of snobbery. "So many different States, each of them a European kingdom in itself," said a *Times* reporter: "here the people are their own sovereigns."[9] Congressmen ranged in character from sophisticated city types and aristocratic planters to unschooled plebians and ill-mannered rednecks. Nowhere else, an anonymous citizen commented in 1857, is "less attention" paid to "mere money . . . and the millionaire, whose magnificent equipage attracts attention in the commercial cities, is surprised at the little influence he exercises here."[10] Laurence Oliphant went to dinner one evening with what he described, in typical English understatement, as a "singular household of people." His host, a senator, was a Methodist preacher who was a teetotaler. His hostess was a "spirit medium, and in constant communication with the nether, though she calls it the upper, world." Oliphant sat next to their daughter, "a Bloomer," who never wore "any other costume." The daughter's husband was "an avowed and rampant infidel, so that altogether it was a very odd if not instructive assemblage. I don't know how they all manage to get on together. For the preacher must look upon his son-in-law as a viper, and the son-in-law must look upon his mother as an impostor, and they must all look upon his wife as a fool—while she takes very good care to show the world that she wears the breeches."[11]

And though the Founding Fathers had abjured titles, "Every body [*sic*] in Washington," John Ellis observed, had one, even if

> it does not legally belong to him, he appropriates it, and that answers the same purpose. . . . "Senator," "Judge," "Secre-

tary," "Mr. Speaker," "Governor," "Marshal," "Admiral,"
"Commodore," "Doctor," "Bishop," "Professor," &c., &c. . . .
The women carry it to excess. In high life the Mrs. Judges,
Mrs. Secretaries, Mrs. Governors, Mrs. Senators are numerous. They are fully aware of the importance of their titles
and parade them upon all occasions. Indeed, they frequently
make more use of them than do the husbands to whom they
legitimately belong.[12]

Almost without exception, the leaders of Washington society were southern women, and none, the *Times* reporter said,
outshone Virginia Clay, "a charming woman" in whom "the
beauteous sentimentality of the South finds form."[13] She was,
her friend Sara Pryor wrote, "the wittiest and brightest of
them all . . . extremely clever, the soul of every company."[14]
Like many other congressional families, the Clays put up at a
hotel—Brown's, in their case—when in Washington for sessions of Congress. They were able to entertain in a spacious
salon that was part of their suite.[15] Other congressional families rented apartments in private homes, while many congressmen who had left wife and family at home took rooms in
boarding houses. Typically, landlords advertised their room-
ing houses as "superior accommodations for members of
Congress" and boasted "elegant parlors and chambers with
gas lights; also bath-room and closets attached."[16] One of the
more fashionable neighborhoods for boarding houses was
Carroll Row, east of the Capitol Building, a block of five
turn-of-the-century houses erected on the northeast corner
of First and A streets. Philip Barton Key's uncle by marriage, Chief Justice of the Supreme Court Roger B. Taney, a
widower, lived in the westernmost of the houses. That neighborhood might have witnessed even greater residential construction because L'Enfant positioned the front of the Capitol
to face east, but speculators early on bought up the surrounding land and held on to it for exorbitant prices. As a result,
most construction was driven to the west. F Street between
Ninth Street and the Treasury Building on Fifteenth Street—
an area known as the Ridge—was popular with year-round

residents, a "pleasant and beautiful village street" though "somewhat sleepy withal," the Rev. Joseph Kelly remembered.[17] Henry Clay and John Quincy Adams had lived along it. A favorite location was the area around Judiciary Square, where elegant rowhouses were erected. Hoping to take advantage of the cachet attached to Senatorial Row on nearby C Street, Stephen Douglas financed in 1857 the building of a row of three pressed-brick Greek Revival mansions in an otherwise vacant area five blocks north of the square.

The most elite residential area of all was Lafayette Square, just north of the White House. The square, once a straggly, unkempt, and uncultivated field, was now the garden spot of Washington. Although across from the president's home, and near the busy buildings housing the State Department as well as the departments of War, Navy, and the Treasury, the park was an oasis of peace and quiet. It teemed with plants and flowers and was surrounded by trees. The spacious square was nearly 420 feet in breadth, and slightly over 725 feet in length, covering in all a substantial seven acres. The streets that bound it were lined with townhouses built in the federal style. Reaching Lafayette Square one early summer morning, Mary Clemmer Ames wrote, "The long summer wave in the May grass; the low, swaying boughs, with their deep, mysterious murmur, that seems instinct with human pleading; the tender pliant of infant leaves; the music of birds; the depth of sky; the balm, the bloom, the virginity, the peace, the consciousness of life, new yet illimitable, are all here, just as perfectly as they are yonder in God's solitude, untouched of man."[18]

The area was very exclusive. Of all the sixty-four senators who served in the Thirty-fifth Congress, only one, John Slidell of Louisiana, lived on Lafayette Square. Originally born and raised in New York City, Slidell, who was a confidant of Buchanan's, had moved as a young man to New Orleans, where he established a wealthy law practice. Of all the 236 representatives who served in that same Congress, only two lived on the square. One was House Speaker James L. Orr of South Carolina; a well-to-do lawyer like Slidell, he was

The Sickles home on fashionable Lafayette Square. Teresa and Barton first made love on a sofa in the study. *Courtesy New-York Historical Society.*

a tenant of John Gadsby's widow in the Decatur House. The other representative, Orr's neighbor a few doors away, was Dan Sickles.

Dan could not have chosen a more prestigious address. The square's encircling streets contained the residences of many of the most important federal officials, military officers, and private citizens in Washington. "Almost within call," Mary Clemmer Ames said, "are men and women whose names suggest histories and prophecies, all the tangled phenomena of individual life."[19] Besides Slidell and Orr, Dan's neighbors on the square included the noted financier and art collector, W. W. Corcoran, and one of the city's most respected residents, venerable Benjamin Ogle Tayloe, who was a distant relation of Barton Key's. Tayloe, whose father had constructed the well-known Octagon House at New York Avenue and Eighteenth Street, was a collector of memorabilia; he possessed Washington's card table, drawing-room chairs once owned by Alexander Hamilton and a portable writing desk Hamilton carried with him during the Revolution, tables belonging to John Quincy Adams, the cane of Napoleon I, and the Sevres plates that Dolley Madison had purchased from the Empress Josephine and Marie Antoinette.[20] Others of Dan's neighbors were Capt. Charles Wilkes, a noted explorer of Antarctica, the Pacific, and the American Northwest, and Lafayette Maynard, a former Navy lieutenant who had distinguished himself by saving the passengers of an Atlantic steamer when it was wrecked on Fisher's Island in Long Island Sound. They all lived in houses that would figure in the coming months in what became known as "The Washington Tragedy."

In colonial times, the square's grounds were once part of a tract called "Jamaica," then in Charles County, Maryland. At the time the District of Columbia was formed, the land was owned by a farmer whose house stood in the northeast corner of the square. The family cemetery was nearby, while his apple orchard covered most of the rest of the site. L'Enfant had not envisioned making the area a separate square at all; instead, it was part of what was called President's Square, which also included the land on which the White House stood and the grounds south of it, later called the Ellipse. A crudely outlined track where local landowners raced their horses ran across its western edge, and a rundown-looking farmer's market occupied part of it until a group of local citizens took it upon themselves in 1801 to organize a more sanitary one on Pennsylvania Avenue, which became Centre Market.

The square took on a life of its own during the administration of Thomas Jefferson, when Pennsylvania Avenue was cut through it, effectively separating the site from the Executive Mansion. At the time, the streets on its east and west sides connecting the Avenue to H Street on its northern border were called 15 1/2 and 16 1/2 streets, respectively. The square by then was denuded of trees and almost totally neglected except for the musters of militia troops held on it. It did not get its familiar name until after the visit of the Marquis de Lafayette to the United States in 1824, though many residents and even guidebooks in the years before the Civil War still referred to it as being part of President's Square.[21]

Although they were wed a second time in a Catholic ceremony and Teresa never abandoned the faith, Dan and she planned to have their daughter Laura baptized by the Rev. Smith Pyne in St. John's (Episcopal) Church on the corner of H and Sixteenth streets, on the north side of the square. The church, designed by Benjamin Latrobe, was the first structure erected on the square and became known as the "Church of the Presidents" because every president since James Madison had either been a communicant or attended services there. Laura's baptism was scheduled for a Sunday in mid-March of 1858—Buchanan was to be the godfather, and John Slidell's wife Mathilde the godmother—but the child came down with a case of whooping cough and the ceremony was never held.[22]

A short distance away from the church, on the southwest corner of H and 16 1/2 streets—across from the northwest corner of the square—was the home, also designed by Latrobe, built for Stephen Decatur in 1819, where House Speaker James Orr lived. Sixteen-and-a-half Street was not yet open when Decatur built the house, but the city council appropriated $150 to gravel a carriageway forty feet wide between Pennsylvania Avenue and H Street. Decatur, a hero of both the War of 1812 and the Barbary War, lived only fourteen months in the house before his death in a duel in Bladensburgh. Subsequently, his widow let out the house to a succession of tenants that included the ministers of France, Great Britain, and Russia and three successive American secretaries of state. John Gadsby, who had operated a famous tavern in

Alexandria, Virginia, purchased the house in 1844 and, while living there with his family, auctioned slaves from a high-walled enclosure in back of the mansion. After his death, his widow rented out apartments on the second and third floors. Orr now occupied one of the apartments, and a friend of Dan's, retired grocer merchant John H. McBlair, the other.

The house Dan lived in, on the same side of the square and halfway down the block between Pennsylvania Avenue and H Street, was built soon after the Decatur House was completed. It was a rather plain, white-stuccoed structure with green shutters. The ground, or basement floor, contained a kitchen and an informal dining area. A high flight of curved stairs with an iron railing ran up to the simple entranceway and first floor. To one side off the front hallway and facing on the square was a small study or library connected by doors to a back parlor; on the other side of the hallway was a long, narrow parlor or drawing room-cum-dining room that ran the entire length of the house, some eighty or eighty-five feet.[23] A staircase led to the second floor, which contained a number of bedrooms. The dormered attic contained the servants' quarters. The house, a modest one compared to some of its neighbors, was erected in 1820 by Dr. Thomas Ewell, who occupied it for four years. After that, it was rented to a number of government officials and was known both as the Stockton Mansion, after Francis B. Stockton, whose wife was a niece of Decatur and who leased it in 1850, and the Levi Woodbury House, after the third of three successive secretaries of the navy who occupied it. Its address was variously given as 7 Lafayette Square, 7 President's Square and, after 15 1/2 and 16 1/2 Streets were renamed Madison Place and Jackson Place, respectively, as 14 Jackson Place.[24] Dan rented the house for $3,000 annually—his total salary as a congressman—and brought with him a nursemaid for Laura, a coachman, a footman, and, to judge by the entertaining he and Teresa did, he must have also had a cook and at least one housemaid, too. The family pet, an Italian greyhound named Dandy, also came along.

Because the trees around the square were not fully grown,

Dan and Teresa could easily see directly across the square the Washington Club where Dan and Barton were once members. The Clubhouse, as it was called, was in the middle of Madison Place. The building was a spacious, thirty-room, three-story red-brick structure built in 1831 by Commodore John Rodgers, who had, among other things, served during the Barbary War of 1805 and the War of 1812 and commanded the first ironclad vessel to cross the Pacific Ocean. Rodgers had acquired the lot on which he built his home from Henry Clay, who swapped the land with him for a prizewinning-breed jackass that Rodgers brought back from a cruise in the Mediterranean. Barton Key's uncle, Roger B. Taney, who was then secretary of the treasury under Andrew Jackson, rented the house for a time after Rodgers's death in 1838. Not long afterward, because it was so expensive to maintain, the building was turned into a boarding house that was especially popular with congressmen. The quarters were eventually taken over by the Washington Club—also known as the National Club—but in time the club folded. Even so, rooms were still available for boarders and the building housed a restaurant "much frequented," it was said, "by the fashionable young bloods of the town and their friends from abroad."[25]

Dan's neighbor Lafayette Maynard lived in the frame house to the south of the Clubhouse, on the corner of Pennsylvania Avenue and Madison Place. The house, diagonally across from the driveway to the White House, had also been built in 1831. Local residents delighted to tell an anecdote about its original owner, Dr. Thomas Gunnell, a dentist. One day, Dr. Gunnell received a summons from the White House saying that the president, Martin Van Buren, wished to see him. Believing that the president had suffered a toothache, the dentist grabbed his bag of implements and medicines and raced across the street. When he reached the White House, Van Buren, much to Dr. Gunnell's surprise, offered him the position of being Washington's postmaster, provided he made Gunnell's brother-in-law, who was a Maryland politician and Van Buren supporter, his chief clerk. The dentist accepted the appointment. His home, which had a renowned landscaped garden and a long, two-story gallery facing the square, was eventually purchased by Maynard and was known afterwards as either the Gunnell House or Maynard's House.

Benjamin Ogle Tayloe, who helped Maynard purchase the Gunnell House, lived in a three-story house on the other side of the Clubhouse. A carriage driveway separated it from the Clubhouse. Tayloe erected the structure in 1828 because his wife was "accustomed from her early life to the pleasures and excitements of society."[26] However he did not move into it after its completion because he found the administration of Andrew Jackson distasteful. He leased it instead for several years before finally taking up residence there.

Charles Wilkes lived up the street, on the southeast corner of Madison Place and H Street—across from the northeast corner of the square—in what became known as the Dolley Madison House. It had been built by her brother-in-law, Richard Cutts, and upon his death, came into her possession. She lived there for more than a decade after her husband's death in 1836, reigning as the queen of Washington society. It was considered part of New Year's Day etiquette for federal officials and the city's social leaders to call upon Mrs. Madison at home after they had first paid their respects to the president in the White House. Wilkes took up residence in the house with his family in 1851. During the Civil War, he created an international ruckus when, as captain of the Union vessel *San Jacinto,* he seized from a British ship two Confederate diplomats enroute to Europe, one of whom was his neighbor on Lafayette Square, John Slidell.

Slidell lived farther along H Street, halfway down the block between Sixteenth Street and Connecticut Avenue, west of St. John's Church, in what was called the Slidell House although the home had been built by W. W. Corcoran. The senator, the leader of secessionist forces in the Senate, moved into it in 1853. The house, whose particular attraction was its projecting center bay and fluted Ionic portico, had been built by Corcoran as a rental property. Corcoran himself lived next door, at the corner of H and Connecticut, in the grandest and most ornate of the homes on the square. A wealthy banker, Corcoran had purchased the structure from Massachusetts statesman Daniel Webster, who had received the house as a gift from admirers in Boston and New York but been forced to sell it because of his extravagant life-style. Corcoran hired New York architect James Renwick, Jr., to enlarge and renovate the structure. The result was a completely different building, a Renaissance-inspired mansion that introduced the Italianate style to Washington. Its rooms were filled with the art and sculpture that Corcoran, a world traveler, brought home with him. Because Corcoran was a southern sympathizer, the federal government might have confiscated his home during the war, but before fleeing to Europe he wisely rented it to the French minister in Washington, thereby gaining diplomatic immunity for it. Corcoran collected so much, and so many people wanted to see his acquisitions, that in 1858 he asked Renwick to design an art gallery a block away to house his collection.

Corcoran was credited with turning Lafayette Square into the tree-shaded and flower-filled park that it became in the late 1850s. At one time, a decade earlier, Congress debated using the land to erect five residences for the cabinet, but that idea was abandoned and instead the land was graded and the park was enclosed with a paling fence. In time, curvaceous walks of flagstone were laid out, trees planted, and shrubs and plants set out. Many of the plantings were purchased in different parts of the world through Corcoran's largesse and were set alongside American plants, the idea being that the American plants would shade and nourish the foreign ones. Unfortunately, except for a few trees, most of the foreign plantings died. One that did survive, a deciduous Spanish dwarf chestnut, was called the "wishing tree," under whose branches young single persons and newly married couples stood and made wishes. The wishing tree was just west of the equestrian statue of Andrew Jackson erected in the middle of the park in 1853. At the same time, Greek vases copied after one that

Corcoran had in his garden were placed in the park, and the old wooden fence was replaced with an iron one. The statue, made from brass melted down from guns captured by Jackson during the War of 1812, faced the Sickles's home on the west side of the square.

❂   ❂   ❂

Dan and Teresa, a contemporary said, "lived in elegant style." The president, who "was always very fond of Mr. Sickles and his wife," was a "frequent visitor at their house." Their dinners and parties "were irreproachable."[27] *Harper's Weekly Magazine* noted that "Mr. and Mrs. Sickles are universal favorites; nowhere is there a more refined or generous welcome."[28] Mrs. Congressman Sickles's receptions, commented the New York *Herald,* were "always attended by the most presentable people in town" and "there was always a brilliant party" at the couple's dinner parties.[29] The balls that she and her husband hosted "at intervals during the season," *Harper's* said, "were always crowded by the best people."[30]

Teresa thus became a vital part of Dan's politicized world. She supervised a household of at least three servants, personally shopped each morning at the Centre Market, purchased gourmet items for her dinner parties at Gautier's, paid house calls each day on the wives of influential lawmakers, hosted her own receptions each Tuesday—became, in other words, the typical spouse of an important and ambitious congressman, one who had, in Teresa's case, the ear of the president. But her world was circumscribed by the role of the woman in the mid-nineteenth century. A woman then had virtually no rights whatsoever. She could not, if married, own property in her own right, make contracts or otherwise conduct business on her own. She was supposed to be modest and submissive. The married woman, in fact, was for all intents and purposes the chattel of her husband. The followers of Amelia Bloomer—who advocated wearing pantaloons instead of hoop skirts for reasons of comfort and health—were considered anathema; bloomers were "only one of the many mani-

festations of that wild spirit of socialism and agrarian radical-
ism which is at present so rife in our land."[31] And married or
not, a woman could not vote. Her education centered on what
social reformer Margaret Fuller critically labeled at that time
"the domestic sphere." Teresa, like so many middle- and
upper-class young women then, was supposed to be "suffi-
ciently instructed and developed to understand the pursuits or
aims of her future husband; she is not to be a help-meet [sic] to
him in the way of companionship and counsel, except in the
care of his house and children. Her youth is to be passed
partly in learning to keep house and the use of the needle,
partly in the social circle, where her manners may be formed,
ornamental accomplishments perfected and displayed, and the
husband found who shall give her the domestic sphere for
which she is exclusively to be prepared."[32]

In what some historians believe was compensation for their
subordinate status, a number of northern women of Teresa's
economic and social ilk became involved in reform causes
such as the abolitionist movement. But Teresa never, to anyone's knowledge, expressed a political sentiment, took sides in
a debate or engaged in a thought-provoking conversation.

She did, however, have admirers.

SIX

First Encounters

Here "English Hunters" run their game to earth,
And strike the "Key" note of their jovial mirth . . .
Lo! little "Riding Hood" with artless grace,
Reveals the sweetness of her childish face;
And if the wolf's not driven from the door,
She knows precisely how to treat a bore;
And they who "pull the bobbin, lift the latch,"
Will find a hostess very hard to match! . . .

I T WAS A CURIOUS but not atypical situation. As the wife of a congressman—an up-and-coming one at that—it was politic of Teresa not only to hold a weekly reception and a dinner party but also to attend the various functions that dominated Washington's social life when Congress was in session. Dan wanted and expected her to do so. On the other hand, he, like so many other congressmen, was often too busy to go with her. So Teresa resorted to doing what the wives of so many other lawmakers did: she asked one of the many available bachelors in the city to accompany her to receptions and parties. He saw to it that Teresa arrived at a party without difficulty and returned home safely. It was a common practice to be escorted about town in such fashion, perfectly respectable, and at first no one paid any heed on whose arm she appeared. But in Teresa's case, the custom took on a foreboding overtone.

For one thing, Dan was often away from home, either at the Capitol or in New York or some other city on private business. When he was in Washington, he was gone most of the afternoon and often into the night. House sessions usually began at eleven o'clock in the morning, but Dan was rarely if ever in the chamber when debate opened. Dan worked in his study at home and ordinarily left for the Capitol between eleven o'clock and noon. He would usually return home between four and five in the afternoon.[1] But now, because of the debate over the Kansas controversy, the House frequently remained in session until late into the night. Moreover, because of his experience abroad, Dan had been named to the House Foreign Affairs Committee. Its work, House debates, and his own legal practice kept him away from home so much that it became unusual for him to be seen in company with his wife in public.

Their lives were moving in separate circles for another reason. Although they kept their personal affairs to themselves, Dan and Teresa were having marital problems. He did not respect her and "often" criticized her for her lack of "superior qualities."[2] Maybe it was because she was too young and immature for him. On the other hand, she was beginning to suspect that he was finding sexual solace in the arms of other women. Teresa had once insisted to her friend Florence that "thank heavens there is *very little* if any jealousy in my composition—and I do not think I could be very jealous of a person I had never seen or known."[3] But now she could not bring herself to question Dan about his "love affairs," though she longed to ask whether they were "love of heart," some physical attraction, "or an infatuation."[4]

Teresa had no shortage of escorts, and she seemed to enter into the custom of having a man accompany her to the various social functions in perfect innocence. Her friend Florence had worried that she would not be able to handle the attention or a compliment. "You need not fear dear F.," she responded. "I know just how much of it to believe."[5] It was a hollow boast. Teresa was young, naïve, inexperienced, so childlike that she was the perfect foil for an unscrupulous rake.

One ardent admirer was eighteen-year-old Henry Watterson, who was born in Washington and, as the son of a local newspaper editor, first gained entrée into political circles as a youngster. He was a childhood playmate of Franklin Pierce's son Benny, had been an unofficial page in the House of Representatives, and would be able to claim before his death in 1921 that he had met every president from Andrew Jackson to Warren G. Harding. Watterson, who was living with his mother in 1858 at Willard's Hotel, held an undemanding job as a clerk in the Interior Department and worked at the same time as an aspiring reporter for a local newspaper called the *Daily States*. He escorted Teresa to dinners during Dan's "frequent absences." Afflicted by weak eyes and delicate health, Watterson fell ill and missed going to a ball one night that spring, but Teresa—one of his "volunteer nurses"—helped him to get well. She was, in his eyes, he later recalled, "an innocent child. She never knew what she was doing."[6]

Watterson was one of her young admirers—younger than Teresa, in fact, and just as naïve. Other escorts were more than twice her age, and sophisticated. One of them was probably the most debonair man in the city: Dan's cosmopolitan friend from New York, Henry Wikoff. Wikoff, who was in his mid-forties, was a frequent traveler between America and Europe, a friend of Joseph Bonaparte, and had been decorated by the queen of Spain, hence his honorific, "Chevalier." Interestingly, one of the few books in Philip Barton Key's library that he seems to have purchased for himself was Wikoff's *My Courtship and Its Consequences,* based on Wikoff's romance with an American heiress living in London in 1851.[7] The day before they were to wed, the young woman changed her mind and ran off to Genoa, Italy. Wikoff followed her there and tried to abduct her. She appealed to the British consul, who had Wikoff arrested and thrown into jail, where he languished for fifteen months. Perhaps it was adventures such as Wikoff's that had prompted Barton to remark to a friend that he was for "French intrigue. A fig for common license! French intrigue and romance, with a good spice of danger in it!"[8]

Wikoff was an inveterate meddler and gossiper. "Ranging through all society," said John Forney, "he can talk of love, law, literature, and war; can describe the rulers and thinkers of his time, can gossip of courts and cabinets, of the *boudoir* and the *salon,* of commerce and the Church, of the peer and the pauper, of Dickens and Thackeray . . . of Buchanan and Pierce, of the North and the South, of the opera and the theatre, of . . . Sickles and Tammany Hall, and of the inner life of almost any capital in the world."

Wikoff was also a personable companion. "He has seen more of the world than most men," said Forney, "has mingled with society of every shade and grade, has tasted of poverty and affluence, talks several languages fluently, is skilled in etiquette, art, and literature, and, without proclaimed convictions, is a shrewd politician, who understands the motives and opinions of others."[9]

Wikoff often escorted Teresa to parties around Washington, but despite his worldly ways, his attentions never aroused any gossip. In fact, it was not the attentions of an escort that started a nasty rumor but someone she met while making her social rounds—Philip Barton Key. Teresa had first met him when she and Dan came to Washington to attend Buchanan's inauguration in 1857. She was introduced to him by her host, Jonah Hoover. Barton, who had a reputation as a lady's man, moved in the same social circle as Teresa did, and they must have encountered each other often. Their meetings were chance at first. They could not avoid running into and mingling together at receptions, dinners, and dances. Some flirtation evidently took place, because they soon began to see each other privately.

Barton's attentions to Teresa did not go unnoticed; indeed, they provoked intense jealousy. One escort of Teresa's was so smitten with her that he became obsessively envious of Barton and caused considerable mischief. He was a young clerk in the Interior Department named Samuel B. Beekman. Beekman, who was from New York, had gotten his job through Dan's influence. He worked with a man who had known his parents in Albany, Marshall J. Bacon, and became intimate with Bacon after meeting him and his wife at the Sickles home. In

March of 1858, Beekman was at Willard's Hotel one evening when Bacon ran into him and took him aside, "so that we could be unheard by the bystanders."[10] Bacon, Beekman said, broached the subject of Barton's "attentions" to Teresa, "making several very indelicate remarks about Mrs. Sickles." Beekman responded "quite guardedly," but "unluckily" he made "several trifling jokes about the female sex in general, and about her."

Ironically, the flurry of rumors that was sparked intimating that Teresa and Barton were lovers was premature. If Teresa is to be believed, she and Barton at this point were still simply friends who enjoyed each other's company. Still, gossip-mongers sensed something unusual about their relationship, and the result was almost as serious as if it had been true.

One evening not long after his conversation with Bacon, Beekman received a note from Dan asking that he stop by his home that night. When Beekman arrived, he was shown into the parlor, where Teresa's mother was seated. Mrs. Bagioli told Beekman why he had been summoned, and Dan himself then entered the room and elaborated on the reason. To what Beekman called his "great surprise," Dan said he had received "a written statement of specific calumnies against his wife and Mr. Key, circulated by me publicly." Although Dan did not identify whom the statement was from, it was written by another federal employee who owed his job to Dan, George B. Wooldridge. About thirty-five years old, Wooldridge was a tall, resolute man whose powerful build resulted from his use of crutches because he had lost the use of his legs in an accident. He was from the Magoff Valley in the Catskills and had been a clerk in Albany when Dan was a legislator. He now worked as a clerk in the map department of the House of Representatives and often visited the Sickles home to sort through Dan's mail for him, setting aside the letters that had to be answered. According to Wooldridge, Bacon informed him that Beekman claimed he had seen Teresa and Barton riding together on horseback three different times while Dan was away in New York. On one of those times, Teresa and Barton stopped at a "house on the road towards Bladensburg [*sic*], and that Mrs. Sickles had a room there and remained one hour and a half." Beekman reportedly told Bacon that Teresa "took off her habit, and that he had no doubt there was an intimacy between Mr. Key and Mrs. Sickles." Bacon insisted, Wooldridge said, that Barton had "boasted that he only asked thirty-six hours with any woman to make her do what he pleased."[11]

Beekman was taken aback. Only "by the liveliest imagination or the most ingenious perversion" could what he said be construed "into anything derogatory to Mrs. Sickles." Key's attentions, in fact, never awakened "any suspicions of any improper intimacy" in Beekman's mind until Bacon had brought up the matter. Beekman protested his innocence to Dan. Yes, he had "noticed a flirtation going on," but he "had uttered no charges, no facts, no inferences even, injurious to Mrs. Sickles, but merely generalities, without the slightest design or malice." What he was accused of saying was "so serious and enormous that no one but a lunatic could think of mentioning them, let alone giving them public circulation." Beekman left the Sickles home—never to enter it again—"excited and enraged beyond control" after telling Dan that he was "personally responsible" only for what he had said.

The charges implicating Teresa and Barton got back to Barton. On Tuesday, March 23, his good friend, Jonah Hoover, who also knew Beekman, appeared at the young clerk's doorstep with a note from Barton demanding to know if Beekman was responsible for "the vile calumnies" that Bacon attributed to him. Beekman immediately answered in the negative, saying that "they were pure fabrications, falsehoods." The result was a flurry of letters that Hoover gathered by going to each one of the men involved so that Barton could dispel the falsehood as quickly as possible. "It is the highest affront which can be offered to me," Barton declared, "and whoever asserts it must meet me on the field of honor, at the very point of the pistol."[12] Barton made copies of all the correspondence in his small, cramped, scratchy handwriting on his personal stationery, buff-colored paper bearing his initials and the Key family crest, the head of a dragon holding a key in its beak. All the letters bore the date March 26, 1858:

Geo. B. Wooldridge, Esq.:—
  SIR—Will you please state in writing what communication you made to the Hon. Daniel E. Sickles concerning me . . .
                                        Phil. Barton Key.

P. B. Key, Esq:
  DEAR SIR: Marshal J. Bacon informed me on Tuesday afternoon, March 23, that Mr. Beekman said . . .
                                        G. B. Wooldridge

Marshal J. Bacon, Esq.:
  SIR: Herewith I send you a copy of a note from G. B. Wooldridge, Esq., which you will be pleased to read and answer in writing, whether you made the statement as contained . . . and if you did make it, state upon what authority you made it. . . .
                                        Phil. Barton Key.

P. Barton Key, Esq.:
MY DEAR SIR: Your note has just been handed to me by Mr. Hoover . . . In reply, I have to state that, in the main, his statement is correct, though some points go beyond what I said . . . Mr. Beekman was my author. . . . I did not believe there was any truth in the statement, and went on in the conversation to give my reasons for such belief, and that I deemed it a fabrication. . . .
                                        M. J. Bacon

MR. BEEKMAN:—
SIR—I send herewith a copy of a note from G. B. Wooldridge, Esq., and also one from Marshall Bacon, which you will be pleased to read and answer in writing, whether you made the statement as contained . . .
                                        Phil. Barton Key.

SIR—I have received yours of to-day through Mr. Hoover, together with notes from . . . I disavow that I was ever their author, and pronounce everything therein as a lie, and also the statement of Mr. Bacon that I was their author. . . .

S. B. Beekman.

HON. D. E. SICKLES:—

MY DEAR SIR: I send by Jonah Hoover a copy of a correspondence had to-day, and you will perceive any effort to fix the ridiculous and disgusting slander on me of the parties concerned, was unsuccessful. Respectfully and truly yours,

Philip Barton Key.[13]

Not long afterwards, Beekman again met Bacon at Willard's Hotel. He was about to harangue him when Bacon promised to retract in writing that Beekman was the source of the rumors, but Bacon never did keep his word. Beekman was so embarrassed by the entire episode that he resigned from the Interior Department and returned to New York.[14]

Dan accepted Barton's denial of the charges, writing him that "so far as that affair was concerned he was perfectly satisfied." He said he "hoped their relations would continue as previously."[15] Dan told Hoover that he "had always liked Mr. Key." He said he "thought him a man of honor," and that the intimation of an affair between Barton and his wife "shocked him when he first heard of it." However, now that both Barton and Hoover had assured him that the charges were fallacious, he "was willing to meet" Barton "as formerly."[16]

Publicly, Dan appeared to be satisfied, but privately he made it clear to Teresa that Barton was no longer welcome in their home anymore unless invited and he was present, too—a stipulation that Teresa soon chose to ignore. Barton confided to Hoover that Teresa said she "wished their relations to be as friendly as heretofore; there was no qualification of the kind."[17]

The Sunday after the package of letters was delivered to Dan, Barton visited the home of Dan's friend, Congressman John Haskin, who lived on Third Street, not far from Barton's own home off Judiciary Square. With Barton was John J. McElhone, a reporter for the Congressional Globe, who knew both Dan and Teresa. Barton started to unburden his mind to

Haskin, though why he chose to do so with a reporter present is unclear. Barton was nearing his fortieth birthday; his four children ranged in age from three to eleven years old. He likened Teresa to them, saying that he regarded her—although she was about twenty-two years old—"as a young person who stood towards him in the relation of a child, and that he was almost in the situation denominated in law *in loco parentis.*" He spoke of "how childlike she was, and how innocent, and what paternal relations he occupied toward her; that she was a mere child," and, he insisted, "that he looked on her as a father." Barton asked Haskin to communicate his "declaration" to Dan in order to "prevent any possible suspicion" Dan might have regarding his motives.[18]

As requested, Haskin told Dan, who perhaps was becoming wary of Barton nonetheless. He was protesting too much. A few days later, Dan was called to New York on business. Before going, he stopped by Haskin's seat on the House floor with a request he had never made before. He asked Haskin to "drop up occasionally" to visit Teresa to "see if she wanted anything." The very next day, Haskin was on his way to Georgetown with his wife and children to buy shoes. As their carriage passed by the White House, Haskin remembered Dan's request. Haskin hastily turned his rig into Jackson Place, pulled up in front of the Sickles house, helped his wife out of the carriage, rushed up the stairs to the entrance and, without knocking, opened the front door, entered the house, turned at the door to the library and, again without knocking, opened it. On entering the room Haskin was startled to find Teresa sitting with Barton beside a round table. On it were two glasses, a half-empty bottle of champagne and a large bowl of salad. Teresa was mixing the salad with a wooden utensil. Haskin quickly excused himself for his "abrupt entrance." Blushing, Teresa rose and invited Haskin and his wife "to take a glass of wine with her." The Haskins rejected the offer and in a moment "hastened away." As his wife got back into their carriage, she commented that Teresa was "a bad woman." Mrs. Haskin never visited the house again.[19]

For some unknown reason, Haskin never informed Dan about the confrontation. Nor did he tell Dan that he later ran into Teresa and Barton while riding through the Congressional Cemetery. Or that he saw them together more than once at the theater and on Pennsylvania Avenue, too. Perhaps because he felt it necessary to act as a kind of chaperon, Haskin that spring joined Teresa and Barton on an excursion to the Great Falls of the Potomac to see the almost completed Washington aqueduct. McElhone, the *Congressional Globe* reporter, was with them.

Because of the incident involving Beekman, Teresa's mother convinced her to attend what was being heralded as the most gala event of the Washington social season that year, a masquerade ball being given by Senator William McKendree Gwin of California and his wife Mary. Mrs. Bagioli was afraid that Teresa would attract undue attention by not going; rumormongers were sure to speculate on the reason she failed to appear. Teresa had dropped her plans of attending the fete because Dan was ill. But her mother prevailed.

For once, Teresa went without an escort. Barton attended, too, alone. The ball was held on Thursday, April 8, at the Gwins's spacious home at the corner of Nineteenth and I streets, a few blocks from Lafayette Square. Gautier catered the affair, providing "a profusion of refreshments" and a "sumptuous supper at midnight." Guests made their appearance in every conceivable costume—as English knight and Italian peasant, gypsy woman and Greek goddess, Turkish sultan and Druid priestess. As the guests entered, an usher announced them "in their assumed characters," and, staying in character, the guests "engaged in humorous conversation."[20] Like many of the women, Mrs. Gwin had sent to New York for her gown, an exquisitely made skirt of white *moire antique* trimmed with flounces of *pointe d'aquille*, a bodice trimmed with lace and a train of cherry satin trimmed with a rouche of white satin. Her coiffure was even more elaborate, in keeping with her title, "A Lady of the Court of Louis Quatorze."[21] Standing by her side, making one of his rare visits to a private home, was the president.[22] Buchanan was not in costume, nor was the senator himself; Gwin, who believed it was undignified for a senator to don one, was wearing his "usual garb."[23]

Teresa was costumed as Little Red Riding Hood, as was a Mrs. Hughes, but it was Teresa who was eulogized in the widely reprinted poem that one of the guests afterwards wrote to commemorate the ball.[24] Barton—dressed in "white satin breeks [sic], cherry-velvet jacket, and jaunty cap, with lemon-coloured high-top boots"—was one of three men who went as English hunters, but he called particular attention to himself by blowing "from time to time" on a silver bugle that hung across his breast.[25] His sister Alice, who was married to Ohio Congressman George H. Pendleton, was dressed as the "Star-Spangled Banner"; a tri-color sash with the words E Pluribus Unum in silver letters hung from her left shoulder, and a golden eagle with wings outstretched covered the corsage on her white satin dress, while on her head she wore a crown of thirteen flashing stars.[26]

The dancing and other festivities continued until the sun rose, but Teresa and Barton slipped out together long before then. About two o'clock in the morning, Teresa asked the Sickles's coachman to take them to the National Hotel. She had him drive down a back street instead of Pennsylvania Avenue, perhaps because she didn't want to be seen with Barton. Once there, however, they sat in the carriage for a while before Barton finally got out and said good night.[27] Had they planned an assignation that night but changed their minds?

Gossipers now had much to talk about. Barton was no longer making any secret of his attraction to Teresa. Jonah Hoover found himself frequently bumping into him at Teresa's Tuesday morning receptions as well as during "spontaneous" visits Barton paid to the Sickles home when Dan was away.[28]

It was just a few weeks later, in April or May—Teresa could not remember the exact date—that Barton and Teresa made love for the first time.[29] They did so on a large red sofa that was next to the door in the study of her home[30]

SEVEN

"Disgrace" and "Disgust"

For know,—whate'er may be the general rule—
'Tis wisdom's part sometimes to play the fool;
And motley here you'll find "the only wear,"
With grave and gay, the homely and the fair. . .

IT IS ASTONISHING how indiscreet Barton and Teresa were. In the months that followed their first making love, they made only the most feeble attempts to keep their relationship private or within social bounds. Friends saw them together, strangers made note of the way they behaved to one another, and servants got so used to their dalliances that the saying in the Sickles kitchen when they saw Barton heading across Lafayette Square was "Here comes Disgrace to see Disgust."[1] Everybody in Washington seemed to know of the illicit affair but Dan.

Their meetings assumed a routine. Barton would show up at one of the receptions that Teresa attended—at the home of the Gwins or the Slidells, for instance. He would join Teresa in her carriage, always making a pretense of social formality by saluting her with a "good morning, Madam," instead of addressing her by name. The two would ride together to other receptions, or sometimes ask the Sickles coachman to drive through back streets. Barton did make some feeble attempts at discretion. He never got into the carriage in front of the Sickleses's home, and he always got out of it before they returned to the house, alighting either at the corner or at the Clubhouse. Barton was also circumspect about entering the

Sickleses's home. He never went into it when Dan was at home, and on reception days he always rang the bell as any other guest would. But when Dan did leave the house, Barton would show up an hour later and slip in without knocking. But his attempts to be prudent, such as they were, were decidedly unsuccessful. John Thompson, the coachman, was one of the many who observed all of Barton's peregrinations. In fact, he witnessed so many of their meetings that he "could hardly mention a day" that Barton did not see Teresa.

Teresa and Barton often met away from the Sickles house between one and three o'clock in the afternoon, when Dan was at the Capitol. She would hand Thompson a list of the houses she wanted to visit. By seeming coincidence, Barton would invariably be at one of them and would promptly join them in the carriage. One of their favorite trysting places was the Congressional Cemetery on the eastern end of the city. Teresa usually rode alone to the rendezvous in her carriage. Barton would soon appear, astride his horse Lucifer, or he would be waiting for her. At the cemetery Teresa and Barton always walked down the grounds, past the rows of cenotaphs of dead congressmen and out of the sight of her coachman, staying away an hour or more. When they returned, Barton would either ride alongside the carriage on Lucifer or he would tie Lucifer to the carriage and get in with Teresa. "Every time Mrs. S. rode out Mr. Key met her," John Thompson could say. "Never a week passed without my seeing him." In fact, when he thought about it, the coachman realized that he saw Barton "pretty much every day."

When Dan was away, Barton got bolder and visited Teresa at her home. The observant Thompson figured out that every time he drove Dan to the railroad depot, "Mr. Key always came to the house afterwards." Barton always came at dusk, and remained shut in the study with Teresa at least until Thompson went to bed, which was usually ten or eleven o'clock. There was one night, though, when Dan was either in Baltimore or Philadelphia, that the coachman would always remember. It was one in the morning and he was still awake.

He was on his way up the hall staircase to his room when he met and stopped to talk with Bridget Duffy, Laura's nurse-maid, who also doubled as Teresa's lady's maid. They were chatting "as one servant talks to another" when suddenly a noise that sounded like the front-doorbell rang out. The study door opened and Barton and Teresa came out of the room and looked outside, but no one was there. They then retreated back into the study. Thompson, who stayed in the hallway with Bridget, heard clicks as Barton and Teresa locked both the study door and the door that led from the study to the back parlor. Thompson then heard them "making this noise on the sofa for about two or three minutes." Commenting to Bridget about it, Thompson said something off-color to her that so embarrassed the young maid that she ran upstairs. Realizing that what he said "was not language suitable for her to hear," Thompson himself ascended the staircase to go to bed. "I knew they 'was'nt' [sic] at no good work."[2]

That June, a friend of Barton's, Albert A. Megaffey, a prosperous Washington contractor, took it upon himself to speak to him. Approaching the subject in gingerly terms, Megaffey said he had "noticed certain conduct" that led him "to suggest" that Barton "was observed to be over attentive" to Teresa. Barton immediately rejoindered with his ready explanation: he had "a great friendship" for Teresa, "considered her a child, and had paternal feelings towards her." Moreover, Barton said he "repelled indignantly the idea of having any but kind and fatherly feelings towards her."[3] Their conversation ended there, but Megaffey later had more cause to bring up the subject again.

◎   ◎   ◎

The first session of the Thirty-fifth Congress ended on June 14, 1858. On July 1, the Sickleses closed their Lafayette Square residence and returned to Bloomingdale. Dan was running for reelection and planned to spend the summer campaigning before the November election. Barton, still in good graces with Dan, visited New York twice that summer, enroute to a vacation of several weeks in Saratoga Springs, and then afterwards on his return. He was in New York on September 1 when a parade and celebration were held commemorating the completion of the Atlantic Cable connecting America and England; they were all at the Metropolitan Hotel, at Broadway and Prince, watching the parade from its "sky parlors"[4]—Barton, Dan, Teresa, Dan's mother and father, John Haskin.[5]

Maybe it was seeing Teresa in Dan's company that prompted Barton to engage in what was for him a sardonic conversation. He met a fellow lawyer one night after dinner, and somehow or other they got around to discussing the constancy of women. Barton defended "with great warmth the opinion that women were naturally inconstant and could always be induced to transfer their affections to the last man who would address them with the requisite flatteries and appliances." To make his point, Barton afterward sent his friend a translation of a Spanish poem he had read:

> One eve of beauty, when the sun
>   Was on the stream of Guadalquiver,
> To gold coaverting, one by one,
>   The ripples of that mighty river.
>
> Beside me on the bank was seated
>   A Seville girl with auburn hair,
> And eyes that might the world have cheated—
>   A Bright, wild, wicked, diamond pair.
>
> She stooped and wrote upon the sand,
>   Just as the loving sun was going,
> With such a small, white shining hand,
>   You would have sworn 'twas silver flowing.
>
> Her words were three, and not one more;
>   What could Diana's motto be?
> The syren wrote upon the shore:
>   'Death—not Inconstancy.'

> St. Francis might have been deceived,
>   With such an eye and such a head;
> Yet one week more and I believed
>   As much the woman as the sand.

Barton told his friend that he "pleasantly" hoped "that he might never practically realize the soundness of his own opinions."[6]

EIGHT

The Anonymous Letters

Our catalogue's not expected to be right,
But 'tis the best that we can now indite [sic].
It may be meagre, and not understood;
But think, at least, that the intent is good . . .

B ARTON FINALLY REALIZED that he ought to find a more private place for him and Teresa to meet. After months of
sham chance encounters and clandestine get-togethers, Barton
started looking in the fall of 1858 for a place to formalize their
assignations. It had also finally dawned on Teresa that con-
tinuing to meet in the Sickles home on Lafayette Square could
attract attention. Belatedly, she was realizing that "there are
servants who might suspect something."[1] Obviously, a hotel
or boarding house was out of the question; Barton was too
well known a figure in Washington. The only recourse, it appeared, was to rent a house. Barton undertook the task while
Teresa and Dan were still in Bloomingdale.

One day that October, Barton spied a vacant brick house at
383 Fifteenth Street. It was on the west side of and in about
the middle of the block between K and L streets, a poor,
mixed neighborhood of blacks and whites. It was just three
blocks north of Lafayette Square—a convenient location
within ten minutes' walking distance of Teresa's home. The
house was a narrow, nondescript, L-shaped two-story structure with shuttered windows. Its front entrance was directly
off the sidewalk. The house's backyard and kitchen entrance
could be approached from an alleyway off Fifteenth Street that

85

The house at 383 Fifteenth Street that Barton rented for his rendezvous with Teresa. Though he had chosen it for privacy, neighbors were soon gossiping about the strange comings and goings at the rundown building and the signal that accompanied them, a white string fluttering from an upstairs shutter. *Courtesy New-York Historical Society.*

ran along the side of the house, or from the rear by crossing through the back lots of houses along K Street; either way, however, was difficult to navigate because, as neighbors found, "walking was very bad, miry and muddy" and "carts could hardly get in."[2] A wood fence surrounded the lot on which the house stood. Besides the kitchen, there were two rooms on the first floor furnished plainly with a carpet, some chairs, tables and a bookcase. On the second floor were two adjoining bedrooms with a door between them; each contained bedsteads and a bare minimum of other furniture.[3]

Nancy Brown, who lived two doors up the street and whose husband Thomas was the president's gardener, was standing by the gate of her home when Barton rode by on

Lucifer. He stopped to ask her whether she knew who owned the house at No. 383. She told him the owner was John Gray, a black man who lived somewhere on Capitol Hill—"the colored people could give him all the information."[4] With that, Barton left.

He returned about three weeks later, knocking at Mrs. Brown's door. Barton had tied Lucifer to a tree in front of her home—in violation of a municipal code to protect trees in the city—and she admonished him for doing so. She had no idea at the time who he was. Barton informed Mrs. Brown that he was renting the house at No. 383 for a friend of his, a "Member or Senator"—she didn't catch which—and then he went away. In the intervening weeks before she saw Barton again, the owner, John Gray, who was receiving $50 a month for renting the house to Barton, delivered a load of wood to No. 383 and piled it in the back yard.[5] Many weeks later, Nancy Brown saw Barton again. She watched as he carried some of the wood inside the house. She soon saw smoke coming from the chimney, and then noticed that he had tied a white string or ribbon to the outside of one of the upstairs shutters "so that when the wind blowed it would swing." Next, she saw a young woman whom she took to be "a servant girl" get out of a carriage and enter the house by the back way. It dawned on Mrs. Brown that every time she saw the white string she soon afterward saw the same young woman enter the house: "I knew it was the signal, of course."

⊙   ⊙   ⊙

Dan was reelected that November to the Thirty-sixth Congress, but his margin of victory was small because of a bitter power split within Tammany. A month later, on December 6, the second, lame-duck session of the Thirty-fifth Congress began, but Dan took his time about returning to Washington. The Sickleses arrived there on December 29, after stopping off for the night at Philadelphia on their way from New York.[6] Dan waited until after the first of the year, when the House reconvened after its annual Christmas–New Year's recess, to enter into its deliberations; his first vote was cast during a fateful last week in February. He apparently was, as usual, traveling a lot.

Teresa learned about the house Barton had rented after the first of the new year. She started going there in the latter part of the month, and it soon became part of her regular routine, as did her almost daily meetings with Barton. He would appear in Lafayette Square, sometimes by the Clubhouse directly across the park with an opera glass in his hand, and sometimes just across the street from the Sickles house. He would wave a white handkerchief, then—if he was by the Clubhouse across the square—look through the opera glass at an upper window of the house, waiting for a response. He sometimes tried to mask his signals, either by pretending he was just nervously fiddling with his handkerchief, or by seeming to play with a passerby's dog. But no matter what he did, the few precautions he took were in vain. He only attracted more attention to himself. One of the first to notice Barton's signaling was a plasterer named John Cuyler, who worked on Seventeenth Street. He walked home for lunch every day through the square. Cuyler, who recognized who Barton was, "often" saw him "loitering back and forth in the square" and "waving his handkerchief."[7]

In fact, if Teresa and Barton thought that their new hiding place provided either privacy or anonymity, they were terribly mistaken. Their attempts at subterfuge were, in fact, so inept that it wasn't long before everyone in the neighborhood knew exactly what was going on. And the unwelcome attention the two lovers prompted proved to be far more dangerous than their earlier trysts.

Moreover, for some unfathomable reason, Teresa took little care to avoid people who might be able to identify her. Nancy Brown got a close-up look at Teresa's face one day while standing at her front door. Teresa was wearing a black bonnet but no veil. As she walked down Fifteenth Street, she passed by Mrs. Brown and they looked at each other straight in the face. Mrs. Brown soon discovered who the mysterious young woman was. Neighbors who had also begun noticing the strange comings and goings identified the woman for her as Mrs. Sickles.

On another day, Mrs. Brown saw Barton and Teresa leave the house together but abruptly retreat the other way when they spotted two policemen standing on the corner, talking with a group of men. Mrs. Brown, who was standing by her gate on Fifteenth Street when Barton and Teresa hurried by, was impressed that "they were so scart [sic], they run away." Meanwhile, a man in the group made "a remark" that prompted one of the police officers, James Ginnaty, to turn in the direction of Barton and Teresa. Ginnaty knew Barton by name, but not "the lady." He thought they were acting oddly. Ginnaty followed the couple as they walked down L Street to Sixteenth Street, then back to K Street and into Fifteenth Street again, circling the block. Barton, who "looked behind," must have spotted him. He and Teresa turned onto L Street and ducked into a little store on the corner. Barton "peeped out, and drew in again." When he finally came out of the store with Teresa, Ginnaty approached them and started idly conversing with Barton, as Teresa stood by his side. A crowd formed around them, and people "both white and black" stood at the doors or by the windows of several houses watching the three of them. One neighbor watching from her window thought Teresa "looked like a person badly frightened." Ginnaty was struck by the fact that Barton had a small brass key that he kept "twisting in his fingers."[8]

The rear windows of John M. Seeley's home on L Street looked out on the backyard of Barton's rented house. He saw Barton and "a lady" going into the house "frequently." Barton usually wore "a steel-mixed gray sack, and on other occasions a plum colored coat." Seeley recognized Barton, but not Teresa. However, a short time later he did get a good look at her face. One day he was leisurely walking up Fifteenth Street behind them when Barton and Teresa stopped at the door of No. 383 and started to enter the house. As Seeley strolled by,

Teresa, who was wearing a veil this time, drew it up, turned and looked at Seeley. An hour and a half later, Seeley saw Teresa leave the house, followed, five minutes later, by Barton, she going in one direction, he in another.

In the next few weeks, Seeley saw Teresa "three or four times" in all and she made "no effort" at all to conceal her features. Both his wife Sarah Ann and his sixteen-year-old daughter Matilda saw her as well, noticing her clothes and her demeanor. Sarah Ann could describe in exact detail how Teresa was dressed.[9]

On February 8, Dan hired a new coachman, John Cooney, and the very next day Cooney was "on the box," driving Teresa, when suddenly she rang the coach bell. Cooney immediately reined in and Barton hopped into the carriage. Like John Thompson, the coachman he replaced, Cooney found that "pretty much every day," when he drove Teresa from the Sickles home sometime after 1:00 P.M., they would meet Barton. Barton's routine never varied. He did not get into the carriage within sight of the Sickles home, and he always got out before they returned home. Most of the time, Cooney drove Teresa to a greenhouse operated by Henry Douglas on Fifteenth Street opposite the Treasury Department, or to Taylor & Maury's Bookstore on Pennsylvania Avenue, where they would find Barton. But once in a while Cooney drove "in some of the back streets" to meet him.[10]

◎   ◎   ◎

Dan was so busy with his own extracurricular activities, he apparently did not have the time or the inclination to notice what was going on. But for all his faults, he was certainly more sophisticated than Barton when it came to the art of discretion. For one thing, he did not frequent any local brothels or places of amusement. He was "never seen in any of those questionable places of resort with which Washington abounds, and by his deportment generally [showed] that he had thrown off the vices of his early manhood," a magazine

writer could accurately report.[11] But, of course, that was because Dan went out of town on his escapades.

One day in early January, Dan walked up to the front desk
of Barnum's City Hotel, at the corner of Calvert and Fayette
Streets in Baltimore, signed the register and went up to his
room. A little later, a woman entered the hotel, signed the
register as "Mrs. Sickles" and was directed to the same room.
But it was not Teresa, and it was not the only time Dan and a
"Mrs. Sickles" spent the night there.[12]

In Baltimore again on Sunday, January 16, Dan left the hotel and went to the railroad station, where he met a woman
arriving from Philadelphia. The two returned to the hotel.
The woman stayed overnight in his room, where they "had
adulterous intercourse."[13]

           ◉   ◉   ◉

Meanwhile, on the surface, Barton and Dan's relationship
appeared normal. On Thursday, February 10, Barton's sister
Alice and her husband, Congressman George Pendleton,
joined Dan and Teresa for one of their customary evening dinner parties, and, because they resided at Barton's home on C
Street, Teresa took the occasion to invite him, too. One of the
other dinner guests, William Badger, the agent for the Philadelphia Navy Yard, thought the relations between Dan and
Barton were, as far as he could see, "of the most intimate
character." Badger and his daughter were staying at Brown's
Hotel and the next night they invited the three of them—Dan,
Teresa and Barton— to a hop in the ballroom there.[14] Badger's
daughter and Dan's friend "Manny" Hart later accompanied
Dan and Teresa to hear the Italian coloratura Maria Piccolomini give an opera recital. At the theater they ran into Barton,
who was alone, and the Haskins. John Haskin, who had never
mentioned to Dan anything about the champagne-and-salad
incident the previous April, noticed that a friendly "recognition" passed between Dan and Barton as "they bid each other
the time of day."[15]

◉   ◉   ◉

The wave of the hankie, the secret rendezvous, the carriage rides, the white string hanging from a window shutter, the clandestine trysts—the pattern grew more frequent as time passed. Dan went to New York for three days in mid-February.[16] The first day he was away, Monday, February 14, an acquaintance of Barton's, Charles G. Bacon, took ill at his office and was walking home in mid-morning when he spotted Barton opposite the Sickles house, waving his handkerchief "two or three times." In the next few days, Bacon saw Barton again, "on the President's side of the avenue near the west gate, waving his handkerchief." Bacon figured out that someone at the library window of the Sickles house could readily see him. "He seemed to clasp his handkerchief, let if fall, clasp it again, and catch it before it could fall any distance."[17]

On Wednesday, February 16, while Dan was still away, teenager Matilda Seeley was looking out a second-floor rear window at the house on Fifteenth Street when she suddenly called her mother's attention to Teresa and Barton. It was the first time Mrs. Seeley saw the two of them together, and on that day she saw them three times in all—at about eleven o'clock in the morning, between three and four in the afternoon, and at dusk. "She always wore a splendid shawl," she recalled. "Black velvet, silk fringe, with bugle trimmings. It was a large shawl. It came down low on her person."[18]

By this time, their affair was causing so much talk that Albert Megaffey decided to talk to Barton again about its consequences. Megaffey repeated what he had said the previous summer—that Barton was being "over attentive." Megaffey "suggested" that Barton "might get into danger or difficulty over the matter." But Barton dismissed his concern. He was no stranger to the idea of violence. An older brother of his, Midshipman Daniel Key, was killed shortly after his twentieth birthday in a duel with another midshipman in 1836.[19] "I am prepared for any emergency," Barton told Megaffey, suggestively patting the left breast of his coat as though he kept a weapon inside it.[20] If anything, Megaffey's warning only served to make Barton bolder and even less discreet.

◎   ◎   ◎

Dan returned to Washington on Thursday, February 17, in time for the farewell ball being accorded Lord and Lady Napier before their return to England. It was the most impressive such event ever held in Washington; some eighteen hundred guests crowded into Willard's Hotel, including Buchanan and members of the cabinet, though the president did not stay for supper because of a "violent" head cold. He caught it, one newspaper jocularly diagnosed, three days earlier, when "Democrat Romeos came wooing him, to share their joy over the admission of Oregon" as the nation's thirty-third state.[21]

Dan and Teresa were at the ball. Virginia Clay saw her dancing with the handsome, courtly son of James Gordon Bennett.[22] The evening may have exhausted her, or perhaps Dan decided to work at home, because the next day, Saturday, Barton was in Lafayette Square between noon and one o'clock, trying to catch her attention without any apparent success. John Cuyler, the plasterer, was entering the square when he saw Barton walk in from the center gate and sit down on an iron bench in front of the Jackson statue. Barton rested his head on his left hand, then took out a pocket handkerchief and waved. Fascinated, Cuyler hid behind the statue, watching. When nothing further happened, Cuyler went home for his lunch. When he returned to work through the square about an hour later, Barton was gone.[23]

That night, Dan and Teresa attended a "brilliant reception" at the White House, Dan "dressed faultlessly and with a beauty upon his arm," according to one of the participants.[24]

◎   ◎   ◎

The next day, Sunday, February 20, Barton and Teresa exchanged signals in the middle of the morning in broad view of everyone in the square. Dan must have been away from home at the time, because the incident was so overt. Barton had walked "very rapidly" past Southey S. Parker on Pennsylvania Avenue. When Barton reached Nairn's drug store at Fifteenth Street, he turned toward Lafayette Square. Parker happened to be going the same way and saw him the enter the square. Barton was standing at its southwest gate, hat in hand, waving his handkerchief toward the Sickles house with his other hand. Teresa came out the front door with her daughter Laura and stood by the railing at the top of the stairs. With one hand she held onto Laura's shoulder—"apparently," to Parker, "trying to keep her from falling over the steps"—and with the other she waved back to Barton. Barton put his hat on his head, "bowed to Mrs. Sickles," and twice waved his handkerchief again.[25]

Later, at about one o'clock that afternoon, John Seeley saw Barton enter the house on Fifteenth Street. Seeley immediately went up to a third-floor back room in his home and peered out the window. Obviously, he was fascinated by the comings and goings of the secretive couple. Sure enough, "the same lady" as usual walked through the alley to the rear entrance of the house across the way. Barton came to the back door and joined her at the gate and they went into the house together. Teresa stayed about an hour or so, then came out alone and returned by the alley to L Street. It was "the only Sabbath" that Seeley ever saw them together.[26]

◎   ◎   ◎

On Monday, February 21—when Dan was at the Capitol, taking part in the vote on an appropriations measure—Barton was back at the square, signalling as usual. This time he was seen by the coachman who worked for Colonel William Freeman, a former member of General Winfield Scott's staff who lived on H Street, on the north side of Lafayette Square. It was a brisk but pleasant day[27] and the coachman, a man whose Christian name was, oddly, Major—Major Hopkins was his full name—was on the box of Freeman's carriage with the

colonel's footman.[28] They were waiting for the colonel to appear, when Barton walked past them "five or six times," each
time waving his handkerchief. Finally, Teresa came out of her
house and joined Barton at the corner of H Street and Madison Place, by the house where Dolley Madison used to live.
She was wearing a black dress and dark cloak bordered with
red and white, but her veil was "up," so Hopkins "distinctly
recognized her"—"she is not very large nor very small, but of
middle height, light hair, a little stout." Hopkins watched as
Teresa and Barton walked up Fifteenth Street. A little later,
after dropping off the colonel at a friend's home nearby, Hopkins again spotted them together but lost sight of them "on
the steps of John Gray's house."[29]

That day, during their tryst, Barton and Teresa agreed to
meet again on Wednesday at the house on Fifteenth Street. In
the meantime, they saw each other on Tuesday, February 22,
at Teresa's regular morning reception, which was crowded
with more than a hundred guests. A reporter for *The New-
York Times* who attended it saw Barton there, "his horse waiting for him at the door." The rooms in the Sickles home, he
remembered, "were filled with a pleasant company; the soft
Spring sunlight poured in at the open windows; and Mrs.
Sickles herself in all her almost girlish beauty . . . seemed the
very incarnation of Spring and youth, and the beautiful promise of life."[30] Daniel Dougherty, a Philadelphia lawyer and politician who was a good friend of both Dan and Buchanan, was
at the reception with his wife, as was the wife of Jonah Hoover. So, too, was Virginia Clay, who guessed that half the
guests were men. "The girl hostess," as she called Teresa,
"was even more lovely than usual." Teresa, she noted, "was
dressed in a painted muslin gown, filmy and graceful, on
which the outlines of the crocus might be traced. A broad sash
of brocaded ribbon girdled her slender waist, and in her dark
hair were yellow crocus blooms." It was the last time Virginia
Clay ever saw Teresa and she never forgot the impression
"Mrs. Sickles" made on her: "the picture of which she formed
the centre was so fair and innocent, it fixed itself permanently

upon my mind." And she could not believe the gossip she was hearing about Teresa: "She was so young and fair, at most not more than twenty-two years of age, and so naïve, that none of the party of which I was one was willing to harbour a belief in the rumours which were then in circulation."[31]

This time, of course, the rumors were true. What was remarkable and unusual was not only that Teresa and Barton flouted the rigid restrictions of an America in the midst of the prim, proper, inhibited Victorian era but also that they did so with so little effort to be prudent or cautious. Teresa and Barton could not seem to be apart for one day; in fact, they were soon meeting as often as three times a day. Their sense of propriety, their flirtation with danger, their astounding record of being observed, watched, and followed only seemed to make them more reckless. What drove them to such extremes? Infatuation? Sexual obsession? Love? Had Teresa given up on her marriage? Was she revenging Dan's extramarital affairs? Or was Barton, the notorious womanizer that he was, the seducer of a naïve young woman whom he now had under his control?

Whatever propelled them, the affair was about to come to a shattering conclusion.

◎   ◎   ◎

Teresa and Barton made love at the house on Fifteenth Street on Wednesday, February 23, the day after her regular Tuesday morning reception. They were not only observed that day, both alone and together, by a number of people as usual but also, incredibly, Barton took Laura in hand and dropped her off at the Hoovers' home before his rendezvous with Teresa. Barton appeared in the square that morning somewhere between ten and eleven o'clock. Standing close by the Jackson statue in the middle of the park, he took out his handkerchief and "twirled" it two or three times.[32] Shortly afterward, Barton escorted Teresa and Laura down Pennsylvania Avenue, and sometime between eleven o'clock and noon, he rang the bell at the Hoovers' home on G Street, between

Fourteenth and Fifteenth streets. He had Laura with him, and asked Hoover if he could leave the child with Hoover and his wife for several hours.[33] He then caught up with Teresa at a reception that the wife of Senator Stephen Douglas was giving at her home on I Street, several blocks west of Lafayette Square. Later, Nancy Brown saw Barton unlocking the door to No. 383. He was carrying a shawl with a gray and red border on his left arm.[34] Teresa's arrival was noticed by the Seeleys, who spotted her coming through the back alleyway. Mrs. Seeley took particular notice of how she was dressed: "in black silk; the square in the silk was dark brown with narrow stripes somewhat darker." Teresa also had "a large velvet shawl, with twisted silk fringe and bugles, black bonnet and feathers, and a short black lace veil."[35]

While Barton and Teresa were inside the house, making love, an ominous incident occurred. A man closely muffled in a shawl came down the street and asked a black woman who was passing by whether the house at No. 383 was occupied. "Yes, sir," she answered, to which he responded, "Very well, that's all I want." The man loitered in the neighborhood until he saw Barton leaving the house. He went up to him, spoke a few words, then hurried away. Apparently, it was the man who handed Barton a letter that he received that day.[36] The letter was in cipher. The code was simple, one letter substituting for another, but it undoubtedly took time to decipher, and Barton apparently did not have the opportunity to deal with it. Between two and three o'clock he returned to the Hoovers to pick up Laura[37] and about an hour later, when he was with Teresa again in the square and might have had the chance to speak to her, a young woman and a man had joined them. The woman was an eighteen-year-old girl whom the Sickleses had befriended—Octavia M. Ridgeley. Octavia, whose father had been killed in the Mexican War, was a frequent guest at receptions and dinner parties in the Sickles home, and she often stayed overnight, though her mother lived only a block away.[38] Dan apparently encouraged her keeping Teresa company, especially when he was away, but Teresa never shared any confidences with Octavia, who had no inkling of the liaison between Teresa and Barton.

That Wednesday evening, Barton missed another chance to talk to Teresa about the letter. The House had adjourned at 4:07 in the afternoon, but Dan must have had pressing business to take care of because that night he left Teresa in the company of both Barton and Henry Wikoff, who escorted her to the theater.[39] If Barton had decoded the letter by that time, he undoubtedly had no quiet moment alone with Teresa to discuss its contents.

⊚   ⊚   ⊚

Dan left his home early and was back at the Capitol the next day, February 24. Taking advantage of his early departure from home that morning, Barton and Teresa met and together with Laura went to the Centre Market, where they stopped at the butcher stall operated by George W. Emerson. Emerson noted the time—between eight and nine o'clock— "an unusual hour for her," because Teresa ordinarily came by between ten and eleven in the morning. Moreover, she treated Barton familiarly. Teresa gave Emerson her order—she was hosting her regular Thursday evening dinner that night— asked how much it cost, and then handed her "portemonnaie" to Barton, saying, "Pay Mr. Emerson."[40]

Later, after Teresa visited a cabinetmaker's shop on Pennsylvania Avenue, Barton showed the letter to Teresa and started reading it to her. Their behavior must have seemed peculiar because it attracted the attention of two men standing together across the street. One was Frederick Wilson, a wood-and-charcoal dealer who had witnessed Barton waving his handkerchief in Lafayette Square "nearly every day" for the last nearly two weeks.[41] The other was his friend, William Rapley, a blacksmith. From what Rapley could see, the letter appeared to be on ordinary stationery, but he couldn't make out how many sheets it encompassed.[42] Wilson was more curious. He had by now seen Barton near the Sickles home such "a great number of times" that "it appeared to be quite a regular business." Wilson purposely crossed the street to get a closer look at the letter. He followed Teresa and Barton as they walked up the Avenue from Eighteenth Street to Twentieth Street. When they switched from the north side of the Avenue to the south side, he did, too. All Wilson could make out was that the envelope was yellow.[43] As it turned out, the contents of the letter never became known, though it apparently concerned the illicit relationship between the two lovers.

Whatever the letter said did not deter the two lovers. That afternoon, Teresa went to a number of receptions, driven by the Sickles coachman, John Cooney, with the family's groom, a young Irishman named John McDonald, acting as footman. With her was Octavia Ridgeley. First they visited Catherine Thompson, wife of Secretary of the Interior Jacob Thompson; then they went on to the home of Cynthia Brown, wife of Postmaster General Aaron V. Brown. At each residence, Barton showed up alone fifteen minutes later, a pitifully inadequate ploy intended to dispel any talk about them. Finally, though, he joined them in the carriage when they rode to the home of Rose O'Neal Greenhow on Sixteenth Street. Mrs. Greenhow, a one-time ardent supporter of Buchanan, was the aunt of Stephen Douglas's wife Adele and had split with the president over the Kansas controversy and because of Harriet Lane's apparent dislike of Douglas[44]; later, during the Civil War, she became a spy for the South, was credited with the Confederate success at the First Battle of Bull Run, was arrested, was released, and subsequently drowned returning from a Confederate mission to France and England. The three of them—Teresa, Octavia and Barton—stayed at Mrs. Greenhow's home for about an hour and a half, until 4:15 P.M. Cooney, the coachman, was accustomed to Barton's presence and he paid little attention to what transpired between Teresa and him, but it was the first time that McDonald, the footman, saw the two together and he was paying close attention to the way they behaved to one another. They were outside Mrs. Greenhow's home, Barton "half in and half out," his hip "on the carriage and his legs out," looking "straight in Mrs.

Sickle's [*sic*] face." Barton first asked Teresa whether she was going to the hop at Willard's Hotel that night. Teresa said "she would go if Dan would allow." Barton then said that he "expected to meet her there." He next commented on her eyes, that they "looked bad." Teresa responded that she did not feel well. Barton then got into the carriage and Teresa told McDonald to drive to the corner of Eleventh Street. The footman hopped up alongside Cooney and told him where to go. As they reached K Street, between Fifteenth and Sixteenth streets—near their house of assignation—Teresa ordered Cooney to stop so that Barton could get out. They then drove down to Gautier's confectionary shop, where Teresa did some shopping, before ordering the coachman to drive home "rapidly."[45]

◎   ◎   ◎

The House remained in session until 10:23 that night, but Dan left in the late afternoon and was on hand for the dinner party at his home. The Pendletons—Barton's sister and his brother-in-law—came to dinner again, also Daniel Dougherty and his wife. Octavia Ridgeley was staying, too, for both dinner and as an overnight guest. After eating, everyone retired to the drawing room and about 10:00 P.M., they all went to Willard's Hotel for the hop. Because there wasn't room in the Sickles's carriage, Dan followed later, arriving about an hour after the others. Before he left home, someone delivered a letter to his house, but in the rush to catch up with the others, Dan thrust it into his pocket, unopened. Meanwhile, at Willard's, Octavia became aware that Teresa was spending all her time with Barton, and Dougherty, on his own because his wife "was promenading the room," also noticed the two of them conversing together before Dan arrived.[46] As soon as Dan did appear, Barton "abruptly" left Teresa's side.[47]

Dan, Teresa, and Octavia returned to the Sickles home about two o'clock in the morning and while the two women went upstairs to prepare for bed, he finally opened the letter in his pocket. Unlike the letter that Barton had received on

The original anonymous letter received by Dan. He tried to find out who "R.P.G." was by placing a personal ad in two local newspapers. But neither he nor anyone else was ever able to determine who sent it. *Courtesy New-York Historical Society.*

Wednesday, this one was not encoded, though it was later suspected to be written by the same person:

Washington, February 24th 1859

Hon. Daniel Sickles

Dear Sir with deep regret I enclose to your address the few lines but an indispensable duty compels me so to do seeing that you are greatly imposed upon.

There is a fellow I may say for he is not a gentleman by any

means by the [name] of Phillip Barton Key & I believe the
district attorney who rents a house of a negro man by the name
of Jno. A. Gray situated on 15th Street btw'n K & L streets for
no other purpose than to meet your wife Mrs. Sickles. he
hangs a string out of the window as a signal to her that he is in
and leaves the door unfastened and she walks in and sir I do
assure you he has as much the use of your wife as you have.
With these few hints I leave the rest for you to imagine.

Most Respfly
Your friend R. P. G.[48]

That night, Dan did not sleep.[49] "After we returned from
the hop," Octavia Ridgeley vividly recalled, "I noticed a
change in his manner . . .

"Mr. Sickles had a very wild, distracted look."[50]

NINE

The Cuckold

Foreign Relations may admit his skill,
But in domestic he is minus still . . .

W HO WAS "R. P. G."? Dan had no idea what the initials
stood for. Was this another crank letter? Could young
Beekman, wherever he was, be behind this ugly rumor, too?[1]
Or was it some spurned lady friend of Barton's, a jealous
Washington matron?[2]

Shaken by the revelation in the anonymous letter, Dan decided to take it upon himself to verify its contents. But first he
wired his friend Manny Hart in New York, asking him to
come to Washington as soon as possible. He apparently gave
Hart no reason for the urgency, and Hart, who was now,
thanks to Dan's influence with Buchanan, surveyor of the
Port of New York, responded that he was too busy to get
away.

Meanwhile, Dan went to Fifteenth Street and interviewed
some residents who lived on the block. They confirmed seeing Barton, but those he spoke to did not know the name of
the woman who met him at No. 383. Some could describe the
clothes she wore, and the descriptions seemed to match
dresses, coats, and shawls that Teresa owned, but the identification was not positive. With the matter unresolved, and still
troubled, Dan proceeded from there to the offices downtown
of two newspapers, the *Daily States* and the *Evening Star*, and
placed a notice in their personals columns for publication on
Saturday. He was as circumspect as possible. The writer of the

anonymous letter would know whom to contact, and the reason:

> R. P. G., who recently addressed a letter to a gentleman in this city, will confer a great favor upon the gentleman to whom the letter was addressed by granting him an early immediate confidential interview.[3]

Dan then went to the Capitol. The House convened at eleven o'clock that day to take up a post-office bill before proceeding to legislation dealing with navy yards. Dan planned to speak on the latter issue, but he was so distracted that he could think of nothing else but the anonymous letter he had received. He sent a messenger to the House map department asking George Wooldridge to meet him. The crippled clerk found Dan about one o'clock that afternoon in a small anteroom behind the speaker's chair in the House chamber.[4] "George, I want to speak to you on a painful matter," Dan said as Wooldridge hobbled up to him on his crutches. "Late last night I received this letter."

Dan began to read the anonymous letter but doing so made him so upset that he could not control himself and he burst into tears. He handed the letter to Wooldridge. Ordinarily, he threw away anonymous letters, Dan said, but inasmuch as "in this the facts could be proved or disproved so easily," he thought he would investigate it. He described his going to Fifteenth Street that morning. He did not say to whom he had spoken, but he had ascertained that Barton had indeed rented a house there from "the negro man Gray" and that "a lady was in the habit of going there." His hope, Dan said, "is that this is not my wife, but some other woman." Dan asked Wooldridge, "As my friend, you will go there, and see whether it is or not." Then Dan put his hand to his head and sobbed. Ashamed by his sudden outburst, Dan jumped up from the sofa on which he was sitting and rushed into the corner of another room, away from the curious stares of other congressmen. "Get a carriage," he finally told Wooldridge, who had followed him. "We'll go, and I'll show you the house."

Neither man spoke as they drove down Pennsylvania Avenue. Wooldridge didn't even ask any questions. It was clear to him that Dan "did not seem to wish to converse." At Fifteenth Street, Dan pointed out the house at No. 383 but said nothing further. Wooldridge got out of the carriage several blocks away and, as Dan continued back to the Capitol, the clerk decided that he would rent a room in the vicinity of No. 383 "to see whether it was Mrs. Sickles or not."

The night was dark and stormy. It was snowing and cold by the time Wooldridge, sometime "after gas light," about 7:00 P.M., returned to the vicinity of No. 383, obviously unaware that the liaisons took place during the afternoon. He stayed about an hour in the neighborhood without seeing any movement in or about No. 383, but he did find out an important piece of information. A light-skinned boy named Crittenden Baylis, the son of a black woman who owned a house on the opposite side of the street from No. 383, had seen both the man and the woman visiting the house. He knew who the man was but not the woman, though he could describe her. Crittenden insisted that he had seen her there the previous afternoon, *Thursday*. Convinced that the boy "was full of knowledge," Wooldridge persuaded the youngster to accompany him to the Capitol despite the raging storm.

The House was still in session. Late in the afternoon, Dan made his address on navy yards and sometime shortly after six o'clock he made a motion for the House to adjourn, but it was defeated. The sergeant-at-arms was then ordered to bring in absentee members, and a tiresome argument broke out about who should be excused from further debate. The members finally agreed to adjourn at 8:35, just as Wooldridge arrived. On entering the building, Wooldridge left Crittenden in an outer hall and went to find Dan. But Dan did not want to interview the boy, "in fact he did not want to see anybody." Wooldridge, nevertheless, was eager to divulge what he had discovered. He told Dan what Crittenden had said, and that the boy had last seen the woman on Thursday. With that, Dan's mood changed. It could not have been Teresa, not on

Thursday. He and Teresa had hosted a dinner party that night, and that afternoon Teresa was supposed to have been out visiting—at the Thompson house, at the Browns', and at Rose Greenhow's. It definitely could not have been Teresa. Dan was relieved.

◎   ◎   ◎

Dan was back at the Capitol the next day, Saturday, February 26. The storm still hovered over the city. It was cold and rainy, and the streets of Washington were covered with snow, the trees with sleet, with the temperature hovering around the freezing point.[5] The Senate was engaged in a fight over the acquisition of Cuba—a favorite Buchanan subject—while the House debated a number of appropriations bills. Dan took part in votes dealing with a post-office bill and an agricultural measure, and again planned to speak, this time specifically on behalf of the Brooklyn Navy Yard. His newspaper appeal to "R. P. G." appeared in the morning newspapers, but so far no one had responded to it—and, in fact, the mystery of who "R. P. G." was would never be solved.

◎   ◎   ◎

Before Dan left for the Capitol at his usual time that morning, Barton appeared in Lafayette Square. Daniel Dougherty had just left Jonah Hoover's home and was on his way to pay his respects to Dan and Teresa before returning to his home in Philadelphia when he met Barton on Pennsylvania Avenue. The two men walked together. Dougherty thought Barton was going to visit the Sickleses, too, but as they passed the Clubhouse on the opposite side of the park, Barton "very abruptly" turned into the building. After visiting Dan and Teresa, Dougherty was returning on the Avenue and passed Barton, who seemed once again to be headed toward the Sickleses's house.[6] As far as is known, however, no one else saw Barton in the square that day, and he and Teresa never met at the house on Fifteenth Street because George Wooldridge would have seen them.

◉   ◉   ◉

Wooldridge was keeping a vigil on No. 383. He had arranged to take a room in the Bayliss home across the street
and took up his post there about ten in the morning. He
stayed there until about three in the afternoon, seeing nothing.
The only thing of note that happened was that Crittenden described in detail how the woman was dressed—which Wooldridge jotted down—and then corrected himself about seeing
the woman on Thursday. It hadn't been Thursday, the boy
realized now. It was Wednesday. Wooldridge, who did not
understand the importance of that piece of information, returned in mid-afternoon to his boarding house on Twelfth
Street, about a ten-minute walk east of Lafayette Square.[7]

He was there, having a late lunch, when a message arrived
from the Capitol. Dan, who had not told Wooldridge to aban-
don his investigation, wrote him to be "cautious" about using
Teresa's name "as the suspicion, if not proven or not true, was
worse than the dreadful reality." Dan may have spoken to his
coachman or perhaps his footman. He said he had "made in-
quiries that assured him that it was not his wife who had been
there on Thursday." Wooldridge now realized that Crittenden's correction might be important. "Depressed" at the
thought of having to tell Dan that "it was Wednesday, and not
Thursday, that the lady was seen there," Wooldridge took a
coach to the Capitol.

Summoned from the House chamber, Dan came out into
the hall outside to meet his clerk friend. He had just addressed
the House on the navy-yard subject. "He appeared different
from what he had been the day before," Wooldridge noted.
"He appeared more like himself." Reluctantly, Wooldridge
told Dan that he had made "a mistake." But first he read
the description of the dresses the woman wore—it was "always one and the same lady." Dan "at once recognized the
apparel of his wife." Wooldridge went on, telling him that
"the lady had come there two or three times a week," that
Barton "would come first, go into the house, leave the door

on a jar, and then she would slip in," that "previous to this, a towel or something white would be put out" and that neighbors knew when they saw the signal that "the lady would come."

Dan still seemed optimistic. He repeated his "hope" that it was not Teresa, because he knew she could not have been there Thursday. At this point, Wooldridge at last told Dan that Crittenden had corrected himself: "it was Wednesday." Put together, the description of the dresses and the correction regarding the day, "completely convinced" Dan. "He was quite prostrated." The news "unmanned him completely." Dan's "exhibitions of grief" were so "violent" that the two men retreated to a "retiring room." Wooldridge tried to pacify Dan. Finally, after about ten or twelve minutes, the clerk left.

◉   ◉   ◉

Francis Mohun, a contractor who had once been introduced to Dan, was standing in front of a house he owned on Pennsylvania Avenue when Dan came walking by "very rapidly" from the Capitol. Mohun had heard "rumors about the city," so he closely observed him. Even though it was dusk, about 5:30 P.M., Mohun could see how disturbed Dan was. He was "in a very excited condition," his appearance "wild," a "strange movement about his person and head." Mohun himself was shaken. "His whole appearance," he said, "did affect me very seriously." Dan, he thought, looked "crazy or insane."[8]

Apparently unable to hire a hack, Dan hastened down Pennsylvania Avenue. He reached Lafayette Square, over a mile from the Capitol, as the Reverend Smith Pyne and his son were riding by on their way home. Pyne, the pastor of St. John's Church was supposed to have officiated at the baptism of Laura Sickles in 1858, he had visited the Sickles home at Teresa's request the previous Lent to arrange the ceremony. Because he was driving their rig, Pyne didn't notice Dan, but his son called his attention to him. Dan, his head "thrown back," looked at the minister but did not seem to recognize him. He acted so "peculiar" that Pyne found it hard to describe him. "There was a wildness about Mr. Sickles' appearance" that impressed him. "He seemed to be like a man who was in some great trouble of some kind or other." Pyne remarked to his son "how very strange" Dan looked. "There was a kind of mingled [sic] defiant air about him; a desolate air."[9]

◎　　◎　　◎

Bridget Duffy knew as soon as Dan arrived home that there was "some unhappy feeling" between him and Teresa.[10] Octavia Ridgeley was staying to dinner. Dan joined her at the dinner table but did not eat anything. The "wild, distracted look" Octavia had observed on Friday was now "especially" noticeable. Agitated, Dan finally got up and excused himself from the table. He went upstairs, asking Bridget to bring him something to eat in his bedroom. The maid thought his "manner and appearance seemed troubled." And he was crying.

Teresa had stayed home that day and now was ensconced in the couple's bedroom. Their door was partly open when Bridget returned upstairs to tend to Laura in the nursery room she shared with the young girl; it adjoined the Sickleses's front bedroom. Octavia was in the downstairs parlor. Bridget heard "loud talking" coming from the Sickleses's bedroom. The young Irish girl listened "a few moments," then went downstairs to the kitchen. When she returned about twenty minutes later, Dan and Teresa were still in the bedroom, their voices ringing with recriminations. They stopped shouting and fell silent when Bridget knocked at their door and went in to fix the fire and take away Dan's dinner tray.

Sometime about 8:30 that evening, Dan asked both young women into the Sickleses's bedroom. Teresa was seated at a desk, writing. Octavia sat down on a small sofa in the room, waiting for her to finish. Dan was restlessly pacing around the room "as if crying." Neither Octavia nor Bridget noticed that Teresa was not wearing her wedding ring. Dan had taken it from her and broken it. When Teresa finished, she asked Oc-

tavia and Bridget to witness her signature. Teresa had actually
signed the document three times—after the main statement
and then after two postscripts—and each time with her
maiden name. The reason for the second of the two postscripts—that Barton had dined with the Sickleses two weeks
earlier—is puzzling; perhaps Dan wished her to make it clear
that he was disassociating himself as a friend of Barton's.

The document was shocking. It spoke of things—nudity
and sex—that no decent woman, or man for that matter, ever
mentioned in public, or even in many cases in private, in Victorian America:

> I have been in a house in Fifteenth street, with Mr. Key. How
> many times I don't know. I believe the house belongs to a
> colored man. The house is unoccupied. Commenced going
> there the latter part of January. Have been in alone and with
> Mr. Key. Usually stayed an hour or more. There was a bed in
> the second story. I did what is usual for a wicked woman to
> do. The intimacy commenced this winter, when I came from
> New York, in that house—an intimacy of an improper kind.
> Have met a dozen times or more, at different hours of the day.
> On Monday of this week, and Wednesday also. Would arrange
> meetings when we met in the street and at parties. Never
> would speak to him when Mr. Sickles was at home, because I
> knew he did not like me to speak to him; did not see Mr. Key
> for some days after I got here. He then told me he had hired
> the house as a place where he and I could meet. I agreed to it.
> Had nothing to eat or drink there. The room is warmed by a
> wood fire. Mr. Key generally goes first. Have walked there
> together say four times—I do not think more; was there on
> Wednesday last, between two [and] three. I went there alone.
> Laura was at Mrs. Hoover's. Mr. Key took and left her there at
> my request. From there I went to Fifteenth street to meet Mr.
> Key; from there to the milk woman's. Immediately after Mr.
> Key left Laura at Mrs. Hoover's, I met him in Fifteenth street.
> Went in by the back gate. Went in the same bedroom, and
> there an improper interview was had. I undressed myself. Mr.
> Key undressed also. This occurred on Wednesday, 23d of Feb-
> ruary, 1859. Mr. Key has kissed me in this house a number of

times. I do not deny that we have had connection in this house, last spring, a year ago, in the parlor, on the sofa. Mr. Sickles was sometimes out of town, and sometimes in. I think the intimacy commenced in April or May, 1858. I did not think it safe to meet him in this house, because there are servants who might suspect something. As a general thing, have worn a black and white woollen [sic] plaid dress, and beaver hat trimmed with black velvet. Have worn a black silk dress there also, also a plaid silk dress, black velvet cloak trimmed with lace, and black velvet shawl trimmed with fringe. On Wednesday I either had on my brown dress or black and white woollen dress, beaver hat and velvet shawl. I arranged with Mr. Key to go in the back way, after leaving Laura at Mrs. Hoover's. He met me at Mr. Douglas'. The arrangement to go in the back way was either made in the street or at Mr. Douglas', as we would be less likely to be seen. The house is in Fifteenth street between K and L streets, on the left hand side of the way; arranged the interview for Wednesday in the street, I think, on Monday. I went in the front door, it was open, occupied the same room, undressed myself, and he also; went to bed together. Mr. Key has ridden in Mr. Sickles' carriage, and has called at his house without Mr. Sickles' knowledge, and after my being told not to invite him to do so, and against Mr. Sickles' repeated request.

TERESA BAGIOLI

This is a true statement, written by myself, without any inducement held out by Mr. Sickles of forgiveness or reward, and without any menace from him. This I have written with my bed-room door open, and my maid and child in the adjoining room, at half past eight o'clock in the evening. Miss Ridgeley is in the house, within call.

TERESA BAGIOLI
LAFAYETTE SQUARE, Washington, D.C., Feb. 26, 1859.

Mr. and Mrs. Pendleton dined here two weeks ago last Thursday, with a large party. Mr. Key was also here, her brother, and at my suggestion he was invited, because he lived in the same house, and also because he had invited Mr. Sickles to dine with him, and Mr. Sickles wished to invite all those from whom he had received invitations; and Mr. Sickles said "do as you choose."

TERESA BAGIOLI

Written and signed in presence of C. M. Ridgeley and Bridget Duffy.
Feb. 26, 1859.[11]

It was almost midnight when Octavia went to sleep. Teresa spent the night in her young friend's room, on the floor, her head resting on a chair. Bridget went to bed about the same time in the nursery room. She could still hear "exclamations and sobbing" and both Teresa and Dan crying.

TEN

A Matter of Honor

And one there was whose eyes would murder more
Than that dark "Bravo" from her native shore.
Sly "Gipsies" lurk, with larceny in their eye,
Though pilfering hearts is not a felony . . .

ABOUT 8:30 THE NEXT MORNING, Sunday, February 27, Octavia Ridgeley awoke, dressed, and went downstairs to have breakfast with Laura, who had spent the night sleeping in her father's bed. She left Teresa upstairs, still prostrate. While sitting at the dining table, Octavia suddenly heard sobbing. Dan was going upstairs, moaning and groaning pitifully. Octavia "could hear him all over the house. He uttered fearful groans. They seemed to come from his very feet. They were unearthly."[1]

Dan passed Bridget Duffy on the stairs. He was holding his face in his hands, crying and sobbing. Earlier, the maid came upon Teresa in Octavia's room, on the floor, where she had lain all night. Bridget was so "very sorry" to see Dan "in trouble" that she started crying herself.[2]

Soon afterwards, George Wooldridge showed up at the house. Dan had sent a message to him the night before, asking him to come to his home if he received the note in time, "and if not, to go up next morning."[3] Wooldridge did not get home until midnight, so he waited until about ten o'clock to answer Dan's summons. He found Dan in the library, his eyes "bloodshot and red," pacing back and forth like "a man in great sorrow and distress." Wooldridge thought "there was a

strange manner about him." Dan would go upstairs, then return downstairs, would talk to Wooldridge "about matters,"
then go upstairs again. Every time Dan returned to the library, "he pressed his hands to his temple, and would go over
to the secretary and sob." Sometimes Dan's fits would cause
him to "bow down his head as if his stomach was giving way,
and he would be hardly able to reach the secretary for support." Wooldridge urged him "to give vent to his tears, as
they would relieve him."[4]

◎   ◎   ◎

Unaware that Dan now knew all about his affair with his
wife, Barton stopped by the barber shop at Willard's Hotel for
a shave and trim that morning before heading toward
Lafayette Square. The weather had taken a turn for the better.
The day was pleasant and mild for February—the temperature
would reach fifty-four degrees in the afternoon—but the city's
streets were still muddy from the recent storm.[5] Barton was
dressed fashionably in gray-striped trousers and matching
vest, a white shirt, brown tweed jacket and brown overcoat.[6]
He was carrying two brass keys, one of which was for the
front door of 383 Fifteenth Street, and an opera glass in a case
inside a side pocket of his coat.[7] Although he did not know
about Teresa's confession, Barton must have sensed something, because he made a brief allusion to the situation to two
men he ran into outside the barber shop. One was Southey
Parker, who had witnessed Barton doffing his hat to Teresa
and Laura in Lafayette Square the previous Sunday. The other
man was Washington's mayor, James G. Berret. Barton
bowed to Parker and spoke to the mayor for a few minutes.
He started to say something about "Mr. Sickles killing him"
before walking off in the direction of the square.[8] Yet Barton
certainly did not act as though he was worried about Dan's
discovering his wife's infidelity. He audaciously appeared so
frequently in the square during the next three hours that no
less than ten persons saw him there at one time or another,
and some persons saw him more than once.

Bridget Duffy was the first to spot Barton that day. She left the Sickles home to attend 9:30 church services. She returned about 10:40, went upstairs to make the Sickleses's bed and found Dan in the room crying and tearing at his hair. He was wringing his hands and "calling on God to witness his troubles."[9] Bridget next went into the nursery where she and Laura slept. It was a corner room, with windows overlooking both the park and Pennsylvania Avenue. Glancing out the window, Bridget saw Barton walking on the Avenue, headed towards Georgetown.[10]

Downstairs, in the library, Wooldridge spotted him, too. He had watched Barton cross the street from the park to the Avenue.[11] Returning from Sunday morning services, a parishioner at St. John's Church, saw Barton stop "on the edge of the pavement," looking toward the Sickles home.[12] A Treasury Department architect walking in the square with a friend also recognized him.[13] Twenty minutes later, when Bridget was down in the kitchen, she saw Barton again. This time he was in the park, headed toward the Clubhouse.[14]

Shortly afterward, a man who was to play a controversial role in the events of the next few hours appeared at the Sickles doorstep. He was Samuel F. Butterworth, an intimate of Dan's who happened to be in Washington, staying with the Gwins. A Tammany cohort, Butterworth was superintendent of the U.S. Assay Office in New York. Like Manny Hart and George Wooldridge, he owed his position to Dan. That morning he received a cryptic note from Dan: "*Dear B. Come to me right away!*" Butterworth could not imagine what he wanted. He showed the note to Senator Gwin and another man he was talking with at the time the messenger arrived, former governor of Kansas Robert J. Walker. "What can Mr. Sickles desire?" he wondered.

Butterworth found Dan in his bedroom "lying on his face on his pillow, overwhelmed with grief." Dan told him the whole story—about the anonymous letter, the house on Fifteenth Street, confronting Teresa, who "perceived she was discovered" and confessed. What, he asked Butterworth, should he do now? Butterworth advised Dan "to send his wife to her mother at New York—that, as it was now near the close of the session, it would excite no remark." Butterworth also suggested—"for the honor of his little daughter"—that after the session ended, and before the Thirty-sixth Congress met the following December, Dan should take a trip to Europe while a separation was arranged.

Butterworth left Dan in the bedroom and went downstairs. "This is a terrible affair," he said on meeting Wooldridge in the library. The clerk handed him Teresa's confession to read. Shaken by the events, Butterworth said he was going out for a short while, but he would be back soon if Dan needed him. He then walked across Lafayette Square to the Clubhouse where he met a friend and joined him in drinking a glass of ale.[15]

Meanwhile, Barton appeared in the square again. Both the Sickleses's coachman and groom saw him about noon.[16] So again did both Southey Parker and the St. John's parishioner.[17]

He reappeared after 1:00 P.M. Colonel Freeman's coachman with the unlikely name Major Hopkins spotted Barton "walking back and forth two or three times to the Jackson statue."[18] While Barton was doing so, he was approached by a Buffalo, New York, lawyer. The man, "a passing acquaintance" of Barton's, "passed the time of day with him" before they parted, the lawyer heading to Sunday dinner at Willard's Hotel, Barton leaving the square by its southwest gate, near the Sickles house, "whirling a handkerchief as he went along."[19]

For the third time that day, Bridget Duffy, sitting by the kitchen window on the ground floor of the Sickles house, saw Barton; now he was walking across the street with a young couple coming from church with Bibles in their hands. He seemed so serious talking to them. The premonition Barton appeared to have earlier in the day when speaking with the mayor outside Willard's Hotel had turned into a general depression. "I am despondent about my health and very desperate," he complained to the man and woman. "Indeed, I have half a mind to go out on the prairies and try buffalo hunting.

The excursion would either cure me or kill me, and, really, I don't care much which."[20]

Suddenly, the Sickleses's dog, Dandy, ran across the street and playfully jumped up at Barton. Bridget couldn't imagine how the wiry Italian greyhound had gotten loose. As Dandy "fawned" on him, Barton took out his handkerchief and "whirled" it three or four times, pretending he was playing with the dog. He continued to wave it in "a slow, rotary movement" after the dog ran off.[21]

In the library above the kitchen, Dan had momentarily left Wooldridge to go upstairs once more. The clerk looked out of the window and saw Barton with the couple "in a direct line" across the street. Wooldridge noticed that as Barton waved his handkerchief, he averted his eyes from the couple, trying to conceal the fact that he was searching for a response from a second-floor window of the Sickles house. Wooldridge then saw Barton part from the couple and walk into the park in the direction of Madison Place.[22]

Somehow Barton and Butterworth missed meeting one another. The latter had "slowly" walked across the park from the Clubhouse on his way back to the Sickles house. As soon as he entered the library, Wooldridge excitedly told him that Barton had passed the house several times while he was away, and had just been seen waving his handkerchief "three times as a signal." Even the servants saw him. Just then, Dan—"very excited"—entered the room. "That villain has just passed my house," he declared.[23] He had been at his bedroom window and "seen the scoundrel making signals," he told his two friends. "My God!," he exclaimed frantically, "this is horrible!"[24]

Butterworth tried to placate Dan, saying that "only themselves knew it." But Dan shook him off. "The whole world," he said, "the whole town knew it."[25]

"Mr. Sickles," Butterworth pressed on, "you must be calm, and look this matter square in the face. If there be a possibility of keeping the certain knowledge of this crime from the public, you must do nothing to destroy that possibility. You may be mistaken in your belief that it is known to the whole city."

"No, no, my friend," Dan instantly replied. "I am not! It is already the town-talk."

"If that be so," Butterworth solemnly said, "there is but one course left you as a man of honor. You need no advice."

Dan paused, apparently weighing the import of what Butterworth meant: a duel. It was a critical moment. Should he challenge Barton to meet on the Duelling Ground in Bladensburgh? Or was there another option? Dan thought and thought. Finally, he said that it was surprising that although his wife had confessed her guilt, she had denied that Barton used the Clubhouse for their rendezvous. It was a curious comment for Dan to make, because he now knew all about the house on Fifteenth Street. Dan walked into the front hall, Butterworth following. Outside of Wooldridge's earshot, Dan suggested that the two of them walk to the Clubhouse and inquire of a mutual friend, a man named Stuart who lived there, "whether Key has a room there, and for what purpose he uses it." Butterworth agreed and walked out of the house and down the steps, thinking that Dan was behind him.[26]

But Dan did not follow Butterworth; he had something else in mind. Instead, he turned up the staircase, went to his bedroom and armed himself with the two derringers and a revolver he owned. Then he went downstairs, grabbed a hat and frock coat from the hall rack, and left the house. He turned left, toward H Street, heading around the north side of Lafayette Square to reach the Clubhouse.

Sitting in an easy chair by the library window, Wooldridge had seen Butterworth walk in the opposite direction toward Pennsylvania Avenue, but missed seeing Dan. The clerk was "so much affected" by Dan's "grief" that he felt the need to distract himself. Without thinking anything about what Butterworth might be up to, Wooldridge reached for his crutches and went into the adjoining back parlor to get a stereoscope to look at some pictures.[27] He was in the back parlor when Dan left.

At almost the same time, Barton was on Pennsylvania Avenue, approaching the southeast corner of the square. Coming from the opposite direction, Butterworth met him on the street in front of Lafayette Maynard's House, at the corner of the Avenue and Madison Place, across from the White House. Barton unsuspectingly opened the conversation. "Good morning, Butterworth—what a fine day we have!" he said. Butterworth inquired if Barton had come from the Clubhouse. He said he had. Was Stuart in his room? asked Butterworth. "Yes," said Barton, "and he is quite unwell." Butterworth then said, "I am going up to see him," and bid him good morning. Butterworth turned toward the Clubhouse, and as he did so, he saw Dan walking "rapidly" toward them from the north side of the square. Approaching, Dan suddenly called out.[28]

◎   ◎   ◎

It was now about two o'clock in the afternoon of that bright, unseasonably warm day, a welcome change from the chilling snow, sleet, and rain of the past two days—the kind of weather that invites people to take a stroll on a Sunday afternoon. Seven persons were converging at that moment on Lafayette Square, walking leisurely, taking in the sun. James H. Reed was on the south side of Pennsylvania Avenue, directly opposite Maynard's House on the corner. Ahead of him was Joseph L. Dudrow, and farther up the Avenue, near the east gate of the White House, strolling separately, were Edward Delafield, Jr., and Eugene B. Pendleton—no relation to Barton's brother-in-law. A young boy, J. H. W. Bonitz, a White House page, had just left the Executive Mansion and was coming out of the gate onto Pennsylvania Avenue. At the same time, Philip V. R. Van Wyck was walking from New York Avenue, a half-block away, and was nearing the corner of Maynard's House. Behind him, also walking westward toward the square, was Richard M. Downer. On Madison Place itself, Thomas E. Martin, a Treasury Department clerk, was just leaving the Clubhouse, after visiting there with three friends who also worked for the federal government—Edward L. Tidball, Francis E. Doyle, and Abel Upshur. And C.

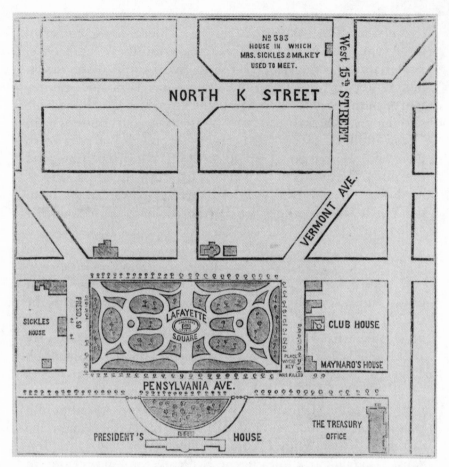

The scene of the murder: The shooting took place near the corner in front of Maynard's House on the east side of the square. Sickles's home was on the west side of Lafayette Square, facing the Club-house on the east. Dan's friend Samuel Butterworth left the Sickleses's home and walked along the southern walk of the park on Pennsylvania Avenue in front of the White House, until meeting Barton near Maynard's House. Dan approached the site after taking the northern route around the square on H Street. Note how close the square was to the house at 383 Fifteenth Street, where Teresa and Barton held their secret trysts. *Courtesy New-York Historical Society.*

H. McCormick was sitting in a room by a second-floor window overlooking the street in a house two doors up from Maynard's House.

What happened in the next few minutes was witnessed by these twelve persons, each of whom heard or saw all or part of what occurred. Their recollection of specific details sometimes differed slightly, but they all agreed on the essentials.[29]

           ©   ©   ©

"Key, you scoundrel," Dan shouted, "you have dishonored my house—you must die!" Dan had a gun in his hand. He was face to face with Barton. The two men were near the corner lamppost by Maynard's House.

Barton "thrust his hand" inside his coat and took a step in Dan's direction. At the same moment, Dan fired. The shot grazed Barton. "Murder!" he cried. Dan raised his arm to fire again. Barton jumped at him, seizing Dan by the collar of his coat with his left hand. It looked like Barton was trying to strike Dan with something in his right hand. The two men grappled. Dan backed from the sidewalk into the middle of the street, dropping his gun onto the sidewalk in the struggle. He turned and started to pull away but Barton grabbed him from behind with both arms around his waist as they stepped onto a flagstone walk that led into the park. Dan was able to pull himself from Barton's grasp. As he swung around toward him, he pulled another gun from his overcoat pocket and pointed it at Barton.

"Don't murder me!" shouted Barton, backing off in the street, Dan following him. As he retreated backwards up the middle of the street toward the Clubhouse, Barton reached inside his coat and tossed his opera glass at Dan. It seemed to float slowly through the air, hit Dan and fall to the ground. At the same time, and when within ten feet of Barton, Dan fired. This time the bullet penetrated Barton's body. It struck him two inches below the groin, missing a main artery, passed through his thigh and exited in the groove between his thigh and his buttock.

"I'm shot," Barton gasped. He staggered towards the sidewalk. "Don't shoot me," he cried out. Dan kept shouting, "You villain, you have dishonored my house, and you must die!"

Barton leaned briefly against a tree, trying to hold onto it, then fell to the ground, lying on his right side, one hand over his groin. Pleading "Don't shoot me," he tried to raise himself up, using his elbow for support, as Dan came up to him and pulled the trigger, but the gun merely snapped, misfiring. "Murder! Murder!" Barton kept yelling. "Don't shoot me!" Dan recocked the weapon, put it to Barton's chest and fired again. This time the gun worked. The bullet hit Barton between the tenth and eleventh ribs on his left side, under the edge of the spleen, and tore through his body and lodged near the hip bone. Mortally wounded, his chest filling with blood, Barton seemed to wilt or swoon as he fell back, his hand pressed to his side. Dan put his gun to Barton's head and pulled the trigger once more, but again it misfired.

By this time, Thomas Martin—who had rushed back inside the Clubhouse, yelled what had happened to his friends and raced back outside—was able to get between the two men. Standing there, the revolver in his hand, Dan asked, "Is the scoundrel dead?" Martin stooped by Barton's side and, taking him in his arms, "looked inquisitively" into Dan's face. "He has violated my bed," Dan said. Francis Doyle, who had followed Martin from the Clubhouse, put his hand on Dan's shoulder and begged him not to fire again. Dan jerked his arm away and drew back several steps. "He has defiled my bed," he said. Edward Tidball, who had also raced from the Clubhouse, came up on Dan's other side and touched his shoulder, too. "He has dishonored my bed," repeated Dan. He said it loudly, but Tidball nevertheless thought Dan was "rather cool and deliberate" though "his face was somewhat pale, of course."

Butterworth—who had stood only a few paces away, leaning against the railing of a house, watching the terrible scene—now approached, took Dan by the arm and started to

The fatal shot: Dan again fires, and point-blank, at the wounded, pleading Barton. In the background, Samuel Butterworth looks on. His role in the slaying was never satisfactorily explained; and, peculiarly, he was not called to testify at Dan's trial, although he was obviously a witness to the murder. *Courtesy New-York Historical Society.*

lead him away, toward the corner of H Street and Madison Place. Putting the gun in his pocket, Dan walked quietly up the street.

Why didn't Butterworth stop Dan? Why did he just stand there, watching the horrifying confrontation without doing anything? Had he purposely stalled Barton at the corner so that Dan could catch up with him? What exactly was his role?

◉   ◉   ◉

Barton was still alive, barely breathing, as several of the bystanders and servants from the Clubhouse took him up in their arms and carried him into the Clubhouse. They placed him on the floor inside one of the rooms off the front hall. Tidball tilted a chair over so that Barton's head and shoulders were slightly raised. He then left to get a doctor. Thomas Martin put his hand over Barton's heart and felt his pulse. He was still alive, but barely. Martin asked Barton whether he had anything to say about what happened "or a word for his children," but Barton "did not seem to understand, and made no response."

Dr. Richard H. Coolidge, who lived nearby on H Street, had heard the shots and rushed to the Clubhouse. An Army surgeon who was well acquainted with gunshot wounds, Coolidge opened Barton's shirt and trousers, trying to locate his wounds. He soon realized that the chest wound was fatal. Barton breathed one last time and died.

◉   ◉   ◉

Within two hours of Barton's death, the District coroner, Thomas Woodward, appeared at the now-crowded Clubhouse. There were nearly a hundred people inside the building, and a group of fifteen to twenty men stood beside Barton's body. Woodward immediately called a coroner's jury into session by swearing in individuals who hadn't witnessed the shooting, and with Barton's body lying on the floor in front of them, his head and shoulders still resting on the overturned chair, Woodward heard testimony from witnesses.

Richard Downer, who had picked up one of Dan's derringer pistols from the sidewalk outside, offered it into evidence. Belatedly, Barton's clothing was searched. A handkerchief, two brass keys, the case for an opera glass, fourteen dollar bills and some coins were found, but a number of people had already made off with other items. Incredibly, Constable Jacob King, who was also the District jailer, watched—with-

The coroner's inquest in the Clubhouse, with Barton's body lying in the foreground. His head was propped up on an overturned chair when he was brought into the club still, but barely, alive. *Courtesy New-York Historical Society.*

out taking any steps to prevent it—as persons without any authority went through Barton's pockets. A Treasury Department clerk who was in the Clubhouse at the time of the shooting seemed to be taking charge "a good deal." King saw him take a small white-handled knife, a memorandum book and a purse from the clothing, and some papers from a "fob-pocket of the pantaloons."[30] The clerk handed the items to a physician who knew Barton and had them delivered the following week to Barton's brother-in-law, Congressman George Pendleton.[31] One of the papers was the anonymous enciphered letter Barton received several days earlier. Someone found a pair of kid gloves in an outer pocket; Pendleton finally received them, too. Barton's relation who lived next door, Benjamin Ogle Tayloe, took a ring from Barton's finger and a pair of cufflinks.[32]

Summoned from the Sickleses's house across the park, Butterworth showed up before the coroner's jury, but he was a reluctant witness and his statement was brief. Obviously trying to protect Dan from scandal about his wife, Butterworth refused to answer whether he was aware of "an intended collision." It was "sufficient," he said, "to state simply that Mr. Sickles shot Mr. Key, who fell dead."[33]

The verdict of the coroner's jury was no surprise:

> That the said Philip Barton Key came to his death from the effect of pistol balls fired by the hands of Daniel E. Sickles, while standing near the southeast corner of Lafayette Square, one of the balls entering the left side of the body, passing through to the corresponding point on the opposite side, lodging under the skin; one through the right thigh near the main artery; the third striking the right side, glancing from the body and inflicting a bruise; said wounds causing his death in a few moments.[34]

J. H. W. Bonitz, the young page, ran back to the White House to tell the president about the shooting. Buchanan listened to the grim news, then told him a lie, perhaps because he did not realize that there were other eyewitnesses. He warned Bonitz that he would be jailed and held without bond as a witness unless he left Washington immediately. Frightened, Bonitz took some money that Buchanan offered him as well as a personal souvenir from the president, a razor. He packed his bags and left immediately for his home in Wilmington, North Carolina. He was never heard of again.[35]

The president would continue to help his friend Dan in an even more crucial way.

ELEVEN

"The Washington Tragedy"

But this is not the time to moralize;
The buzz and glitter claim our ears and eyes.
We but attempt the merit of the dog,
Fidelity, in this our catalogue. . .

THE CHANGE IN DAN'S BEHAVIOR was dramatic. He was calm for the moment, the frenetic rage spent. But he was on edge and his mood would abruptly reverse; one minute he would act normally, the next fulminate. The swift shifts in his behavior were reminiscent of the way he acted almost twenty years earlier when his mentor, Lorenzo L. Da Ponte died: his hysterical outburst at Da Ponte's gravesite, his lightheartedness afterwards. Except that Dan was not flippant now. He may have appeared calm at times, and he may have felt justified, but he was fully aware of the gravity of the situation: He was a murderer; his marriage was shattered; his political career was a shambles.

The persons he encountered that Sunday—people who knew him as well as strangers who met him for the first time—perceived his behavior in sharply different ways. Their perceptions would soon have an important bearing on a new and untried legal issue.

Leading him away from the scene of Barton's murder by the arm, Butterworth suggested that Dan go straightway to Attorney General Jeremiah Black's house and turn himself in. Black lived two blocks away on Franklin Square, north of Lafayette Square, the direction in which they were heading. They slowly walked there together.

◉   ◉   ◉

It is incredible how swiftly the news of the murder swept through Washington. Less than four blocks away on F Street, Senator Clement C. Clay, Jr., of Alabama burst into his wife's room. "A horrible, horrible thing thing has happened, Virginia! Sickles, " Clay blurted out, "has killed Key; killed him most brutally, while he was unarmed!"[1] Nearby at Willard's Hotel, Felix McClusky, a friend of Dan's from Brooklyn, joined a growing surge of people hurrying toward Lafayette Square. A mob was in front of the Clubhouse, everyone confused about what was happening. Off in the distance, he could see Dan and Butterworth headed for Black's home, trailed by a swarm of people. McClusky followed them.

Butterworth left Dan at the stoop in front of Black's home. Dan entered the house alone. A servant showed him into a back parlor where two fellow Pennsylvania friends of Black's were seated, conversing, waiting to see the attorney general. One was the editor of a Democratic paper in Harrisburg named Haldemar, the other former Senator Richard Brodhead. Neither man guessed that Dan was in any trouble. He started to talk to Haldemar about Pennsylvania politics. Brodhead called his attention to some mud on his boots, and he left the room to wipe them off. No sooner did he return than they heard footsteps on the stairs and Dan went outside into the hall to meet Black. They spoke a few minutes, then Black—"scared and excited"[2]—entered the back parlor to tell his friends what had happened. Dan joined them. Brodhead and Haldemar offered to go with him to a magistrate's, and Brodhead asked whether the offense was a "bailable" one, but Dan did not know though he thought that, "if all the facts were known, it would be." Then he added, "For God knows I would be justified."

Butterworth came in. He had gone back to Madison Place and picked off the street the opera glass that Barton had thrown at Dan. It was dirty with mud. He handed it to Dan. One of the men asked if Barton was dead. "Yes," Butterworth answered simply. "One wretch less in the world," Dan muttered.[3]

Felix McClusky was standing with a crowd of people outside Black's home when Dan, accompanied by Butterworth and two police officers, came out and got into a carriage to return to the Sickleses's home. Dan's mood must have changed because, unlike Brodhead and Haldemar, who did not find Dan's behavior unusual, McClusky thought he seemed "like a man frightened to death, you know, with his hair over his face."[4]

The streets were now so clogged with men, women, and children that carriages could not get by, and McClusky was able to walk back to Dan's home before Dan and Butterworth could get through in their carriage. Behind them trooped the crowd of people who had followed them from Black's home.

Wooldridge was stunned by the news. "I never want to see such another day," he said.[5] Throughout everything, the clerk had sat by the library window, his crutches by his side, idly looking at pictures through the stereoscope. He noticed people running across the square but was not curious enough to find out why. McClusky was telling him about Dan's shooting Barton when Dan entered the house. Dan's mood had changed once again, this time from the fright McClusky observed only moments before outside Black's home to a rage that made McClusky sure that Dan "would kill every man, woman and child in the house. I thought, even, that if he went up stairs [sic] he might injure his wife."[6]

Outside, people who saw Dan return spread the word where he was and a large crowd now began to form on Jackson Place. Inside, one after another, friend and official, turned up—the friends to console and offer their help, the officials to take Dan into custody. Soon the house was filled with "a great buzzing and confusion," people huddled together in small groups, talking.[7] Two of Dan's friends, retired grocer John McBlair and Senator John Slidell of Louisiana, both neighbors on the square, arrived together. McBlair thought Dan was "extremely calm," though it might have been "the calmness of desperation."[8] Robert Walker had the opposite reaction.[9] Walker—to whom Butterworth that morning had shown Dan's summons—arrived by carriage with Senator William Gwin of California. Walker was troubled when he entered the back parlor and found Butterworth there, alone and "deeply distressed." A "long and intimate" friend of Barton's, he nevertheless commiserated with Butterworth: "It is deplorable, but Mr. Key deserved his fate." At that moment, Dan entered the room, greeted Walker—"A thousand thanks for coming to see me under these circumstances"—and suddenly threw himself on a sofa in a state of the "deepest distress" Walker ever witnessed. Dan covered his face with his hands and broke into "an agony of unnatural and unearthly sounds, the most remarkable" Walker ever heard—"something like a scream, interrupted by violent sobbing." His body would go "rigid," then he would writhe and go into convulsions "in a state of perfect frenzy."

Dan kept on talking "about dishonor having been brought on his house, his wife and child," in particular "on the disgrace brought upon his child." He told Walker that "he might have tried to suffer in silence, without home or hope in this world, but after the signals and the disgrace became public, he neither asked nor wanted advice as to his course." Listening to his anguish, watching his "spasms," Walker "feared he would become insane." He and Butterworth tried to calm Dan down and "at length" they were able to do so. But Walker was afraid that the "paroxysms of grief and despair" would recur, so he decided to accompany Dan to jail.

Meanwhile, Mayor James Berret showed up, together with Police Chief John H. Goddard. In the library, Dan, calm once more, handed Goddard the opera glass, which was still smeared with mud.[10] He then left the room and started up the staircase. Two police officers stopped him. Teresa was upstairs, alone as far as they knew. Dan said he only wanted to get some papers. The policemen hesitated. He could go if he promised "not to harm his wife." Dan said he had "no such intention."[11]

He came upon Teresa in Octavia Ridgeley's bedroom, still

Dan confronts Teresa to tell her the news: "I've killed him!" She had
spent the previous night on the floor in her friend Octavia Ridgely's
room, weeping uncontrollably after confessing to Dan about her illicit relations with Barton. *Courtesy New-York Historical Society.*

lying on the floor, overcome with despair. No one seemed to
be attending her, and it didn't appear as though she had eaten
anything. Octavia and Bridget Duffy were evidently in the
ground-floor kitchen, taking care of Laura. Dan stood before
Teresa "like a marble statue." He uttered only one sentence:
"I've killed him," then he left.[12]

When Dan returned downstairs, the mayor told him that he
"ought to be composed," that "he had better go to jail, where
a preliminary examination would take place." Dan said that

that was what he wanted to do.[13] But before they left the room, Dan invited everyone, including the police officers, to have a drink. Only Butterworth accepted the offer. Dan went to a sideboard and poured them both glasses of brandy.[14]

The police officers were worried about the mood of the crowd outside. They "apprehended some of the mob would shoot Mr. Sickles." But one officer said he intended to protect Dan no matter what. He put his hand on his pistol, saying that he "could shoot as well as any of them."[15] The mayor was also concerned when Dan walked down the steps outside his house in the late-afternoon sunshine and started to salute the people gathered on the sidewalk. Berret warned him not to draw the crowd's attention, and the two men were able to get into a carriage with Robert Walker and Senator Gwin and drive away without incident.

Dan was taken to a jail that could not have been a more depressing structure—"a miserable old building," as one contemporary put it[16]; a "paltry structure," said another, that "is as deficient in all the interior requirements for enabling its faithful officers to perform their duties with an equal regard to the demands of the law and of humanity, as it is devoid of the exterior embellishments to permit us to describe its architecture."[17] It was a three-story building made of brick that was plastered over and scored to resemble stone; it earned the sobriquet "The Blue Jug" when its walls were painted with a wash during the Civil War. Built in 1839 in a feeble attempt at the Gothic Revival style, it was habitually overcrowded with an assortment of criminals, runaway slaves, insane persons, and debtors.[18] "It combines," one visitor said, "all the disadvantages which have been gradually removed from every other place of confinement in Christendom. It swarms with vermin; it has no sewage, no bath, no water, no ventilation; and frequently contains twelve prisoners in one close, narrow cell."[19]

The prison—known both as the Washington Jail or County Jail—was situated on the southeast corner of G and Fourth streets, a block and a half from City Hall, north of Judiciary Square—only three blocks from the house on C Street where, ironically, Barton had resided and where his funeral would be held.

The police examination was brief. Dan did not deny what he had done. In fact, he asked to be put on trial immediately. He was escorted to a dark, dingy cell reserved for prisoners charged with murder. It was crawling with insects.

◎   ◎   ◎

Neither Dan nor Teresa slept much that night. Dan suffered several fits of sobbing and crying, but nothing as severe as he exhibited at his home. The Rev. Dr. William D'Arcy Haley, pastor of the Unitarian Church a block west of City Hall, did not sleep at all. The minister, who had never met either of them before, took it upon himself to act as a go-between for the couple. He went back and forth, from the jail to the Sickles home, from the home to the jail, then back to the home again, all night long, so exhausting his coachman and horses that by early Monday morning he finally took to walking the more than a dozen blocks between the two places. Implausible as it sounds, Haley evidently believed it possible that he could reconcile Dan and Teresa. But he did succeed in accomplishing one thing. He pleaded with Dan to return Teresa's wedding ring to her—"to abate her grief, which had become so violent and remorseful as to threaten her life." Dan finally agreed to the minister's appeals, provided, he said, that doing so would not look like he was forgiving her of adultery or would in any way prevent him from seeking a legal separation.

Dan told Haley he could dispose of the ring any way he saw fit. He was determined never to see Teresa anymore. She had "sundered the bonds it pledged too cruelly."[20]

◎   ◎   ◎

"The Washington Tragedy," as newspapers called it, provided a field day for the nation's press. Before the Civil War, no single other incident captured front-page headlines or attracted the extent of coverage for such a long period of time as did that of the murder of Philip Barton Key and the ensuing legal travail of Daniel Edgar Sickles. It shoved off the front page reports of war threatening Austria and France, Garibaldi's movements in northern Italy, civil war in Mexico, salacious details about polygamous Mormons in Utah. At one point, *Frank Leslie's Illustrated Newspaper*, which sent both a reporter and an artist to Washington to cover the story, proudly boasted to its readers that "Our presses have been going night and day without cessation." Even though the weekly newspaper claimed that, because it considered itself "a fit paper for a family," it was omitting "the details of evidence which only go to prove the improper relations which existed between Mr. Key and Mrs. Sickles,"[21] *Leslie's* first issue "far exceeded two hundred thousand copies; and could we have met the demand by an immediate supply, it would assuredly have reached half a million."[22] The Washington *Star* said its circulation "ran up enormously," adding some three thousand permanent readers to its subscription list, but at the expense of "extra labor and redoubled exertions" on the part of its staff.[23]

All the sordid details of the murder found their way into print, the gossip about Teresa and Barton finally surfacing in public. The press fed on any rumor, quickly echoing it without any attempt at substantiation: that Teresa was "*enceinte*" with Barton's child[24]—not true; that Dan had a separation agreement drawn up a year earlier, after the imputations linked to Beekman—there is no evidence of this; that Dan had dictated Teresa's confession[25]—although no one could prove this, the tone and wording prompted George Templeton Strong, among many, to believe that "it is manifestly Dan Sickles' work, copied by his wife, and tells damagingly against him"[26]; that Teresa and Buchanan had been intimate in London—ridiculous; that Dan had encouraged Barton's attentions to Teresa—preposterous, though some people, like Virginia Clay's husband, believed that Dan "forced his wife into Barton's company"[27]; that Dan attempted to commit suicide after shooting Barton[28]—he never even hinted at it; that Barton's younger brother Charles threatened to avenge him by killing Dan[29]—not only was no attempt ever made, but their uncle,

Chief Justice Roger Taney, urged that the case be settled properly in court; that upon learning about the affair between Teresa and Barton, the president immediately set about to dismiss Barton from his position as district attorney[30]—undocumented; that the president visited Dan in prison[31]—he didn't, but he did send a note of consolation and would try to hamper the case against him.

For many newspapers, the issue in the case went far beyond murder and adultery and the flaunting of convention. To them, and others, the entire affair symbolized everything from the widespread corruption of American politics to the decadence and destruction of American morality. "Can any of us be surprised?" asked *Harper's Weekly Magazine:*

> When the newspapers declare, and private testimony asserts, that no capital in the world is more rotten than ours, is it remarkable that a wife should be faithless and her husband shoot her seducer? When it is perfectly well understood among intelligent people that corruption of every kind prevails in Washington, reaching even to the bribery, or the pecuniary persuasion, of the men who make the laws, which the rest of us are punished if we do not obey, shall we turn pale and profess to be horror-stricken by a crime? If a whole system of practical politics be a conflict of job and jobbers, of course at the very centre [*sic*] of the struggle there will be no social honesty, no individual honor left. A man who is false or corruptible in politics is false every where.[32]

The Philadelphia *Inquirer* went further, viewing the murder as another example "of lawlessness and individual revenge which, from time to time, have been exhibited in various parts of the country, as if in defiance of the law and above the administration of justice."[33] That city's *North American* bemoaned, "Alas! for the morals of the nation when murder haunts the thoughts of its representatives, and crime even baser finds shelter under the robes of the law."[34]

A number of people were particularly concerned that the murder would set a precedent for assassination in general. Sitting in his study in Philadelphia, Samuel Rush, son of Revolutionary patriot Benjamin Rush, decried the "copious Tragedy" and "fiendish assassination": "Oh just Heaven guard our most misdirected Laws." Rush wondered whether "even this deserve the cold-blooded murder inflicted on him? Yes, if Law is forever ended in the land—and there be no other remedy—perhaps so."[35] In New York, George Templeton Strong wrote in a similar vein in his diary.

> This right of assassination is now practically so well settled that legislation has become necessary to regulate and define it and prevent its abuse. As the law now stands, Othello can shoot Michael Cassio at sight and be sure of acquittal, because he did so on his best information and belief derived from Iago. . . . So far the law is plainly defective. Moreover, none can avail themselves of this right at present without a certain amount, more or less, of address in the use of the knife or revolver. It is practically denied to a very large class of the community. And what is to be done if Cassio be forewarned [sic], if Othello's first shot chance to miss, and Cassio respond with another that does execution? How are we to dispose of his plea of "Se defendendo"?[36]

Others despaired, worried about the effect of the incident on the nation's morals. "What is the world coming to?" Congressman Lawrence O'Bryan Branch of North Carolina wrote his wife.[37] "Society itself has suffered a grievous wound," the New York Courier said. "It is a disgrace to the civilization and Christianity of the country, that such hideous abominations should occur in the high life of its metropolis."[38] The Reverend Henry Ward Beecher, who would be no stranger to scandal himself, uttered a "fearful objurgation":

> Out of this boiling and uneasy crater, just now comes a fiery flash, a rain of mud; and black clouds, full of sound and bolts, hang about it. Pride has reached forth a hand of lust, and vanity has clasped it. Then comes assassination to destroy the guilty plight. The papers are loaded down with the matter.

There is not a hamlet or ranche [sic] on the continent in which this sore of depravity is not about to drop its ichor.[39]

To some cynics, the murder was far from unusual. The Washington correspondent for *The New-York Times* said, "The vulgar monotony of partisan passions and political squabbles has been terribly broken in upon . . . by an outburst of personal revenge, which has filled the city with horror and consternation"—a vendetta, he admitted, that did not come as an "absolute surprise."[40] The outcome did not surprise *Harper's* either. Washington, it declared, "is, in a certain sense, an epitome of the moral condition of the country; and the worst of the late tragedy is not the individual adultery or murder; it is a secret tendency in the popular mind to justify the one crime by the other. . . . It is the moral, not the legal, aspect of the matter with which we are concerned. Let the law have its course—but let us not forget that crimes are still crimes, however sharp the provocation."[41] The fact was, the magazine added, "that the legal practice in this country will secure impunity to any husband who, on conclusive evidence, takes the life of the destroyer of his domestic peace."[42]

Although most people appreciated what provoked the slaying, Dan's past attitude and actions prompted second thoughts about how justified he was to take another person's life. "Mr. Sickles has never been regarded as a model of all the domestic virtues," the Springfield, Massachusetts, *Republican* wryly observed. "The character of the husband too often corrupts that of the wife," declared the New York *Post*.[43] "We cannot acquit the husband of all blame for her ruin," said the Washington *Evening Star*. "Such ruin rarely, if ever, invades the threshold of the husband who strictly discharges the duty of a head of a family."[44] The Albany *Evening Statesman* was quick to point out that Dan "has a reputation for everything *but* integrity, honor, morality and manhood."[45] The New York *Evening Post* quoted that city's *Weekly Day-Book* as saying:

We can recollect no one act of his life that should bring him even the well wishes of any mortal. . . . Mr. Sickles has allowed his wife, it would seem, free latitude to go out with Mr. Key, who escorted her to the theatres, upon riding excursions, &c. That such improprieties should finally culminate in her downfall is not the most surprising thing in the world, and they will go far to take from Mr. Sickles that sympathy which otherwise would have been quite universal."[46]

The Baltimore *Exchange* believed that "no matter what the provocation may have been, in the eye of the law, the wilful and premeditated killing of a man, cannot be less than murder, and murder in the first and highest degree."[47] The New York *Courier* thought the slaying was better suited to the lawlessness of the frontier: "Mr. Sickles did precisely that which a Sioux or a Pawnee would have done under similar circumstances."[48] The New York *Herald* shared the same thought: "In some of the border Territories, where, from the laxity of society and the weakness of infant governments, the theory of violent remedies for violent social evils is necessarily recognized, he may commence a new career, unstained by social ban."[49] He might just as well, *Harper's* said, because "he, as a politician, may be ruined."[50]

As expected, George Templeton Strong was especially critical. "The news of the day is that the Honorable Dan Sickles has attained the dignity of homicide," Strong sardonically declared. "Were he not an unmitigated blackguard and profligate, one could pardon any act of violence committed on such provocation. But Sickles is not the man to take the law into his own hands and constitute himself the avenger of sin."[51]

On the other hand, the *South Carolinian* of Columbia, South Carolina, believed that "public sentiment fully sustains Mr. Sickles. This is natural. We would pity that public sentiment which is so lost to the sanctity of the family relation as to denounce as an infamous murder that which, terrible though it be, was but a proper punishment for so heinous an offence."[52] Two newspapers that supported Dan politically also sided with him. "We cannot but sympathize with him," said the New York *News*. "Mr. Sickles," said the New York *Sun*, "may, in his conduct, have paid little attention to principles of honor and virtue; but he is not upon trial for all the acts of his life, and we think it unbecoming to enter into matters which have no connection with the present case."[53] And even *Harper's* observed that "if Mrs. Sickles was guilty, her husband held the life of her seducer in his hands. This has been the law and the practice from the earliest periods of which we have any historical record. Under the Jews, and subsequently under the civilized nations of the ancient world, the adulterer might lawfully be put to death if he were caught in act."

Harper's went on to say that there were three ways "an injured husband" could react. There was the "French method": "He may laugh at it, or he may challenge his enemy"—but the first "affords but little consolation" and the second "may superadd physical to moral injury." Then there was the "English plan": he could sue the adulterer for damages—but that involves "patience, delay, exposure, disgrace" and "seldom yields substantial profit; and when it does, it must be painful to use money obtained at the cost of the virtue of a wife." The third way was the "American system": "taking the life of him who has injured him"—and as "terrible as homicide is, this method must, on the whole, be admitted to be the most effectual, the wisest, and the most natural revenge of an outraged husband."[54]

"You have my entire sympathies," a New Yorker wrote Dan. "May they with those of other friends and well wishers, and with the main helpers time and yourself, give you the comfort perhaps the future does not now seem to afford you and yet may have in store. With God all is possible."[55]

The vehemence of the reaction to the liaison between Barton and Teresa can be attributed to the contemporary view of marriage. Marriage was central to society's stability, and reflected God's laws. A threat to marriage was a threat to society. And, taking into account the illogical double standard of the time, that threat was more likely to be realized if it was the wife, rather than the husband, who was unfaithful. A philandering man might not be accepted in polite society if he was caught, but the adulterous woman was condemned and ostracized. She was the worst sort of sinner and betrayer of the family. Ergo, the adultery committed by Teresa was an unpardonable sin, and newspapers, and the public in general, expressed little sympathy for her and then only obliquely: "It is a singular coincidence," *The New-York Times* noted, "that this little girl [Laura], Mrs. Sickles and Mr. Sickles himself, were all three only children, over whose miserable fate three living mothers now hang broken-hearted."[56] Worse, Teresa became the focus of cruel banter and the butt of snide remarks. An anonymous lyricist penned a song entitled "Mrs. Sickles," to be sung to the tune of "Villikens and his Dinah":

> In Washington city, that town of great fame,
> There lived a lady, Mrs. Sickles by name;
> She was the cause of a murder or a sad tragedy,
> Between her husband and a villain whose name was Key.

> This lady was false to her husband, its [sic] true;
> She went with another, and this she did rue;
> He hired a house for this lady of fame,
> The purpose he had, I'm ashamed for to name.

> On the twenty-seventh of February, in the year fifty-nine,
> This crime was committed by this man in his prime;
> But in stating the case, I would be to blame,
> If the truth I don't tell of both parties the same.

> In the first place this Key he was a false friend,
> Sickles he thought that on him he'd depend,
> But the false-hearted villain, his honor betrayed,
> He took his wife away, and Sickles him he slayed.

> What in this world is more sacred to man,
> Than the right of his bed, to protect if he can?
> The man that invades it, I count him a snake,
> He is not fit to live, so his life he did take.

O! woman, frail woman, you were much to blame;
Yet I cannot consider all women the same;
I maintain that women are virtuous and true,
It would not be right to condemn all for few.[57]

That theme, a concomitant of the double standard that prevailed in mid-nineteenth-century America—that woman was
frail and easily taken advantage of—would echo throughout
discussions of Teresa's involvement with Barton. Man held
woman on a pedestal, which was no more than a convenient
way to control her life. She was a goddess with attributes of
virtue and purity, but severely restricted powers. Her place,
which made reformer Margaret Fuller so despondent, was in
the home, her role to have children, her life devoted to the
happiness of her husband and her children. Not only did she
not have any rights—legal or political—she did not need any.
Her husband's job was to take care of her. Brought up in a
man's world, most women accepted this, their role. They did
not challenge any of the premises on which their lives rested—
and they often resented those of their sex who did. The New
York *Herald* perhaps best summed up the prevailing attitude
when it reported, "The general impression among the female
sex seemed to be that there was no excuse for Mrs. Sickles;
that she had position, attention, and a confiding husband—all
that a woman could wish for—and that she deserved the most
stringent fate for her violation of the dictates of virtue. In this
censure they hardly thought of the punishment the unfortu-
nate woman will suffer for the remainder of her life."
The *Herald*, however, acknowledged that there were some
"extenuating circumstances." Teresa, it declared, "was to be
pitied more than blamed":

She was young when she was married—too young to be
trusted in promiscuous society; too innocent and guileless to be
subjected to the arts of designing men; too thoughtless, perhaps, to have realized fully the enormity of her crime until she
had gone too far to retract, or too infatuated with a dishonor-
able man, who took advantage of her weakness.[58]

In a revolutionary statement for that time, *Leslie's* urged that women heed the moral lesson that Teresa's behavior taught and take a stand for all womanhood:

> We feel convinced that the cure lies with the ladies themselves. Their sex is the victim, and the vindication of their own honor rests in their own hands. A true woman should resent every wrong to her sex as one offered to herself; she should partake of an *esprit de corps* such as that which leads every highspirited American to consider disrespect of his country as an insult to himself . . . we are convinced that nothing would have so great an effect upon the morals of society, as a determined stand made by woman herself against countenance to this foulest of crimes. Away with a conventionality which permits to man what in the opposite sex is the signal for instant fall! . . . let the scorn of united womanhood be the swift avenger of the dastard's crime, and we will engage that the remedy will prove more effectual against such infamous betrayals, than all the scaffolds and penitentiaries in the Union, or all the assassinations in a century.[59]

Few persons, mostly friends and family, sympathized with Barton. "It was quite a shock to me," wrote Washington diarist Benjamin Brown French, "Key having been my personal friend for several years, and always esteemed by me as an upright, honest gentleman. . . . Poor Key—I can hardly realize that he is dead."[60] Barton's sister, Alice Pendleton, expressed her gratitude to their relation Benjamin Ogle Tayloe "for standing by poor Barton in all this dark misery. He was worthy of it, and either here or hereafter time will solve the mystery and vindicate his name." Alice asked that Tayloe thank those who had offered their condolences "for him whose memory I love, honor, and cherish . . . and tell them that *I*, who knew his heart, believe that 'God who knoweth all things' saw that he was more sinned against than sinning."[61]

Almost alone among the newspapers, the New York *Daily Tribune* expressed compassion for the dead victim:

Mr. Key's fate has been a hard one. Cut off from life and its enjoyments in an instant, without warning or opportunity, and without a chance for a single word in explanation or self-vindication, the newspapers have been filled . . . with statements calculated to blacken his memory and plunge the survivors who love him into keener anguish and bitterer sorrow. Culpable in the premises, he doubtless was; but *how* culpable, who shall say? His side of the story can never be heard in this world; all who survive him and have any knowledge on the subject have a common and obvious interest in putting him as deeply in the wrong as possible. Add to this, the anonymous tales that have been circulated of his general levity and libertinism of thought and language—stories resting on no authority and corroborated by no previous public reputation—and it must be realized that, if his offense was grievous, grievously hath he answered it.[62]

Other persons were less forgiving about Barton. As the *Evening Star* put it, "We have nothing whatever to say in extenuation of the conduct of Mr. Key; as when a man invades the marital rights of another, he carries his life in his hand." The newspaper said its "chief sympathy, we frankly admit, is with his orphan children."[63] The *Herald* spoke in the same vein: "Here are two families desolated at one blow—one life sacrificed and others made forever miserable."[64]

Perhaps the most strident criticism of all was leveled at Butterworth. The Washington *Evening Star* thought his actions deserved "rigid scrutiny" on the part of law-enforcement officials.[65] The Baltimore *Exchange* agreed, saying that his guilt "is not one whit less" and "should be equally made the subject of judicial investigation."[66] George Templeton Strong had already made up his mind about Butterworth. He was "in a yet worse position" than Dan: "He had no wrong to avenge and no passion to cloud his sense of right and wrong, but he seems to have gone forth at Sickles's request and engaged Key in conversation till Sickles could get his pistols and come up and use them. He clearly deserves hanging."[67]

As for Dan, *Harper's* believed that "if the guilty connection of Mr. Key with Mrs. Sickles be proved, it is difficult to expect that any jury will find Mr. Sickles guilty."[68] Similarly, the *Herald* was certain public opinion would "be almost unanimous in favor of Mr. Sickles." After all, "he had admitted Mr. Key to his fireside and his table, to the society of his wife and children—to that magic circle where the man, wearied and baited in political discussions, could seek and find the only repose he might know on the face of the earth." The *Herald* did not even believe that a grand jury "could be found" to indict Dan.[69]

The *Herald* was wrong.

TWELVE

Incarcerated

Our Pegasus is but a sorry nag;
He stumbles oft times, and perchance will flag . . .

E IGHTEEN HOURS AFTER HE WAS SLAIN, an autopsy was performed on Philip Barton Key. Dr. Richard Coolidge,
the Army surgeon who was with Barton when he died, performed the postmortem with Dr. Robert K. Stone, one of the
city's most prominent physicians and later Abraham Lincoln's
doctor. Because Washington did not have a city morgue at the
time, the autopsy was apparently performed at Barton's
home, on the north side of C Street between 3d and 4 1/2
streets, where his body was carried Sunday night.

The doctors' findings confirmed Coolidge's initial examination regarding the path of the bullets that struck Barton; the
doctors found between three and four quarts of blood in the
left side of his chest, where the fatal wound occurred. But
there was one surprise. Despite Barton's complaints about his
health, "the structure of the heart itself," Coolidge reported,
"was healthy."[1]

The funeral service for Barton was held at 2:00 P.M. on
Tuesday, March 1, in the parlor of his home.[2] For two hours
before it began, "a motley crowd" of people came to pay
their respects—"boy and man, rich and poor, black and
white, free and slave." The service was officiated by two Episcopal clergymen and attended by his sister's family and members of the District Court and local bar. Conspicuous by their
absence were Barton's four young children. They were being

shielded from the tragedy in Baltimore, where Barton's
mother lived. People wondered how she would bear his death;
he was the fourth of six sons that Mrs. Key, now in her seventies, had lost, and the second of them to be shot dead.

There was an elegant simplicity about the way Barton's
body was displayed. His features were "so life-like," said one
mourner, "as to make it difficult for the spectator to realize
that that once noble form lay in the stillness of death." Barton
rested in a mahogany coffin with silver trimmings that was
covered with black cloth. He was clothed in full dress—a
black cloth coat and pants and a white vest. His hands were
covered with white kid gloves and in them a bouquet had
been placed. Japonicas, geranium leaves, and other flowers
were strewn inside the casket. On its lid was a plaque bearing
Barton's name, the date of his death and his age.[3]

After the service ended, the coffin was placed in a hearse
and, followed by the mourners, taken to the B & O depot
nearby. There, with seven pallbearers in attendance, it was put
aboard the three o'clock train to Baltimore. Late that afternoon, Barton was buried next to his wife Ellen in the Presbyterian burial ground in Green Street. Barton's sister Alice took
custody of his orphaned children, taking them with her own
two children to her home in Cincinnati later in the week, after
Congress adjourned.

◎   ◎   ◎

That same Tuesday, Dan was transferred from his vermin-
infested cell to the jailer's own office, which adjoined the
guard room on the ground floor. It was an arched room about
twenty feet square that had a fireplace and contained a desk,
two bureaus, and chairs and stools. On one of the walls was a
rack containing a few old, useless muskets. The jailer, Jacob
King—"a good tempered, benevolent-looking man, whose
height seemed lost in the clouds"[4]—had the room fumigated
and its walls whitewashed. He also had a cot brought in for
Dan to sleep on.[5] Dan had a window to look out, though it
was barred, of course. He also enjoyed a modicum of ventila-

Dan in the jailer's room in the Washington Jail that was fixed up especially for him. He was permitted to have some unusual privileges, including an unlimited number of visitors, many of whom were distinguished cabinet members, congressmen, and politicians. Here the crippled clerk George Woolridge is shown conferring with him. Dan was also allowed to have his playful pet Dandy stay with him. *Courtesy New-York Historical Society.*

tion by means of a makeshift tin ventilator that was inserted into the window glass; however, it rattled so much that one visitor thought it "almost" led "one to the belief that the dungeon is part of an immense train jogging comfortably along at the rate of twenty miles an hour."[6] Dan was allowed to exercise in the narrow corridor outside the room, and to have as many visitors as he wished, with no restriction as to hours. He even had his pet dog Dandy to stay with him. He put the books and flowers his friends brought him on the windowsill.[7] He was also permitted to have his meals sent from home.[8]

Dan soon developed a daily routine. He rose early each day, smoked a cigar, took a sponge bath, had a barber shave him, ate breakfast, then read the usual "pile" of letters delivered overnight to the jail. The letters came from cabinet ministers and congressmen, Tammany allies from New York, and even political enemies—and the president.

The rest of the day was spent entertaining visitors, many of them some of the most illustrious names in national and New York politics. The visitors included, among many others, Attorney General Jeremiah Black, Secretary of the Treasury Howell Cobb, John Forney, "Chevalier" Wikoff, Police Superintendent Fred A. Tallmadge of New York; and A. Oakley ("Elegant Oakey") Hall, a future New York mayor under Boss Tweed. Dan's own father kept him constant company, and Reverend Haley came by so frequently that Benjamin Brown French, who was one of his parishioners, complained to his diary that the Unitarian minister was "attempting to do too much *out-of-door* work, and thus paying too little attention to his *inside* duties as a Pastor."[9] Two local clergymen in addition to Haley came to offer consolation: the Reverends F. C. Granberry of the Methodist Episcopal South Church and Charles J. White of St. Matthew's Roman Catholic Church.

Perhaps the most touching of Dan's visitors was his "elderly, bald-headed" father-in-law, Antonio Bagioli.[10] The old *maestro* was especially disturbed by the turn of events and sympathized with Dan. "You have heaped on my child *affection, kindness, devotion, generosity*," he was quoted as writing to Dan. "You have been a good son, a true friend, and a devoted, kind, loving husband and father."[11]

"And so the day wears on apace, and another night in prison commences," a visitor noted. Dan expressed "poignant regret for the circumstances which, in his judgment, forced him to the deed, but has not yet expressed any faltering or doubt as to the propriety of his course *under the circumstances*."[12]

After the first night in prison, Dan slept quietly for four

hours or more each night, and appeared to his visitors "cool and self-possessed" except once when some friends made "indiscreet remarks" about Teresa and Laura that "drove him nearly frantic." Dan had hung several photographs of his daughter on the wall above the desk in his cell[13] and was particularly upset whenever he thought about his reaction to the public hue and cry. He "tore his hair and gave way to passionate expressions of grief."[14] In fact, it was when Laura and other members of his family came to visit that Dan was most visibly shaken.

George Sickles had arrived from New York on the night after the murder and held a "painful interview" with him. His mother came the next morning, escorted by Manny Hart, and was so overcome that she fainted.[15] Their visits upset Dan terribly. But nothing and no one affected him as much as a visit that his daughter Laura paid him. Under the law, Dan had every right to retain custody of Laura, but he agreed to let Teresa keep their six-year-old daughter if Teresa returned to New York and her father's custody. In the meantime, he ordered that no one was to be allowed inside his house on Lafayette Square without his written permission. The only exception was Manny Hart, who was minding both Teresa and Laura. Part of that restriction was probably intended to forestall constant interruptions by newspaper and magazine reporters, but curiosity seekers were also a problem; "token hunters" had already torn "great chunks" from the tree on Madison Place where Barton fell wounded,[16] and others visited Fifteenth Street to view the house where the fateful trysts were held.

Laura came by on Wednesday, March 2, accompanied by Teresa's mother. Dan had written notes to his daughter but initially refused to see her. But Manny Hart was planning on taking her and Teresa back to Bloomingdale and Dan did not want the girl to go without seeing her. Laura gazed in wonder as she was led through the prison and, entering Dan's cell, "was at a loss to know what to make of her father's surroundings." She asked why he did not come home. Dan tried to explain that he had "a great deal of work to do, and could not leave." She then asked whether he would be going to New York with her and her mother. That and "a hundred" other questions were too much for Dan to bear, and he started to become unnerved. Sensing something she could not understand, Laura started weeping, tears streaming down her face, and even when she stopped crying, she still sobbed. Finally, Dan, tormented by her grief, gathered a few flowers from a bouquet that had been sent to him and gave them to Laura as she left. Then he hid his face in his pillow and wept "the most bitter tears he has shed since he has been in prison."[17]

Teresa was writing him, though newspapers were quick to point out that he was not answering her letters—which, it would have surprised them, was not true. She reportedly made "heart-rending declarations of repentance for having plunged him into so much sorrow" and expressed her gratitude "for his uniform kindness toward her." Teresa, according to one newspaper account, said Dan's "only fault" was that "he was too kind and over-indulgent. Had he been less so, and guarded her more carefully by the exercise of a husband's authority . . . her present lamentable position would have been avoided."[18]

Perhaps out of a sense of guilt, Dan turned down offers that friends made to bail him out of jail. Anxious to be put on trial, he waived a hearing before a magistrate, hoping that he could be immediately tried. But the District's criminal court met only three times a year and was currently in recess until the third Monday in March. Moreover, no trial could be scheduled until a grand jury officially sat and handed up an indictment.

However, municipal officials realized the enormity of the case, and the publicity it was already attracting, and quickly summoned a grand jury. Among its members was Barton's distant relation, Benjamin Ogle Tayloe, who lived next to the Clubhouse and took possession of several of Barton's personal effects,[19] but no one questioned his presence on the panel. The grand jury began hearing testimony on Monday, March 14, and ten days later indicted Dan for murder. By strange coincidence, the clerk of the court, Erasmus J. Middleton, wrote up the indictment with a gold pen he had never used before and had forgotten about—a gold pen he had carefully laid aside in a private drawer. Middleton was reminded of the pen after Barton's murder. It was the same pen that Barton had given him as a gift on New Year's Day.[20] He used it for the first time to write:

> The jurors of the United States. . . do present that Daniel E. Sickles . . . gentleman, not having the fear of God before his eyes, but being moved and seduced by the instigation of the devil, on the 27th day of February, A.D. 1859, with force and arms . . . in and upon the body of one Philip Barton Key, in the peace of God and of the United States . . . did kill and murder, against the form of the statute in such case made and provided, and against the peace and government of the United States.[21]

Dan's trial was set for Monday, April 4—a remarkably short thirty-six days from the Sunday in February when he shot Barton.

      ©   ©   ©

While Dan was in jail, his friends were busy devising strategies for his defense. For one thing, they were cooperating with the police, a strange development in a murder case, but there was good reason for their doing so. Dan's friends deplored the slaying of Barton but felt it was justified; they were intent on amassing as much information as they could about Teresa's immoral behavior and Barton's treachery as a friend.

The police were losing no time in gathering evidence and rounding up witnesses—there was no lack of either. They were assisted by two Washington lawyers Dan had quickly hired. On the day after the slaying, the two attorneys—Daniel Ratcliffe and Allen Bowie Magruder—accompanied a police officer in a search of 383 Fifteenth Street.[22] Crittenden Baylis went with them to show them the house, though Ratcliffe, a native South Carolinian and former Alabama congressman, refused to allow him in the carriage they took once he discovered that the light-skinned boy was black. The policeman had to force his way into the house. He climbed over the back fence and, with Crittenden's help, hoisted himself through an unlocked rear window of the house, then opened the front door for the attorneys. Upstairs they noticed that the bed in one room was "all in confusion" while the bed in the adjoining room "looked as if it had not been made up for a week or two." There were "soiled towels lying about." They found an odd assortment of miscellaneous items that had been left in the two disheveled rooms—a comb, a pair of gloves, some cigarettes, and a man's shawl. Ratcliffe, who knew Barton Key— he had entertained him and his wife in his home—thought the shawl looked like one that he had seen Barton wearing. He instructed the policeman to take it and the other items they found into custody.

In the days ahead, four persons who had seen "the woman" entering the house on Fifteenth Street to rendezvous with Barton were escorted by police to the Sickles's home to ascertain whether the woman they saw was Teresa. Without hesitation, all of them—Nancy Brown and the three Seeleys—identified her. After they had done so, Teresa and Laura, in company with Manny Hart, left for Bloomingdale on Thursday, March 10. There was "no possibility," *Harper's* reported, "that Mr. Sickles will be ever be reunited to his wife."[23]

Meanwhile, Samuel Butterworth consulted with a friend of Dan's, one of Washington's most able attorneys, Reverdy Johnson. Johnson was a constitutional lawyer and, though he believed slavery was wrong, he was credited with successfully arguing the Dred Scott case in the Supreme Court. Acting on Johnson's advice, Butterworth made public a disclaimer denying that he knew about Dan's intentions toward Barton or was a part of any conspiracy to murder him. He insisted that he "took no part in the contest" because he "believed them both to be armed." His relations with Barton, whom he had known for ten years, "have ever been of the most friendly character" and he had no thought, he said, "of meeting or seeing Mr. Key" that day. Butterworth said he carried "no arms" and "did not know that Mr. Sickles intended to take arms with him." But he admitted that he thought a confrontation was inevitable: "I did not anticipate a collision on the Sabbath, though I did not doubt but that it would take place at an early day."[24]

But was that the truth? Butterworth, according to George Templeton Strong, told one of his friends that he "advised Sickles to challenge Key or else to give him notice and kill him in a street 'collision,' but that Sickles avowed his preference for an *ex parte* assassination."[25]

Whatever the truth, Butterworth abruptly left Washington and returned to New York. No complaint was ever filed against him. He was not examined by the grand jury investigating Barton's murder, nor was he subpoenaed to be a witness before it. And, unbelievable as it may seem, he was never called to testify in Dan's trial although he was within a few yards of the fatal shooting and witnessed the entire tragic incident.

As the weeks passed and the day of the trial neared, Dan's defense team took shape, and it was a formidable one. Dan was going to be represented by no less than eight lawyers. Three of them were friends from New York who were serving "without fee or reward"—James T. Brady, John L. Graham, and Thomas F. Meagher.[26] The burden of the defense would fall on the shoulders of Brady and another of Dan's friends— Edwin McMasters Stanton, an Ohioan who now practiced law in Washington and specialized in cases before the Supreme Court.

Brady, who was nearing his forty-fourth birthday, was one of the nation's leading criminal lawyers. A onetime New York corporation counsel, Brady, a bachelor, was also a champion of women's marital rights and had handled the divorce of the wife of the noted Shakespearean actor Edwin Forrest. He had already won fifty-one of fifty-two murder cases. Brady was easily identifiable by his "massive head, with its corona of curls, his graceful form, electric wit, ready rhetoric, and Irish enthusiasm."[27] He was known for being "studiously polite to Judge, jury, counsel, and witnesses . . . Even where he thinks the Judge is wrong in the decision of small matters, he prefers to submit gracefully rather than consume time and exasperate feelings in disputation." He was also considered "unsurpassed in the examination of witnesses" and so logical in his presentations that "the soundest judges on the Bench listen to his exposition of knotty legal points with deference seldom awarded to so young a man." Moreover, Brady had made a special study of the subject of insanity. His only fault was verbosity.[28]

Stanton, who was to play a large part in Dan's future, was chiefly a civil and constitutional lawyer, but his closeness to both Dan and Buchanan suggests that he might have taken on the case as second in command at the president's request. Stanton had only recently returned to Washington from California where, at the instigation of Attorney General Jeremiah Black, he successfully settled fraudulent land claims antedating the Mexican War. He lived on C Street, within a short walk from both the Washington Jail and the courtroom, and became Dan's communication link with the rest of the defense team. Like Brady, Stanton stood out physically. He was dark-complexioned, with a "head which Titian would have loved to paint, so massive were its proportions, and so sweeping were its long locks and beard."[29] But unlike Brady, he was direct and blunt. "What Mr. Brady lavishes in the *suaviter* Mr. Stanton makes up in the *fortiter*. There is no ceremoniousness about him. He comes up to the point with a sledge-hammer earnestness which stands out in contrast to his colleague's extreme politeness."[30] His one fault was that he talked too fast.

Another of Dan's friends from New York who would be sitting at the defense table, Graham, was perhaps best known as a lawyer of considerable oratorical ability. He would be making the opening statement for the defense. Graham was the older brother of Charles K. Graham, the surveyor who helped Dan in the legislative battle for Central Park and was

now, due to Dan's influence, civil engineer of the Brooklyn
Navy Yard. Interestingly, in a scrapbook John Graham kept,
he wrote on the penultimate page: "Honour and shame from
no condition rise / Act well your part there, all the honour
lies."[31]

The third friend from New York was Meagher, the revolutionary who had escaped from a British penal colony—"a glorious specimen of a rollicking Irish barrister,"[32] though George
Templeton Strong considered him an "expatriated wind-bag."[33]
Only thirty-five years old, Meagher was expected to content
himself "with suggestions to his seniors."[34]

To handle matters of local law, Dan had four Washington
attorneys, including the two who had assisted the police to
search the house on Fifteenth Street—Daniel Ratcliffe, who
had a reputation of being "a keen lawyer, up to all the arts of
the profession,"[35] and young Allen Magruder, who would be
assisting in the selection of the jury. In addition, Dan would
have the services of Magruder's partner, Samuel Chilton, "a
highly respectable and intelligent-looking elderly gentleman,
whose very appearance is calculated to have a favorable impression on the jury,"[36] and Philip Phillips, a former Alabama
Congressman, "an Israelite in faith," who would also participate in the jury selection.[37]

It was an awesome team, but it faced a seemingly insur-
mountable task. There was no doubt, no question, that Dan
had shot Barton. Yet their plea would be: Not guilty.

                    ◎   ◎   ◎

Meanwhile, friends of Barton Key and his family were so
disturbed by the progress of the investigation—the lack of any
legal action with regard to Butterworth, for example, and the
joint efforts of the police and Dan's lawyers—that they started
to take matters into their own hands. They believed there was
no excuse for the cold-blooded murder of Barton, no matter
what the provocation, and especially in the case of Dan, a notorious libertine; they were determined to press for Dan's conviction by squelching evidence of the liaison between Barton

and Teresa. Instead, they started to ferret out what they could about Dan's own immoral ways.

Barton's brother-in-law, George Pendleton, turned over the cipher letter found on Barton's body to another of Barton's brothers-in-law, Charles Howard, husband of Elizabeth Phoebe Key, the eldest of Francis Scott Key's daughters. Howard took the letter home with him to Baltimore and set about trying to decipher it. A few days later, Pendleton decided to search the house on Fifteenth Street himself.[38] He and Col. Charles Lee Jones, a friend of Barton's from childhood, were met there by the owner, John Gray, but he did not have a key and they had to summon a locksmith to open the front door. While Pendleton and Lee went through the house—and, of course, found nothing of Barton's still there—the locksmith proceeded to pry off the lock to the front door and replace it. Dan's lawyers would later pounce upon the tampering with the lock as an attempt to suppress evidence.

What troubled Barton's family and friends most, though, was the president's attitude. In another ironic twist, Buchanan chose Barton's assistant, Robert Ould, to take his place as district attorney—and to prosecute Barton's killer, Dan. Ould was a thirty-nine-year-old native of Georgetown who had studied to be a minister before turning to law and still spoke "with a somewhat clerical air."[39] The problem was, as one reporter pointed out, Ould "looks more like a friend to be honorably trusted than like a lawyer to be depended upon."[40] Ould had been a lawyer for seventeen years and a member of the committee that codified the District's laws, but he was inexperienced as a trial prosecutor, and his choice as district attorney to handle such an explosive case was unusual. Barton's family entreated Buchanan to at least appoint an experienced assistant to help Ould, but the president rejected the idea. Ould was to prosecute on his own. Buchanan, it seemed, was trying, in the least overtly intrusive way possible, to support Dan.

The Key family and Barton's friends refused, however, to let the matter rest. They decided to hire an assistant for Ould themselves—James M. Carlisle, sometime city attorney for Washington and, by another strange coincidence, the lawyer for the owner of the Sickles's house with whom Barton negotiated for Dan. "Wiry, and restlessly active," the same reporter remarked about Carlisle, "nothing seems to escape his attention." Dan's defense counsel would have "more difficulty to expect from him than from the Government prosecutor."[41] "He is sharp, forcible and cautious," commented another observer. "Nothing escapes his argus eyes."[42]

Carlisle and a lawyer friend of Barton's[43] went to see the president, to ask for his official approval about providing legal aid to Ould, but Buchanan, it was reported, "expressed his surprise at this singular attempt to draw him into an interference with the usual course of justice."[44] Despite the rebuff, Carlisle decided to go ahead with his intention to help the prosecutor. In addition, Charles Lee Jones, who was also an attorney, offered to join him at the prosecutor's table to assist with legal citations.

◎   ◎   ◎

As far as the public knew, Dan would have nothing to do with his wife. He did not write her nor ever respond to any of her plaintive letters. He was the injured husband, too shattered by Teresa's infidelity, too hurt to forgive. A popular magazine illustration showed him kneeling, his hands clasped in prayer, his eyes rolled up in torment.[45] How could he forgive her? Adultery was a sin, a violation of the Seventh Commandment. It was unthinkable that he could pardon her because, if he did, how could he justify his own sin, his violation of the Sixth Commandment? And if he excused his wife's infidelity, why couldn't he have excused Barton's? Why kill the man? No, there was no reason, no cause, to forgive. No husband would have acted— should have acted—differently.

Dan's apparent attitude won the sympathy of most Americans, but it was a sham. It is clear from the letters that Teresa wrote that he was indeed corresponding with her, that in his heart he had forgiven her. He told her that he prayed for her,

An anguished Dan is depicted in his prison cell as kneeling in prayer, seemingly begging for forgiveness, in this linecut published in *Harper's Weekly*. The truth was very different. He never regretted killing Barton, nor did he turn his back completely on Teresa, despite what everyone believed. *Courtesy New-York Historical Society.*

enclosed verses in his letters, sent her symbolic kisses. He, like she, obviously believed there was much to repent.

On the eve of the trial, a month to the day that Dan shot Barton, Teresa wrote:

> Good morning, dear, dear Dan—Mr. Fields has just left. He brought me a kind, good letter from you. Thank you many times for all your kind expressions and God bless you for the mercy and prayers you offer up for me. Do not ask if I never

think over the events of the past month. Yesterday, at each hour by the clock, I thought, "One month ago this day, at this hour, such and such things were going on in our once happy home." That fearful Saturday night! No one has any idea what I suffered. If I could have foreseen the scenes of the following day I would have braved all dangers, all things, to have prevented them. Oh that Manny Hart could have been with us! . . .

I have been out of the house but three times since I came home; and you know how much exercise I have been in the habit of taking. . . . Last night I walked with Manny Hart; but my body trembled, my legs seemed to give way under me and my heart beat violently.

The verses you send me are very beautiful. I will keep them always, and I thank you sincerely for them. . .

No, dear Dan, I cannot say you ever denied me what was necessary, and you gave me many things I did not deserve—everyone knows this. . . . I shall commence a pair of slippers for you in a few days, my dear Dan. I will not stop working on them until they are finished. Will you wear them for me? Or would you dislike to wear again anything that I have made? . . .

Write when you can, and think and feel as leniently as possible of me and my unhappy position. God bless you for the two kisses you send me—and with God's help and my determination to be good, true and faithful to you and myself hereafter, those kisses shall never leave my lips while *I* am called *wife* and *you husband*. I swear it by Laura.[46]

And a few days later, she wrote:

You say that any object you have loved remains dear to you. Do I now stand upon a footing with the other women I know you have loved? I have long felt like asking you what your love affairs have been—love of the heart, or love of their superior qualities such as you have often informed me I did not possess, or attraction of face and form, or an infatuation? If during the first years we were married my good conduct did not keep you true to me, can I suppose for the moment the last year has? *Ask your own heart who sinned first, and then tell me, if you will.*[47]

It is just as well that no one knew what they were writing to each other. It might well have changed the course of the next few weeks.

◉   ◉   ◉

Congress adjourned shortly after midnight on March 3. Not one member in the four days between the murder of Philip Barton Key and the last day of the final session of the Thirty-fifth Congress said a single word on the House floor about what had occurred or mentioned the name of their fellow congressman, Daniel Edgar Sickles. The shooting was a matter of gossip, not of official congressional notice; it would have been considered unseemly to say anything in a public forum, although members were no strangers to violence and indiscretions.

Within a few weeks, the city of Washington was already lolling into its annual summer hibernation, and *Harper's* Washington correspondent reported that "this skeleton metropolis" reminded him of Oliver Goldsmith's "Deserted Village":

The stars and stripes no longer float from the Capitol, to announce that honorable gentlemen are in session; the broad trottoirs of Pennsylvania Avenue are no longer swept by the trailing products of Lyons looms; a corporal's guard of melancholy waiters mount guard over the vacant rooms at the hotels; hackneycoach horses are gaining flesh as they rest from their labors; and even 'ye gallant gambaliers,' who serve as the *garde royale* of King Faro, have closed their barracks and left, to pitch their tents at the seaside or where the healing waters flow. Washington has, in fact, no fashionable or political existence just now.[48]

No, it didn't have any fashionable or political existence, that is true. But it did have what what was shaping up to be a most unusual murder trial, one that the entire city—and the nation as well—would follow with the strictest attention:

> The peculiar nature of the case—the fact of the accused being a member of Congress, and having been formerly Secretary of Legation at the British metropolis . . . the fact of the killing having been done in a public square, in open day, before several witnesses, and without attempt at disguise or concealment—the prisoner's immediate surrender of himself to the authorities—the intolerable provocation which incited to the deed of blood, and the whole train of circumstances which led to the denouement of this domestic tragedy—combine to take it out of the ordinary catalogue of criminal trials, and to render it one of the *causes célèbres* of history.[49]

◎   ◎   ◎

A *Herald* reporter interviewed Dan in his cell on the eve of the trial. He had not seen Dan since his arrest more than a month earlier and was amazed to find him "looking so well." Dan's father was with him, together with two friends. Dandy was sitting on Dan's knee when the reporter entered the jailor's room where Dan was incarcerated, but then the frisky little dog jumped away and got between the sheets on Dan's bed. The reporter found Dan's manner "pleasantly natural. There was little or no talk about the event in which so deep an interest is felt; at the same time there was no apparent desire to evade the subject. Conversation was kept up on a variety of topics, and the accused bore his part in it with such ease that no one would imagine that he bore a great and abiding grief in his heart."[50]

THIRTEEN

The Trial

As things of value they are not esteemed—
A mere rag currency that's ne'er redeemed.
So give fair play to "Bowlin" and "Beach,"
And let them steal—we'll promise not to peach . . .

THE BUILDING where Dan was tried, City Hall, was on a steep hill that fronted on Judiciary Square, facing south. It was an imposing Greek Revival edifice with two three-story wings that extended beyond its central, columned portico. Visible to the southeast some six blocks away on another hill, Capitol Hill, was the domeless Capitol Building. The courtroom was in the east wing of the building, which had been recently completed, paid for by both municipal and federal funds and thus crowded with a variety of offices of both governments—that of Washington's mayor, board of aldermen and city council, as well as federal courts and the depository for the District's property titles, bills of sale, mortgages and other records. Unfortunately, the building was not properly guarded, and records "of vast public and private importance," said one local observer, "are daily *and nightly* exposed to the pilfering, or confided to the honor, of any scoundrel who may choose to enter a public, unguarded passage-way, and decide whether or not to mutilate them."[1]

The courtroom itself was a high-ceilinged but "dingy little room"[2] with several tall, arched windows over which were huge, cumbersome louvered blinds. Long, weighted pull cords drew the blinds up and down. A wooden "Yankee

162

clock" with a brass pendulum that ticked loudly rested on the wall opposite the judge's bench, directly over the double doors leading into the room. There were two barrel stoves nearby, but drafts were such a problem that heavy wooden screens were placed on either side of the judge's chair. One of the screens fell against the back of the chair, but fortunately the judge was not in court at the time. The weather for early April was unusual, more like "capital March weather—raw and cold, with copious piercing rains" that destroyed most of the peach crop around Washington and half of the apple blossoms.[3] As a result, the stoves were fired all the time, giving out "a heat," one reporter moaned, "unqualified by water, slightly qualified by fresh air, more than qualified by the breath of the crowd that stands between and about them, and leans over the high bar which halves the room." Another correspondent likened the courtroom to an "apartment," while yet another thought the room was "badly aired, looks damp and smells musty." So many people jammed into it during the trial that it became stiflingly hot, and one afternoon the judge adjourned the trial because of its "oppressive atmosphere."[4] Acoustics was another problem. The judge's bench was "so high and broad that the Judge cannot, without much difficulty, make himself heard over it." Edwin Stanton would complain that "his client had not heard half the testimony given where he was on trial for his life, and he [Stanton] had not heard one-fifth of his Honor's observations."[5]

To the judge's right were the witness box and the jury panel. To the judge's left, near a window, was the prisoner's dock, but it was so far from the table where the eight-man defense counsel sat that after the first day they asked that it be moved. As Allen Magruder pointed out, Virginia, Alabama, Pennsylvania, and New York allowed a prisoner to join his counsel at the defense table, and the defendant was furnished with pens, ink, and paper "although he was arraigned for the worst crime known to our laws—high treason."[6] The judge agreed to have the dock moved to the rear of the bar, behind the defense table, but Dan and his lawyers were still too far apart for them to confer easily, so Stanton stationed himself next to the dock to keep Dan appraised of legal matters.

The judge presiding over the case was peevish, pinch-faced Thomas Hartley Crawford, who had recently been ill.[7] He was variously described as "venerable and dignified looking," a "white-haired, spectacled old gentleman, rather of the ancient regime, and profoundly governed by English precedents," and "an old gentleman, whose intellect appeared to be somewhat clouded, but who endeavored to conceal a lack of capacity by a testy, querulous manner." Most people agreed, though, as the trial proceeded, that despite his being a "very old man, and a little old fogyish," his decisions were marked by "fairness and dignity."

Considering how clear-cut the case against Dan appeared on the surface, the trial was exceptionally lengthy and contentious. And it was full of surprises. The case, *The New-York Times* pointed out, "has no precedent in the annals of criminal jurisprudence . . . Never before have a Jury been called upon to sit in deliberate trial and declare for or against a man who slew his wife's seducer, that seducer being the guest of his roof, the declared friend of the husband, and the assumed protector of the wife."[8]

The trial began on Monday, April 4—on the eve of what would have been Barton's forty-first birthday—and did not end until Tuesday, April 26, more than three weeks later, taking, in all, twenty court days to complete, with respites only on Sundays. During it, the twelve-man jury was sequestered at the National Hotel, where, incidentally, one of Dan's lawyers—James Brady—was also staying.

The prosecution called twenty-eight witnesses, including all those who had witnessed Barton's murder except for two individuals: J. H. W. Bonitz, the White House page whom the president had frightened off and about whom only Buchanan knew; and, for some mysterious reason, Samuel Butterworth.

From the very first day, the courtroom was crowded with newspapermen and spectators, all men. Because of the scandalous nature of the case, it was not considered decent for a woman to attend the trial and none ever did. The only women who appeared in the courtroom at any time were all summoned as witnesses—neighbors to the Fifteenth Street trysting house Nancy Brown, Sarah Ann Seeley and her daughter Matilda, the Sickleses's friend Octavia Ridgeley, and the family's nursemaid Bridget Duffy.

Anticipating the popular appeal of the trial, the usual courtroom police detail was supplemented and on hand at 8:30 in the morning on the first day. The doors were opened to the public at 9:30 and the hundreds of men lined up outside—some said there were thousands of them—rushed to get inside and find a seat, so many in fact that most had to be turned away.[9] Although the police tried to restrict the number of spectators, a number of people got into the courtroom through a window and, not able to find seats, stood throughout the proceedings on tiptoe in order to see. Because of the crush of reporters with credentials, all the desks inside the bar were removed; in their stead chairs and long benches were brought in from the lobby. Still, there was not enough room for every journalist, and the Associated Press correspondent griped that if it hadn't been for the "imbecility and ignorance" characteristic of the "old fogy officials," there would have been "proper arrangements made by the introduction of tables or temporary desks." As it was, "no more than three or four reporters have been able to get facilities for writing, and those for the Associated Press are not among them, although application was made by them weeks ago."

In addition to representatives of the Associated Press, the press contingent included members of the major Washington and New York papers, the Baltimore *Clipper,* the Philadelphia *Evening Bulletin,* and reporters from as far as away Galesburg, Illinois. Many members of the Washington bar and the diplomatic corps attended the trial, as well. There was always a large turnout of Dan's family and friends. His father, George Sickles, and his father-in-law, Antonio Bagioli, sat together at the opening of the trial. His father—"quite a young-looking man, although his beard is long and gray"[10]—exhibited a copy

of *Harper's* that contained Dan's illustration and seemed grati-
fied when anyone said it was a good likeness.[11] Bagioli, on the
other hand, looked "poor, weakly, heart-stricken" and so
shaken up by his daughter's behavior that he would not be
able to stay for the entire trial. Among the friends who attended the proceedings were Manny Hart, "Chevalier"
Wikoff, and, at various times during the three weeks that the
trial lasted, a legion of supporters from New York, many of
whom owed their jobs to Dan. Others also on hand included
Washington Tax Clerk William J. Donoho; Peter Cagger, the
Albany lawyer Dan had recommended to Barton; and Congressmen Thomas B. Florence of Philadelphia and George
Eustis Jr. of Louisiana—the latter appearing in the courtroom
on the very day that he wed "the well known heiress," William Corcoran's only daughter, Louisa.[12]

As the courtroom buzzed with the excited banter of the el-
bow-to-elbow spectators, Dan, dressed in a dark coat and vest
and light pants, and wearing a frock coat and top hat, left the
jailhouse and, with jailer Jacob King on one side and a police
guard on the other, walked to City Hall less than two blocks
away. It couldn't have taken even five minutes to traverse the
distance. Little Joseph Kelly saw him; in fact, the boy watched
Dan being escorted to and from the jailhouse almost every
day. Kelly lived on the opposite side of the street between the
prison and the courthouse, and he remembered the prison especially well because it was around the block from the city's
only public school, on Fifth and F streets, which had a sign on
its front saying "School" with the "S" turned the wrong way.
Dan, he recalled, "was a tall, soldierly figure, immaculately
dressed, marching with head erect, glancing neither to left nor
right." There always was "a rabble crowding and running the
street but nothing could disturb the stern serenity of the man
who was on trial for his life."[13]

Judge Crawford entered the courtroom at 10:15 A.M., had
the case—No. 124 on the docket—called, and asked both
sides if they were ready to proceed. He then had the clerk—
Erasmus Middleton, who had drawn up the indictment with

A not-very-accurate rendition of the scene in the courtroom in Washington's City Hall during Dan's trial, from *Frank Leslie's Illustrated Newspaper*. Crowds did fill the room, and many people had to stand, but other than as witnesses, no women attended the proceedings. Dan—at right—stood in a dock throughout the trial, but the enclosed pen is difficult to make out here. *Courtesy New-York Historical Society*.

the gold pen Barton had given him—call out the names of witnesses. At 10:40, Dan was led into the courtroom and entered the dock. He looked, one reporter said, "a little pale, but otherwise as usual, calm and self-possessed"[14]—"remarkably calm," another reporter thought. "Mr. Sickles," *The Times* correspondent noted, "preserves a *sang froid* that is absolutely miraculous. And yet, if my judgment do not materially deceive me, he is engaged in a continuous struggle with himself. His head and his heart are [engaged in] a violent war."

The dock that Dan was put in was a peculiar, three-foot-square enclosure with a waist-high railing that one observer thought looked like "the old-fashioned, square, high church pews."[15] Another likened it to a "cattle-crate," and yet another described it as "a chicken-koop [sic] with a chair placed inside it." After Middleton read aloud the indictment, Dan was asked how he pleaded and, upon his responding "Not guilty," the trial began.

A major difficulty was finding an impartial jury. The selection process took three days to complete. One hundred and sixty talesmen were questioned before twelve were finally selected. Even though, as one newspaper pointed out, "the qualification of jurors in the matters of impression and bias as to the guilt or innocence of the prisoner is much less stringent than that adopted in criminal cases in the Courts of New-York,"[16] it was a problem to find jurors who believed they could render a fair and impartial verdict. Almost a third of those questioned[17] said they had already formed an opinion and could not be objective. One prospective juror said he could not be fair "because of the relations which he bore to the prisoner at the bar as a married man."[18] Another talesman shocked the courtroom when he candidly remarked that he "should acquit the man if he were placed upon the jury."[19] Ten others expressed the same opinion. Even several of the jurors who were chosen said they had formed an opinion, though they believed they could render an impartial verdict. One of them subsequently asked to be excused, but the judge would not permit him to leave.[20]

A poignant moment occurred when one of the prospective jurors—the only one to raise the specter of the penalty for murder—claimed that he was not biased "but if the prisoner was guilty," he "would say hang him as high as hell."[21] The man was excused from serving and as he left the courtroom he passed by Antonio Bagioli. "I heard you just now say something harsh of the prisoner," the old Italian said, "but let me ask you if you had lost your wife, or had your daughter sacrificed, would you have been able to control your feelings and be governed by your reason?" The man answered, "I don't know, but who is asking me this question?" Bagioli replied, "I am the father of Mrs. Sickles." The talesman "expressed his sorrow" for his remark and admitted that "with the same provocation" he "might have done likewise."[22]

Another difficulty that delayed the jury selection was Ould's insistence on a property qualification. The prosecutor said that anyone who served on the jury had to be worth $800. Despite defense objections, the judge upheld the requirement, saying that a law of Maryland—of which Washington had once been part—necessitated it and was valid in the federal District of Columbia.

The twelve jurors who were chosen represented a cross section of the District's year-round residents: four grocers, two farmers, a shoemaker, a tinner, a merchant, a coachmaker, a cabinetmaker, and a dealer in "gent's furnishing."[23]

⊙   ⊙   ⊙

The first of many surprises was the decision of the defense not to offer an opening argument until after the prosecution called all its witnesses. It was a move obviously calculated to accomplish two things: throw the prosecution offstride and hide from it the strategy of the defense until the last possible moment. The legal maneuver was skillfully done: Robert Ould did not learn of the defense's plan until the fourth day of the trial, after the jury was selected and he had already made his opening address.

Ould's speech was a relatively brief one for a time when it was common for legal pleas to last for days. It took him less than an hour to make his opening argument, but it was emotionally charged nonetheless. Barton's murder, the prosecutor said, was done "in the soft gush of that Sabbath sunlight . . . when the echoes of the church bells were lingering in the air." Dan, he said, "was a walking magazine. He was not only fully provided in the number of his firearms, but had also taken care to supply himself with their different varieties, each one of which, doubtless, possessed its peculiar excellence for the murderous work." To defend against "this moving battery," Barton had only "a poor and feeble opera-glass." Dan, Ould charged, "must have known" that Barton was unarmed "when the first shot was fired at the corner; and that he must surely have known it when, subsequently, the exclamations of the deceased were ringing in the air; and that, if possible, more certainly still he must have known it when he stood bravely over his victim, revolver in hand, seeking to scatter the brains of one who had already been mortally wounded . . . and whose eyes were being covered with the film of death." Dan's actions were nothing less than "remorseless revenge." Ould said he did not know "what will be the peculiar line of defence [sic] in this case," but that if it was not a legal one, the jurors "owe to yourselves, to your God, and to your country, to smite the ready hand of violence everywhere by your verdict."[24]

The prosecution case moved swiftly. The eyewitnesses, the coroner, and the Drs. Coolidge and Stone took but a day and a half to complete their testimony. Ould handled the direct examination, James Brady the cross for the defense, but he left it to both Edwin Stanton and Samuel Chilton to raise legal points and objections. When Ould announced that his case "in chief" was completed,[25] Daniel Ratcliffe took up the defense baton to chide Ould for not calling Butterworth to testify. After all, Butterworth had testified before the coroner's jury, and it was upon his testimony, among others, that Dan had been committed to prison. But the prosecutor said "he had good reasons why" he had not even summoned Butterworth before the grand jury—"and these reasons he intended to keep within his own breast now and hereafter," though "he imagined, however, that these reasons were very well known to the gentlemen of the defence."[26] What did Ould mean? The prosecutor's attempt to explain Butterworth's absence was so vague and enigmatic that it defies understanding. He never expanded on his remarks, and no one inside or outside the court was ever able to explain what he meant. One can only speculate that it was perhaps a matter of self-incrimination,

that Butterworth could not be made to testify about a situation in which he might be culpable or charged with complic-
ity. But if that were the case, why not say so? Why hide the
reason? Did the president have a hand in the failure to summon him? Like the identity of the anonymous letter-writer
"R. P. G.," Butterworth's absence as a witness for the prosecution remained forever a mystery.

                    ⊙   ⊙   ⊙

Once the prosecution case was ended, it didn't take long for
Ould to discover the defense's strategy. His ignorance was
quickly dispelled on the sixth day of the trial, Saturday, April
9, when the defense began its case. More in keeping with the
then-current legal oratorical tradition, John Graham spoke all
day that day and into the afternoon of the next trial day, Monday. He quoted the Bible, he quoted Shakespeare, and he
quoted legal precedent. His argument came down to three
major points—that Dan's wife and his friend were carrying on
an adulterous relationship; that Dan, within rights under both
the Bible and the "principle of the old rule that palliates the act
committed by the husband," had every right to act as he did
considering "the heinousness of the crime"; and, finally, and
most importantly, that Dan's mind was obviously "affected"
and there had not been "sufficient time" for "his passion to
cool."[27] That last point was a new one in American jurisprudence, a plea that had never before been made: temporary
insanity. Insanity was a valid defense; in fact, it was a long-
established principle. Madness—total derangement—had been
recognized as a defense to a criminal charge in the Justinian
Code in Roman times, and the Jewish Talmud also cites imbecility as a legitimate defense. King Edward affirmed the con-
cept in England in the fourteenth century. Ironically, Barton's
father, Francis Scott Key—although he was the prosecutor—
had recommended in 1835 that the deranged housepainter
who attempted to assassinate Andrew Jackson plead insanity
as a defense. The elder Key, himself then District Attorney cf
Washington, urged that the court follow the criteria for delu-

sion set in 1800, when a former British soldier who had suffered severe head wounds in battle attempted to slay George
III. Such reliance on English law was common. American
courts, both federal and state, tended to follow the British example, particularly after 1843, when fourteen English jurists
established the so-called M'Naghten Rule. M'Naghten was a
deluded Scottish woodcutter who assassinated the secretary to
Prime Minister Sir Robert Peel in the mistaken belief that the
secretary was the prime minister, whom he believed was responsible for his personal and financial failures. Sometimes referred to as the "right-and-wrong test," the M'Naghten Rule
held that persons could not be convicted if at the time they
committed a criminal act they were laboring under such a defect of reason due to a disease of the mind that they did not
know what they were doing—that is, they did not know right
from wrong.

Such a principle was well established. But no one had ever
raised the notion of someone being only temporarily mad.
The idea was undoubtedly James Brady's. He was an expert in
the field and had successfully argued insanity in a number of
murder trials where the defendant was deranged. But no one
was saying that Dan was deranged. His lapse was a sudden,
temporary one—like the time he collapsed at Lorenzo L. Da
Ponte's funeral. C. H. A. Bulkley, who witnessed that hysterical outburst, would testify about it, and others would also
detail how Dan reacted once he found out about his wife's
affair, heard her confession and saw Barton signalling to his
wife. It was up to the prosecution, Graham declared, "to
prove that the prisoner was at the time in sound mind and
memory." That declaration was also revolutionary. The law
until then presumed everyone to be sane, and the burden of
proving otherwise was up to the defendant. More important
from a legal standpoint, however, was that there was no precedent with regard to an uncontrollable "irresistible impulse."[28]
"Was Mr. Sickles, at the time of the homicide, such a mere
creature of instinct, of impulse, that he could not resist, but
was carried forward, like a mere machine, to the consumma-

tion of that so-called tragedy?" Graham asked. "It may be tragical to shed human blood; but I will always maintain that there is no tragedy about slaying the adulterer; his crime takes away the character of the occurrence."

Dan's responsibility as a husband was clear, Graham continued. "The connection between parent and child, and husband and wife is founded on divine law," he said, "and she being the weaker vessel, it is his duty and right to defend her; it is his duty to protect her against frailty as much as against the violence of the robber.

"It has been well said, 'Frailty, thy name is woman.' A man who obtains the affections of another's wife is as guilty as him who deflowers her by ravishment."

Dan, Graham declared, had acted "in a transport of frenzy." But Leviticus, 20:10, was clear: "the adulterer and the adulteress shall surely be put to death." And Deuteronomy, 22:22, echoed that mandate: "they shall both of them die." It was, in fact, "Christian to punish adultery with death." And as for the lapse of time between Dan's discovery of the illicit relationship and his slaying of Barton, Graham said that "there is no cooling off after such an offence. Talk about the cooling of the provocation of defiling a man's wife! A mere personal indignity can be cooled over; but if Mr. Sickles is cool now he is more than human." Othello realized this, Graham pointed out, when, upon learning of his wife Desdemona's inconstancy, the Moor cried out: "But (alas!) to make me / A fixed figure for the time of scorn / To point his slow unmoving finger at— / O!!"

And the word "Cuckold!," Graham declared. "Who would live to have the word written on his back? What man is made of flint, that he can walk in the presence of his fellow men and feel that some person was secretly smirking or smiling at him, because he knew, if he did not enjoy, his wife's inconstancy." It did not matter, he said, "how a man becomes insane; is he insane, that is the question . . . A sudden transition will destroy the equilibrium of the body; and it is precisely the same with the mind—the reaction is as strong in the mind as in the body." Dan, he argued, "did not act in cold blood." If anyone was responsible it was Barton. He and Dan had been friends who "stood as close as do those two human beings, the Siamese twins." It was all the fault of "Mr. Key, because he deflowered the wife of his friend, and attempted to keep his guilt from the detection of his friend. Intention is the soul of crime."

A key point was the defense contention that Dan's learning about his wife's adultery was equivalent to having seen Teresa and Barton actually in the act of lovemaking. In other words, the very knowledge of it, his first learning of it, was tantamount to catching them in bed. Thus, it was critical that Dan's counsel convince Judge Crawford to permit evidence of the adultery to be introduced into the trial. A lengthy argument that spilled over from one day to the next broke out over that point. One by one, Dan's attorneys took turns to try to persuade the judge to allow the evidence. James Brady declared passionately that "Mr. Key was killed in an act of adultery, within the meaning of the law."[29] Not so, countered James Carlisle for the prosecution: "the adultery must be an actual and not an imaginary or figurative one; that it must be one in the eyes of the husband."[30] Dan, Carlisle insisted, had recourse to legal redress—adultery was a misdemeanor under District of Columbia law—and the judge himself had presided over such a case in the past. Under prodding by Allen Magruder, Carlisle conceded that the case he referred to had been tried under Maryland law, and punishment for conviction was a fine of one hundred pounds of tobacco—which, taunted Magruder, meant that "the only satisfaction an injured husband could have would be a chew of tobacco."[31] Philip Phillips argued for the defense that "as the law declares adultery to be the greatest of all provocations, there could be no such legal absurdity as permitting evidence of the lesser provocation"—murder—"and excluding evidence of the greater"—adultery.[32] The defense, Phillips pointed out, was "seeking to extend the line of proof already commenced, and if it stops here we leave no doubt, morally or legally, in the mind of any man of the existence of this very adultery which we seek to establish by more positive proof."[33] Phillips insisted that as St. Matthew put it (5:28), "whosoever looketh on a woman to lust after her hath committed adultery with her already in his heart."[34] The question was: when did the adultery first come to the defendant's knowledge? "This is the time it took place, when the husband first heard of it. It then took place before his eyes." Such knowledge, Phillips concluded, "places the deceased in *flagrante delicto* at the time of his death."[35]

Judge Crawford took no time whatsoever to ponder his answer. An "almost painful" silence fell on the courtroom as he gave his decision:

> At the time of the homicide the prisoner declared the deceased had dishonored his house, or defiled, or violated his bed . . . This declaration is a part of the principal fact. It is important to the jury to have it explained, and it is the right of the defendant, in all justice, to have it explained.[36]

The judge's decision was a triumph for the defense. Dan's lawyers had effectively altered the nature of the trial. It was no longer a murder trial. Instead, Barton and Teresa were on trial for adultery. It wasn't even necessary for Dan to defend himself in the witness box at all. His counsel produced forty-three witnesses—the friends, strangers, and servants who had knowledge of some part of the illicit liaison. They testified to Barton's repeated appearances in Lafayette Square, recounted his curious signalling, described the house on Fifteenth Street and the white ribbon that fluttered from its upstairs window, told about the suspicious repast of champagne and salad he and Teresa shared in her parlor, recalled the meaningful sounds the two of them made one night in that locked room. Though often couched in euphemisms, the words clearly detailed a long-standing and frequent round of acts of adulterous intercourse.

The testimony was so shattering that Dan broke down three times and had to be excused from the courtroom. He was wrenched by Nancy Brown's testimony about seeing

Barton and "a woman" at the Fifteenth Street house,[37] and then again when Manny Hart recalled Mrs. Brown's visit to the Sickleses's home several days after the murder to identify Teresa as the woman she had seen.[38] The worst episode, though, occurred as Robert Walker was describing Dan's "terrible convulsions" that he witnessed in the Sickleses's home after the slaying. The images of that dreadful Sunday shook Dan. "Suddenly overcome and racked with a relentless grief," Dan began sobbing and crying. Edwin Stanton asked the judge to allow him to retire for a few minutes. Supported by Manny Hart and Isaac Bell of the New York Board of Supervisors, Dan left the courtroom, "his vision quenched in scalding tears, his limbs paralyzed, his forehead throbbing as though it had been bludgeoned by some ruffian, and his whole frame convulsed."[39] Behind him, "much affected by his condition," came Dan's father.[40] Walker and many of the spectators were so moved by Dan's emotional outburst that they started crying, too. After several minutes, Dan was brought back in, his "countenance still indicating extreme mental suffering, and the desolateness of his whole appearance awakening strong sympathy in the breasts of all who saw him."[41]

The letters precipitated by young Beekman's misplaced remarks in March 1858 were introduced into evidence as part of the defense effort to show how untrustworthy a friend Barton had been. The defense even succeeded with exploiting the unsavory details of Teresa's confession. A dispute erupted over whether to allow the confession into evidence. Agreeing with the prosecution this time, the judge ruled that it could not be introduced because "declarations of a wife or husband, for or against each other, stand on the same footing as though it was testimony given on the stand."[42]

The document nevertheless turned up word for word in the next day's newspapers. Dan's lawyers denied that they had leaked it to the press, but the damage was done. The shocking details—Teresa's statements about her and Barton undressing, of having "had connection" on the sofa in the parlor of her home, of doing "what is usual for a wicked woman to do"—

titilated readers across the country. The graphic descriptions—unheard-of for that time—stimulated both taboo fantasies and moral indignation. Newspapers in San Francisco were censured for obscenity when they reprinted the confession.[43]

The prosecution tried to counter that maneuver with one of its own. James Carlisle's friends in Baltimore traced Dan's activities there and were able to verify his assignations at Barnum's City Hotel with a "Mrs. Sickles" in January as well as "other acts of adultery" that Dan committed "at different times during his married life."[44] The proprietor of the hotel, his register book under his arm, appeared in court one day, but the judge would not allow him to testify: Dan's moral character was not on trial. Foiled, Ould and Carlisle tried to counter the plea of temporary insanity by showing how cool and self-possessed Dan appeared at the time of the slaying. They recalled several of their eyewitnesses and summoned several new witnesses in an attempt to prove that the slaying was a premeditated murder.

Oddly, Carlisle tried to get a translation of the cipher letter Barton received accepted as rebuttal evidence but James Brady fought against it, perhaps because Dan wanted to spare Teresa's feelings. Brady said that "bad as this woman was, there might be some lingering touch of pity or regard for her which would induce the prisoner to save her further exposure."[45] Anyway, Judge Crawford decided the letter was not valid rebuttal evidence, so both the letter and the translation were excluded, and the contents were never disclosed. A curious incident related to it, however, occurred during the last days of the trial. One of the jurors received a letter postmarked New York City in handwriting similar to that of both the cipher letter and the anonymous accusatory letter Dan received. This new letter was said to contain "scandalous assertions against some of the counsel." The letter was shown to the judge, counsel for both sides and even Dan, but no one could identify the handwriting.[46]

Some of the participants received crank letters, as well. James Brady received one from a lady in Vermont who signed her name in Greek characters "Olympia Aiken" and said she was "one of the order of frailty—one of the simple waiters for the wave of some masculine pocket handkerchief." The woman called the counsel's attention "to the following extracts" from a published account entitled "White Lies":

> I'd have no wasps round my honey. If my wife took a lover, I would not lecture the woman—what's the use? I'd kill the man, then and there. I'd kill him in doors or out. I'd kill him as I would kill a snake. If she took another, I'd send him after the first, and so on, till one killed me.[47]

The length of the case evidently wearied the jurors. The foreman, an old farmer named Reason Arnold, feared that his health "might not last him throughout the trial."[48] Another, a young grocer named Henry M. Knight, had brought his fiddle with him and was able to break up the monotony by serenading his fellow jurors "during their long evenings of their seclusion" in the National Hotel.[49] Robert Ould suggested that the court recess on Good Friday, April 21, because some of the jurors might want to be excused to attend church services. But the jurors were eager for the trial to end; they had by this time been sequestered for fourteen days. They responded that they "did not desire to adjourn over to-morrow [sic]; that they had a solemn duty to perform, and would prefer to come here and perform it."[50]

◦   ◦   ◦

The trial began to wind up on Saturday, April 23. That day, with Senator Stephen Douglas sitting at the defense table, Edwin Stanton summed up for the defense. Outside, a storm raged. The worst gale in twenty years swept through the city, so violent that three schooners were swamped in the harbor, and "it required the utmost exertions of all upon them" to save steamers and mail boats on the Potomac River "from great damage."[51] Inside the courtroom, sheltered from the savage winds, Stanton spoke most of Saturday afternoon, expounding particularly on Teresa's immoral behavior, which had destroyed her marriage.[52] As a result, he said, her daughter Laura was "cut off from all kindred fellowship. The companionship and protection of a brother of the same blood can never be her's [sic]. No sister of the same blood can ever share her sorrow or her joy. Alone, thenceforth, she must journey through life, bowed down with a mother's shame." As for Teresa, "the wretched mother, the ruined wife, has not yet plunged into the horrible filth of common prostitution, to which she is rapidly hurrying, and which is already yawning before her." What would any husband have done in the same circumstances, "who, seeing this thing, would not exclaim to the unhappy husband, Hasten, hasten, hasten to save the mother of your child. Although she be lost as a wife, rescue her from the horrid adulterer; and may the Lord, who watches over the home and the family, guide the bullet and direct the stroke." As applause burst through the courtroom, Stanton continued: "The death of Key was a cheap sacrifice to save one mother from the horrible fate, which on that Sabbath day, hung over this prisoner's wife and the mother of his child":

The wife's consent cannot shield the adulterer, she being incapable by law of consenting to any infraction of her husband's marital rights, and that in the absence of consent and connivance on his part every violation of the wife's chastity is, in the contemplation of law, forcible and against his will, and may be treated by him as an act of violence and force on his wife's person . . . By the contemplation of law the wife is always in the husband's presence, always under his wing; and any movement against her person is a movement against his right and may be resisted as such . . . The theory of our case is, that there was a man living in a constant state of adultery with the prisoner's wife, a man who was daily by a moral—no, by an immoral power—enormous, monstrous and altogether unparalleled in the history of American society, or in the history of the family of man, a power over the being of this woman—calling her from her husband's house, drawing her from the side of her child, and dragging her, day by day, through the streets in order that he might gratify his lust. The husband beholds him in the very act of withdrawing his wife from his roof, from his presence, from his arm, from his wing, from his nest, meets him in that act and slays him, and we say that the right to slay him stands on the firmest principles of self-defence.

James Brady took over the defense argument on Monday, April 26.[53] "It would have been well," he declared, "if Mr. Key had attached as much importance to the dignity of a banner as did his distinguished sire" when he used a white hand-kerchief to signal Teresa:

> If he had remembered that the star-spangled banner has been raised everywhere . . . he would never have chosen that foul substitute for its beautiful folds. . . . If his noble father incul-cated in lines imperishable the duty of the American people to protect their homes against the invasion of a foe, how does it become less a solemn duty of the American citizen to protect his home against the invasion of the traitor, who, stealing into his embraces under the pretext of friendship, inflicts a deadly wound on his happiness, and aims also a blow at his honor.

What, Brady asked, was Dan to do that Sunday that he confronted Barton in Lafayette Square—"to bid him good morning, to pass him silently by, to avert his eye?" Brady read a dramatic description of Dan's breakdown in court dur-ing Robert Walker's testimony that Thomas Meagher had written:

> Recall this scene. Think of this—think of the tears you shed yourselves as this stricken victim was borne by—think, think of this—and then may we well say to the jury, if your love of home will suffer it—if your genuine sense of justice will con-sent to it—if your pride of manhood will stoop to it—if your instinctive perception of right and wrong will sanction it, stamp "murder" upon the bursting forehead that has been transpierced with the thorns of an affliction which transcends all other visitations.

Robert Ould offered the final argument for the prosecution, and though this time he spoke at length, from Monday afternoon into Tuesday morning, his point was a simple one: "The question, however, is not of adultery, but one of murder, and whatever vice and criminality may attach to adultery does not relieve the other and higher offense of murder from the condemnation which the law passes upon it."[54] If Dan had "found" Barton and Teresa "in the act," the law "says the homicide may be reduced to manslaughter—but if the husband pursue the adulterer, and slay him out of revenge, it was murder."[55]

It was now up to the judge to guide the jury. To make sure they could hear him, Crawford stood up to deliver his instructions.[56] As he did so, a "profound" silence again fell over the crowded courtroom[57]:

> It is for the jury to say what was the state of Mr. Sickles's mind as the capacity to decide upon the criminality of the homicide . . .

> The time when the insanity is to operate is the moment when the crime charged upon the party was committed . . .

> If the jury have any doubt as to the case either in reference to the homicide or the question of sanity, Mr. Sickles should be acquitted . . . the jury must be satisfied, beyond all reasonable doubt, of the insanity of the party for whom the defence is set up . . .

> The humane, and, I will add, just doctrine, that a reasonable doubt should avail a prisoner, belongs to a defence of insanity, as much, in my opinion, as to any other matter of fact.[58]

Although the judge's acceptance of the defense plea of temporary insanity was without precedent, and the case now represented a legal landmark, interestingly it drew no public comment from law experts at that time or from newspapers and interested individuals. The reason, it seems in retrospect, is that the overriding issue of the trial was the repeated and prolonged instances of adultery committed by Teresa and Barton. The violation of the sacred marriage contract, not a legal

nicety, captured the public's attention. Nevertheless, as a result of Dan's trial, the M'Naghten Rule was amended in practice to include the defense of an "irresistible impulse," and the
trial represented the first in a series of cases that established the
principle—enunciated by Judge Crawford—that if a jury has a
reasonable doubt as to the sanity of a defendant at the moment
that a crime such as murder is committed, the defendant is
entitled to the benefit of that doubt.[59]

        ◉   ◉   ◉

Many spectators thought that "from their manner," the jurors'would not even bother to retire to render their verdict.[60]
George Templeton Strong had predicted as much, writing in
his diary that weekend: "Some people think there's a chance of
the jury disagreeing, but I predict they will acquit without
leaving the box."[61] But as "every eye" watched, the jurors
consulted amongst themselves for a few minutes and then
"suddenly they announced their intention to retire."[62]

The clock in the courtroom stood at 1:50 P.M. as the twelve
men headed through a little white door into the marshal's
room to deliberate. Slowly the spectators broke up into small
groups, talking in whispers. Everyone was standing but the
marshal, Col. William Selden, who sat in the witness box,
conferring with Judge Crawford. Dan's attorneys gathered
around the dock. He appeared, one reporter observed, "as
calm and self-possessed as usual and conversed with his
friends." Some of them spoke words of encouragement, but a
few warned him of the chances of an adverse decision. The
Rev. Dr. Byron Sunderland, pastor of the First Presbyterian
Church, took Dan by the hand, saying: "Sir, I have come to
express to you my heartfelt sympathy, and to say that if the
voice of the people of this city could speak at this moment,
your acquittal would be instantaneous. In case, however, an
adverse verdict should be rendered, be assured that you have
hearts around you, and mine not the least warm of them, to
sustain you in your affliction." Moved by the minister's
words, Dan responded, "I am prepared for the worst."

Suddenly a police officer appeared and ordered that chairs

for the jury be taken to the marshal's room. Everyone took that as a sign that the jurors were in disagreement. Confirmation came when the jury sent word that the room was cold and it wanted a stove lit in it. As the minutes passed, people began to wonder whether the speedy acquittal many thought possible was wishful thinking. Samuel Chilton prophesied that if the jury remained in deliberation for more than thirty minutes, it would be a hung jury. Fed by such remarks, rumors swept through the courtroom as swiftly as the minutes passed, and each one seemed to increase the chances of Dan's conviction: the jury stood ten for acquittal, two for conviction—eight for acquittal, four for conviction—six for acquittal, six for conviction—two for acquittal, ten for conviction.[63]

In reality, the jury was divided eleven to one. The lone holdout was in a corner of the marshal's room, on his knees, praying for "Divine guidance." He rose briefly, spoke to his fellow jurors, then retreated to the corner and knelt in prayer again. When he finally got up, he said his mind was "fully made up."

Meanwhile, in the courtroom, many spectators believed that the jurors "clearly" intended "to make a night of it." The crowd grew nervous, but Dan, The Times reporter saw, continued to bear himself "with perfectly unaffected calmness and self-possession though the anxiety and the suggestions of his friends were eminently calculated to upset any man's composure."

Then, just as the clock struck three o'clock, there was a rap from inside the door to the marshal's room. It was a soft tap but it "electrified the crowd, brought the lounging reporters up to their bearings, roused the wearied Judge, silenced the buzzing groups." A deputy marshal called out for the spectators to make room for the jury. People immediately jumped up on chairs, benches and tables. "Here they come," someone shouted. "Down in front!" called another. "Get off the benches!" "Sit down!" The judge was hammering for order, the marshal yelling, "Silence in Court! Order!"

Seventy minutes after the jury retired, the door to the room opened and the jurors filed out one by one, returning to the jury box, the foreman, Reason Arnold, leading the way.

"Gentlemen of the Jury," the clerk, Erasmus Middleton, asked dryly, "have you agreed upon your verdict?"

"We have," Arnold responded in a soft, low voice.

"Stand up, Daniel E. Sickles," the clerk ordered. Dan rose.

"How say you, gentlemen of the Jury, do you find the prisoner at the bar, as indicted, guilty or not guilty?"

"Not guilty."

Pandemonium broke out in the courtroom. Judge Crawford and Marshal Selden tried to restore order, but were totally unsuccessful. Dan's lawyers displayed a mix of emotions. Despite all his experience as a criminal lawyer, James Brady "became pale, nervous and agitated." The ordinarily staid Philip Phillips covered his face with his hands and "wept like a child" as his wife, in the courtroom for the verdict, patted Dan on the back, saying, "Now we have got you off this time. Now you be a good boy."[64]

The irrepressible Irishman Thomas Meagher clapped people on the back, asking over and over again if it was not "glorious." Bumping into jailer Jacob King, who was weeping, Meagher tried to console him "on losing his tenant." Allen Magruder, Daniel Ratcliffe, and Samuel Chilton pressed forward to greet "their liberated client." John Graham joined them at the side of the dock, looking "passive and undemonstrative." In contrast, Edwin Stanton was dancing a jig that "almost rivaled David when he danced before the ark of the tabernacle." He shouted above the tumult to ask the judge to "discharge the prisoner."

Everyone now seemed to be crowded around the dock, congratulating Dan. One friend of his from New York, Captain William L. Wiley, deputy surveyor, under Manny Hart, of the Port of New York, lost all inhibitions. Wiley rushed up to Dan, clasped him in his arms and unashamedly kissed him. George Sickles, meanwhile, "was sobbing like a child." Police officers quickly surrounded Dan to prevent spectators from tearing his clothes from him.[65] Dan slowly made his way through the mass of people towards the jury box, where he thanked the jurors for his "safe deliverance." Dan's lawyers paused at the jury box, too, to thank them.

Alone, ignored, District Attorney Robert Ould said simply that he "thought it would be so." James Carlisle was nowhere in sight.

Outside, the word spread quickly, the shouting from inside the courtroom "instantly caught up and carried from crowd to crowd at every corner" to the "furthest end of Washington." Several persons ran to the National Hotel two blocks away on Pennsylvania Avenue to summon hackney coaches. The reporter for the *Herald* was so excited that he jumped into the driver's seat of one carriage and drove it back to City Hall himself. All the hackmen at the stand in front of the National, and from Brown's Hotel down the street from it, followed the reporters' example. Meanwhile, crowds of people were hurrying in the same direction, their "excitement" as "intense as it was instantaneous."

"Completely overcome with emotion,"[66] Dan stepped down the stone stairs of City Hall amidst his friends. "Three times three cheers" rang out as he entered one of the carriages.[67] William Wiley, John Graham, and Jacob King got in with him. For a moment, Dan looked tired and almost faint, but he revived quickly once in the carriage. Some people tried to unbridle the horses so that they could draw the carriage themselves, but they were pushed aside and Dan was driven away. Several carriages carrying his father and other friends drove after them, and "an immense crowd" followed in their wake. As the "cavalcade" raced "at railroad speed" down Pennsylvania Avenue, men, women, and children on the sidewalks shouted "enthusiastic cheers."

Dan wanted to avoid going home to his deserted house on Lafayette Square. Instead, he planned to stay for several days with his friend and neighbor, John McBlair, in McBlair's apartment in the Decatur House. Somehow the news of their coming raced ahead of them and as they drew up to the house, thousands of people were gathered in front of it to greet him.

Inside the house, Dan turned to Jacob King and, taking the jailer by the hand, said, "I would wish, if I could, to make it known how grateful I feel for all the affectionate and considerate kindness that has made my prison a second home." Just then an old vendor was let into the house. He was carrying a basket of oranges. "Mr. Sickles," he said, "I am a poor man, but I have a wife and child at home, whom I love, and I, if you will take this poor gift, as a token of how I honor a man who has taught me how to defend them, will be made most happy."[68]

◎   ◎   ◎

That evening, James Brady invited all the jurors to his suite at the National Hotel to join him, Stanton, Magruder, and Chilton in a celebration party. "I want you, Sir," one of jurors, coachmaker John McDermott, told him, "to tell the people of New-York that the citizens of Washington are not behind those of any other part of the country in devotion to the family altar." When Henry Knight showed the lawyer the fiddle he played for his fellow jurors, Brady said he wished he had known about it earlier as "we might have made our minds easy, for no fiddler was ever known to find a conviction of murder." Jury foreman Reason Arnold expressed his gratitude that he "had lived to render such a verdict." He said he "hoped and believed the great God would acquit as the jury had done." Another juror, haberdasher William M. Hopkins, left no doubt about how he felt about Dan's justification in killing Barton. He said "he would not for himself have been satisfied with a Derringer or revolver, but would have brought a howitzer to bear on the seducer." After canvassing the jurors, the reporter from *The Times* wrote that "they gave their verdict on the principle that, in the absence of any adequate punishment by law for adultery, the man who violates the honor and desolates the home of his neighbor, does so at the peril of his life, and if he falls by the outraged husband's hands, he deserves his doom."

There was the sound of music outside. The partygoers

leaned from the windows. The Marine Band was on the street below Brady's suite, serenading the victorious lawyers. After playing several tunes, the band, accompanied by several thousand men and women, marched smartly down Pennsylvania Avenue to Willard's Hotel to play for John Graham, who was staying there. Then the band trooped to Lafayette Square but didn't stop—Samuel Chilton had urged them not to call on Dan because "he was overcome by his feelings and sought repose"—and continued on to Philip Phillips's home nearby on G Street. Phillips came to the door and spoke. The result of the trial, he said, was "a new era" in the "jurisprudence of the world."

"An honest, upright, and intelligent American jury," Phillips concluded, had "established a precedent which all civilized nations would henceforth recognize and be guided by . . . that when a man violated the sanctity of his neighbor's home he must do so at his peril."[69]

⊙   ⊙   ⊙

Newspaper reaction around the country was virtually unanimous. The Baltimore *Republican* best summed up what most newspapers considered the meaning of the verdict: "All we feel called upon to say is, that the people of this country *will not convict* a man of murder, under such circumstances of provocation. It is well that this fact should be understood by the libertine. Public opinion is the law in the case."[70]

One of the few newspapers that decried the jury decision was the Philadelphia *Evening Journal*. It was concerned that the verdict represented "not only a revolting, but a most dangerous doctrine to be sent abroad throughout the land, bearing upon it the seal of judicial recognition and authority."[71]

Robert Ould, who would become a Southern agent for the exchange of prisoners during the Civil War and later had charge of the Confederate Secret Service, was vilified for what many thought was his inept prosecution. As "Mr. Ould himself naively admitted," the New York *Daily Tribune* said, "he had been outwitted." The prosecutor's cross-examination was "far from being thorough or searching," and it was clear that he "evidently has no love for his profession. At no time did he manifest a real lawyer's ardor or ambition, and in private he admitted more than once that the case fatigued him, or gave him the headache."[72]

The Baltimore *Patriot* thought it knew the reason behind Ould's lack of zeal: "We may somewhat account for the seeming tenderness and extreme delicacy of the prosecution on remembering the fact that the accused was a fast friend of the highest officer of the nation."[73] Indeed, the president was said to be "delighted" by the outcome of the trial.[74] George Templeton Strong's reaction to the verdict was a curt, "Sickles acquitted, of course."[75]

The *Tribune* thought that even the judge lacked the proper judicial attitude. "It may now be regarded as settled," it declared, "that while Mr. Crawford is Judge, no member of Congress can be convicted of a criminal offense."[76]

Frank Leslie's Illustrated Newspaper was especially appalled at the outburst in the courtroom. "The scene which followed the delivery of the verdict was most disgraceful," it said, and William Wiley's embracing of Dan and kissing him "converted the whole affair into somewhat of a burlesque."[77]

Benjamin Brown French, who was a friend of Barton's, believed that Dan would carry the murder on his conscience for all time: "Sickles, who murdered Key in cold blood, has been acquitted by a Washington jury, and perhaps, in view of *all* the circumstances, rightfully acquitted, but the blood is on his hands, & the 'damned spot' will never 'out' as long as he breathes mortal breath."[78]

A similar feeling was expressed by the *Journal of Commerce,* which expressed pity for Dan: "It is a fearful thing to take the life of a fellow-being, and while the public sympathy will generally approve the verdict of the jury, the prisoner, if he have the heart of a man, cannot fail to carry with him feelings of poignant sorrow in which he finds himself, although acquitted by human tribunals."[79]

◎   ◎   ◎

Not Dan Sickles. He showed no feelings of poignant sorrow. Before he left Washington to return to New York, Dan walked across Lafayette Square to Madison Place with two friends and paused by the spot where he shot and killed Barton Key. He described to them how he and Barton grappled together into the street and up toward the Clubhouse, and pointed out "the localities where the different incidents took place." He had, he said, every intention to kill him.[80]

As unremorseful as he was, Dan had nevertheless won the sympathy of the nation. His wrong had been righted, the murder was accepted as justified, he, the injured husband, was vindicated. Popular opinion was, indeed, on his side. He could now resume his life and career, his head held high, once more a respectable, respected citizen.

But then Dan did the unthinkable.

FOURTEEN

"Hail! Matchless Pair"

But that the Muse, a stubborn, wilful jade,
And somewhat jealous, will refuse her aid . . .

H E FORGAVE TERESA. By that simple act of what ordinarily would be considered Christian charity, Dan produced an incredibly swift—and unforgiving—turnaround in public opinion. The public could condone murder as retribution for adultery, but it could not condone a murderer's willingness to forgive. After all, if Dan were capable of Christian charity and had a forgiving spirit, why did he come to it so belatedly? Murder first, forgiveness second? Temporary insanity—an act of passion—aside, it was all too much for the public to accept.

The first intimation that the public got of the reconciliation of Dan and Teresa came in a brief item in the New York *Herald* on July 12, some two and a half months following the trial. Dan had returned to New York and was living with a friend in Bloomingdale, not far from his own residence.[1] There had been talk of a divorce, but guided by their two fathers and advised by their counsel, so the story went, Dan and Teresa started to see each other again. And now, the *Herald* reported, they were about to "resume marital relations, if they had not already done so." The families had decided that "it would be better for Mr. Sickles and his wife to live together again in peace and mutual affection, burying the past in the grave of oblivion. Both parties have agreed to this step, and it is said their love is greater than ever."[2]

The startling news created an uproar. Public reaction was immediate and hostile. The turnaround was so complete that those who had once denigrated Barton now defamed Dan. Why, people asked, was it necessary for Dan to murder Barton? The Washington correspondent of the Philadelphia *Press* echoed what was on everyone's mind: "If Mrs. Sickles was herself guilty before the death of Key she is guilty still, and if one can be forgiven now Key ought to have been forgiven in February . . . I can only regret, for the sake of Mr. Key, that he [Sickles] had not months ago agreed to forgive his wife, and to spare a human life, which under the circumstances, as now developed, ought to have been spared."

"All the feeling for poor Key has been revived," the correspondent added, "all the grief suppressed by the verdict in favor of Mr. Sickles has been called forth anew by the forgiveness extended by Mr. Sickles to his wife, and Heaven knows where it will end."[3]

"The inquiry everywhere now," the New York *Evening Post* editorialized, "is, why Key was killed at all, or, having been killed, why such extraordinary efforts were made to screen the slayer?"[4] The Washington *Evening Star* said; "In condoning her offence, Sickles proclaims that he was himself the author of her revolting confession; or that a woman such as she describes herself to be, therein, is not unfit to be his wife; that he shot Philip Barton Key unarmed and unaware of his approach with any such intent, for an offence which he does not regard as sufficient cause for more than a temporary estrangement between the woman and himself, she being as much a principal in the affair as the victim whose life he took in so cowardly a manner."

Now that Dan had showed "his true colors," the *Star* continued, he "has opened the eyes of the dupes of his late melodramatic programme, so as to enable them to realize the facts that the aspersions showered upon Key, for his (Sickles's) benefit, were . . . baseless." The *Star* said that "this *denouement* . . . will do some good, we trust, in teaching District of Columbia juries their duty between law and justice on one side and a vulgar bastard public opinion manufactured for the moment by theatrical appliances to cheat law and justice, on the other."[5]

Dan's friends, said the *Sunday Atlas*, "have been completely disgusted by the announcement of the fact that he has taken the polluted female again to his bosom as a wife."[6] *The New-York Times* pointed out that Dan's friends, both personal and political, "honestly believed him to be a man maddened by intolerable wrong, and in that belief interposed their influence between him and the hasty rage of public feeling at the time of his trial at Washington." Those friends now insisted, the newspaper continued, that "they should not be made responsible" for "a step taken entirely on the impulse of Mr. Sickles himself, without their knowledge, and in the face of their positive remonstrance and disapproval."[7] The *Evening Post* took up the same theme. "The friends of Sickles, who stood between him and the gallows, which the *Times* euphoniously describes as 'the hasty rage of public feeling,' were highly delighted with the vengeance, but are not with the forgiveness. They shouted bravo and flung up their caps when 'the most resolute of avengers' shot Key in cold blood, but they turn their faces from 'the most relenting of husbands'."[8]

The Sickleses, the New York *Herald* said, "are just now representatives of a bad state of society, wherein political success and power are to be had at any sacrifice of personal honor and private morality." Dan and Teresa, the newspaper said, "are the types, not the founders, of the school; and in the whole history of the affair, from the first to the last, there may be read a most mournful and dangerous indication of the corruption, demoralization, the dishonor and the debauchery that seem to be inseparable from the political history of the country in these latter days." The *Herald* then raised a question that continues to haunt the political arena to this day: How can one divorce the character of one's private life from his, or her, public life?:

We are quite conscious that the politician by profession claims to have one code of morality for his private life and another for his public career; but this is false, logically and practically. Here and there one may find an exception, but, as a rule, the corruption, the thieving, the lying and general immorality which obtain in political circles are carried into private life, staining alike the senatorial robes, the gentleman's honor and the woman's chastity. The legal maxim, false in one thing, false in all, applies equally, and perhaps with greater force, to this fancied distinction which is hypocritically set up between a man's private and public character. The thief in the lobby, the liar in the forum, the slanderer in the Capitol, must be the same in private life in a common sense view of the matter.[9]

Some newspapers became derisive, even going so far as to print satiric comments. One, the *Sunday Mercury*, published an "Epithalamium"—a lyric ode customarily written for a bride and a bridegroom—"in honor of the union of a distinguished couple, who had been parted for a brief period by circumstances over which neither of them had any control." It went, in part:

> Hail! matchless pair. United once again
> In new born bliss forget your bygone pain.
> Hail! turtle doves, returning to a nest
> Defiled, yet dear—determined to be blest!
> What though the world may say, 'With hands all red,
> Yon bridegroom steals to a dishonored bed.'
> And friends, estranged, exclaim on every side:
> 'Behold! Adultery couched with Homicide!'
> What thought (in dreams) a bleeding spectre flings
> Your curtains backward, like a demon's wings,
> And howls, exulting, as entranced you lie
> Beneath the glare of its sardonic eye:
> 'Live on—live on! each other's proper hell;
> None but yourselves could damn yourselves so well!'[10]

Finally, Dan, faced with almost daily assaults in the press, decided to offer a public explanation. His statement—a letter to the editor of the *Herald*—was reprinted throughout the nation. It was both poignant and self-righteous. In it, Dan urgently appealed for the right to conduct his personal family life in privacy. He was especially concerned about protecting his daughter Laura. The public response to the news of his reconciliation, he realized, only proved to him that he had "rescued the mother of my child"—he never called Teresa by name—from "misery and perils." He knew of no "statute, or code of morals," that prevented him from forgiving her. And he did not care what his forgiving her meant to his career or public life. He expressed no regret, no sign of contrition whatsoever, about his slaying of Barton; in fact, he never mentioned Barton's name either, or said one word about the murder:

> Through the course of sad events, which during the last few months have brought so much affliction upon my family, I have been silent. No amount of misrepresentation affecting myself only could induce me now to open my lips; nor could I deem it worth while [sic] under any circumstances to notice what has been or can be said in journals never regarded as the sources or the exponents of public opinion, for in these it is too often obvious that only unworthy motives prompt the most vindictive assaults upon the private life of citizens holding public stations. But the editorial comments in the *Herald* of yesterday, although censorious, (of which I do not complain, whilst I read them with regret), differ so widely in tone and temper from the mass of nonsense and calumny which has lately been written concerning a recent event in my domestic relations, that I cannot allow a mistake, into which you have been led by inaccurate information, to pass without such a correction as will relieve others from any share of the reproaches which it is the pleasure of the multitude at this moment to heap upon me and mine.
>
> Referring to the forgiveness which my sense of duty and my feelings impelled me to extend to an erring and repentant wife, you observe, in the course of your temperate and dignified article, that, "It is said, however, that the last phase of the affair was brought about through the advice of his lawyers." This is entirely erroneous. I did not exchange a word with one of my

counsel upon the subject, nor with any one else. My reconciliation with my wife was my own act, done without consultation
with any relative, connection, friend or adviser. Whatever
blame, if any belongs to the step, should fall alone upon me. I
am prepared to defend what I have done before the only tribu-
nal I recognize as having the slightest claim to jurisdiction over
the subject—my own conscience and the bar of Heaven. I am
not aware of any statute, or code of morals, which makes it
infamous to forgive a woman; nor is it usual to make our domestic life a subject of consultation with friends, no matter
how near and dear to us. And I cannot allow even all the world
combined to dictate to me the repudiation of my wife, when I
think it right to forgive her, and restore her to my confidence
and protection.

If I ever failed to comprehend the utterly desolate position of
an offending through penitent woman—the hopeless future,
with its dark possibilities of danger, to which she is doomed
when proscribed as an outcast—I can now see plainly enough,
in the almost universal howl of denunciation with which she is
followed to my threshold, the misery and perils from which I
have rescued the mother of my child. And although it is very
sad for me to incur the blame of friends and the reproaches of
many wise and good people, I shall strive to prove to all who
may feel any interest in me, that if I am the first man who has
ventured to say to the world an erring wife and mother may be
forgiven and redeemed, that, in spite of all the obstacles in my
path, the good results of the example shall entitle it to the imi-
tation of the generous, and the commendation of the just.

There are many who think that an act of duty, proceeding
solely from affections which can only be comprehended in the
heart of a husband and a father, is to be fatal to my professional, political, and social standing. If this be so, then so be it.
Political station, professional success, social recognition, are
not the only prizes of ambition; and I have seen enough of the
lives of others, to teach me that, if one be patient and resolute,
it is the man himself who indicates the place he will occupy;
and so long as I do nothing worse than to reunite my family
under the roof where they may find shelter from contumely

and persecution, I do not fear the noisy but fleeting voice of popular clamor. The multitude accept their first impressions from a few; but in the end men think for themselves, and if I know the heart—and sometimes I think that in a career of mingled sunshine and storm I have sounded nearly all its depths—then I may reassure those who look with reluctant forebodings upon my future to be of good cheer, for I will not cease to vindicate a just claim to the respect of my fellows; while to those motley groups, here and there, who look upon my misfortunes only as weapons to be employed for my destruction, to those I say, once for all, if a man make a good use of his enemies, they will be as serviceable to him as his friends.

In conclusion, let me ask only one favor of those who, from whatever motive, may deem it necessary or agreeable to comment in public or private upon this sad history; and that is, to aim all their arrows at my breast, and for the sake of my innocent child, to spare her yet youthful mother, while she seeks in sorrow and contrition the mercy and the pardon of Him to whom, sooner or later, we must all appeal."

Dan's plea drew some sympathetic response. A Lockport, New York, man wrote him "in answer to the many unkind and uncharitable criticisms on your recent act (that of receiving and forgiving your repenting wife)." He explained:

I feel impelled as a duty to express to you my gratification and the gladness for this noble act . . . the whole is softened and wrong greatly mitigated by this one deed of forgiveness.

Although in your political life nor in your (reported) social habits heretofore I can find little to commend you this act has given me more satisfaction than to have seen you (had you been my favorite) succeed to the highest political honors. . . . the course in the matter will not only add to you *true* friends but ever give you great satisfaction. And believing, as I have, that the wife you have so nobly forgiven 'has been more sinned against than sinning' will yield the "grateful fragrance of the crushed flower."12

Another Lockport resident—a "minister of the New Testament" as he put it—said he had "two dear little daughters, the eldest the age of yours:"

> I appreciate your regard for that little one as expressed in your letter to the public. She has suffered early in life, a terrible shock by the acts of the past in her fathers [sic] house. Nothing can save her and those parents dearer to her than all the world beside, but the conversion of her parents by *the Spirit of God* and a determination on their part to lead *a new life* . . . Are you willing to confess to the Savior your sinfulness as Paul did in his day?[13]

But such letters of sympathy and support were few and far between, and, as individual expressions, they were unpublicized and had no effect on public opinion. Most people continued to express unrestricted condemnation of the reconciliation. Never one to harbor an unexpressed ill feeling about Dan, George Templeton Strong wrote in his diary:

> The last and most surprising phase of Dan Sickles's domestic difficulties much talked of. He publishes a well-written manifesto in today's *Herald*. Probably the lovely Theresa [sic] had a hold upon him and knew of matters he did not desire to be revealed. Some say he had promoted her intrigue with Key; others that our disreputable old Buchanan's interest in his welfare was due to relations with her which her husband had encouraged. He must have been in her power somehow, or he would not have taken this step and sacrificed all his hopes of political advancement and all his political friends and allies. He can hardly shew [sic] himself at Washington again.[14]

◎　　◎　　◎

But Dan did return to Washington for the first session of the Thirty-sixth Congress, which began on December 5, 1859. For all intents and purposes, however, he became a shadow figure. He exercised little influence in House matters, took little part in debates and was virtually ostracized by his congressional colleagues. He abandoned the idea of seeking reelection to a third term. His use to the Democratic Party was virtually nil; the pipeline to the White House that he represented—so vital to Tammany Hall—was severed. Buchanan did not dare to be seen with him or connected to him in any way. Southern states were moving closer to secession, the nation closer to war, but Dan literally sat on the sidelines, an observer, ineffectual.

Dan no longer resided in Lafayette Square. Instead, he lived alone in an apartment on Thirteenth Street, a few blocks east.[15] As might be expected, his wife and child remained in Bloomingdale; the Sickleses were now anathema to capital society. The Washington correspondent for the Philadelphia *Press* said there was "very little disposition manifested by any of the representatives to establish intimate relations with Mr. Sickles," though in truth, the reporter added, "he seems to invite no such relations. He seems conscious that public opinion is greatly against him; and although his bearing is full of characteristic ease and coolness, it is singularly retiring and unobtrusive."

Like clockwork, Dan entered the House chamber "every day, about fifteen minutes past twelve, when debate has begun." He was always dressed in "exquisite taste, and has cultivated a large pair of brown whiskers." There was a sadness about his appearance, though. He walked in "quietly from the side-door [*sic*], and takes his seat on one of the sofas on the western side of the House, where, resting his head on his gloved hand, he remains seated, taking no part in the discussions—voting, when called upon, in a low voice."[16]

One day, Mary Miller Chesnut, the wife of newly elected Senator James Chesnut Jr., of South Carolina, was seated in the House gallery with some women friends. Glancing down, she saw Dan "sitting alone" on a bench. The much-traveled and "worldly" woman,[17] a usually acerbic person, took pity on him. "I have seen only two men in all my life who were sent to Coventry thoroughly and deliberately," she later recalled. "One was a fine young officer in all his bravery of naval uniform, travelling with a rich old harridan at her expense." The other was Dan: "He was left to himself as if he had smallpox."

Mrs. Chesnut asked a friend sitting next to her, "What had the poor man done?" She was told that he had killed Philip Barton Key, but "that was all right. It was because he condoned his wife's profligacy, and took her back" that people avoided him. "'An unsavory subject,'" said another friend "with a sniff of disgust.'"[18]

FIFTEEN

"A Sort of Poobah"

No more a rude barbarian is he prized,
But claims his place among the civilized . . .

THE CIVIL WAR saved Dan's career. But his subsequent life—all fifty years and more of it—continued to be an unusual olio of success, misadventure, and scandal. And his marriage never recovered from Teresa's traumatic and devastating affair with Barton.

Why Teresa might want to reconcile is easy to understand. No matter how penitent she might be, a woman besmirched by the vilest gossip would find life near to impossible. And, after all, she had violated the sanctity of marriage by committing adultery, an unpardonable offense in the day of the double standard. Who would support her and her child? Her father? Antonio Bagioli was in his mid-sixties, and though he would live another twelve years, his spirit had been broken by his daughter's sordid affair. An indication of his inability to support her was his decision in 1861 to take in boarders at the house he then owned on Thirty-second Street.[1]

Moreover, there was, as so many others had recognized, a childlike quality about Teresa. She was not the type to be independent, to go her own way, to face a hostile world alone. Her letters reveal this. Dan must have taken her passive nature into consideration when he said that he wanted to rescue "the mother of my child" from the "utterly desolate position of an offending though penitent woman—the hopeless future, with its dark possibilities of danger, to which she is doomed when

200

proscribed as an outcast." Certainly, his forgiving Teresa did
not help his political career. So one has to accept on face value
his simple explanation.

Although Dan exercised little political influence, Edwin
Stanton, for one, appreciated his perspicacity about the way
Buchanan's mind worked and was able to use him at a critical
moment in the nation's history—or so Dan said. As a result,
Dan "personally" claimed credit for the unswerving stance the
federal government took at Fort Sumter as the year 1860
turned into the portentous year 1861. Stanton would prove
such a valued friend as Lincoln's Secretary of War in the politics of the war that followed that a future son of Dan's would
carry his surname as his middle name.

A half-century later, on the fiftieth anniversary of the out-
break of the Civil War, Dan explained to a veterans' association his critical role. Secessionists in South Carolina had already seized Fort Moultrie in Charleston harbor and were
demanding that Union troops on nearby Fort Sumter be with-
drawn. Buchanan, Dan said, "was only anxious that peace
should be preserved while he remained President" and "was
strongly inclined to yield to this demand in order to avoid
bloodshed." Dan, long a friend of many southerners, believed
in peaceful secession, but their threats of violence angered
him. Stanton—then Buchanan's attorney general—was enraged, too, as was Jeremiah Black, now secretary of state, and
others in Buchanan's cabinet who had replaced members from
secessionist states. Stanton, Dan related, "asked me to go up
and talk to the President" about refusing the southern demand. But Dan thought he knew a more feasible alternative:
"how to influence him—not by what I say, but in another
way." What he had in mind was a ruse that came easily to
a veteran of Tammany Hall political battles. "I will pepper
him to-morrow [sic] with no end of telegrams congratulating
him on his heroic fortitude," he told Stanton. "Well," Stanton
replied incredulously, "that is a new way of managing a
President."

Dan immediately got on a train heading north. At Philadelphia, he met with his friend Daniel Dougherty, whose political connections were extensive. "Bring out your guns tomorrow morning early," he told Dougherty, "fire 100 guns in Inde[pe]ndence Square . . . go to all the leading merchants asking them to send him telegrams—long ones—approving his patriotism; go to all the newspapers asking them to print double-headed editorials praising the president." Dan made the same request of friends in Trenton and New York. He personally went to Wall Street, "had the bank presidents, & the leading manufacturers send telegrams to the same effect & went to the editors of the *Herald* and *Sun* and had them print double-headed editorials, all to the same effect."

The hastily manufactured wave of support and approval worked. "Victory—we won," wired Stanton. "Thank you for your kind offices."[2]

Eight days after war broke out on April 12, 1861, when southern guns bombarded Fort Sumter, Teresa, troubled by reports that Dan was "determined to join the Army even as a Private," wrote him from Bloomingdale with an old complaint: "*Please come home dear* Dan—It seems so unsettled, so lonely for us to have you so much away." Her letter was full of gossip—about the rats that had gotten into a storeroom, how "hard at work" she was cleaning up the attic, putting away winter clothes and taking out summer "articles." She wrote that their hens were laying "a fair amount of eggs" and the horses "never looked better," but that "poor *Dandy*" was "a pitiful object to behold." She told about a friend's funeral, the latest doings of neighbors, that Henry Wikoff had visited briefly. Laura "sends you much love & many kisses." There had been talk that Teresa was "desperately unhappy," could not sleep, was taking opiates.[3] "I am pretty well," she assured Dan, "but *very* bilious, have been going it strong on Brandreth's Pills—dont [*sic*] think them *so far* very wonderful." She ended her letter with another fervent plea: "dear dear Dan—Write soon and often. Let me know when we may expect you home. God bless and protect you dear dear Dan—and believe me your sincerely attached wife—Terese."[4]

Dan did return home, to organize the Excelsior Brigade. He and William Wiley took it upon themselves to raise the volunteer unit, and in the process ran up huge debts to pay for uniforms, equipment, food, supplies, and housing. An old ally, Charles Graham, left his post as Civil Engineer of the Brooklyn Navy Yard and brought with him four hundred workers to join the unit. The recruiting drive took up all of Dan's time, and he was not at home to celebrate the Fourth of July. Writing to her old friend Florence, Teresa went into detail in an almost infantile way about the "great time" she had that long holiday weekend with a group of friends and her parents at Bloomingdale. "I can't begin to tell you all the sport we had, went rowing, . . . stilt walking seesawing on the whirligig, pitching quoits, racing, riding, eating & drinking out of doors, etc etc etc—in the evening we had a fine display of fireworks & then a large bonfire." It was as though there was no war going on; there was no mention of it in her letter, nor any indication of her husband's activities. The night following the celebrations, Teresa continued, "we revived an old amusement which you once got enough of—I slapped Ma (in face) and she threw water on me. . . . So pitcher after pitcher of water was thrown." Teresa was so "*drenched*, the hall near my door looked very much like a small lake. I ran to get away from Ma when I slipped near the applewood room & down I went—hurt both of my arms & hands—as for my body it is a mass of black & blue spots." And then, in a childish enumeration of the pets she had acquired, she concluded with a remark that on the surface was strange. She now had, she said, "*two new dogs* . . . I am also to have two peacocks & a monkey.—& what after that I dont [sic] know *not a 'Baby'* I promise you."[5] The inference was that she and Dan were not having sexual relations.

The Excelsior Brigade—Dan, a full colonel, at its head—was summoned to Washington after the disastrous First Battle of Bull Run. He left behind him more than $283,000 in unpaid bills for equipping the brigade. Wiley—the friend who had kissed him in the courtroom when he was acquitted—was dunned for the debts, and, as a result, was forever afterwards embittered toward Dan and refused to talk to him.

Dan and his men fought with distinction in the Peninsular campaign. When he had time he wrote home, to Laura. "Many thanks my darling Papa," his daughter, now nearing nine years old, responded, "for your affectionate letters":

Mamma, Grandmamma, and I, spent the day with Grandma Sickles, on Wednesday, and had a very pleasant time.

How very fine your Soldiers and Horses must appear and how glad I should be to see them. Will you let us all come to see you one of these days.? [sic] Grandma Sickles says she intends to make you a visit.

Oh' how happy we shall be if you can come to us at Christmas! Accept an affectionate embrace and 10,000 kisses dear good Papa, from your Laura.[6]

There is no evidence that Dan returned home for Christmas. His career as an Army officer appears to have dominated all his attention. In time, Dan was breveted to a brigadier general and later a major general. At one point in the spring of 1862, a Tammany friend wondered if it might not be politically advantageous—congressional elections were coming up that fall—if Teresa visited the wounded of his brigade who were hospitalized in New York. Teresa readily agreed at first, then had second thoughts. "Upon reflection," she wrote, "I think it advisable for me to defer the visit. . . until I hear direct from the General. He will write to me if he desires me to call."[7] She never did visit the hospitalized men, so presumably Dan did not want her to do so; he undoubtedly believed that more harm than good would be done. Anyway, he was too busy to think of reviving his political career.

Dan commanded the Second Division, III Corps, at Antietam and Fredericksburg, and was in command of the entire III Corps at Chancellorsville, where he helped to stymy Stonewall Jackson's encirclement of the federal lines. He was

in command of the III Corps when it marched onto the battlefield at Gettysburg on the fateful second day of that battle,
July 2, 1863—and he did a rash thing. The Union commander, George Meade, had Dan station the III Corps to
cover two hills on the left of the Union line known as the
Round Tops. Dan decided on his own that he could best cover
the area by advancing his men to a peach orchard that served
as a salient in front of the hills. When Meade came by to ex-
amine Dan's new position, he was troubled. It was too exposed. Just as the two men were conferring, a Confederate
attack led by James Longstreet struck Dan's corps. The battle
raged for four hours until nightfall. By then more than a
third of Dan's 12,000 men were killed, wounded or missing,
though reenforcements helped to stem the southern attack and
little ground was lost. It was a critical turning point for the
Confederacy.

Afterwards, even though Meade strongly criticized Dan in
his reports for placing the III Corps so far forward, Dan became a hero in the eyes of the public. A wounded hero at that,
too, for as the firing died down, Dan was struck by an artillery shell that shattered his right leg. Jauntily smoking a cigar
to allay fears that he was fatally wounded, Dan was borne on
a stretcher to a field hospital where the leg was amputated.
Dan was awarded the Medal of Honor for the battle. After the
war, the Union's own Philip Sheridan examined the battlefield
"very carefully" and said he had "no hesitation whatever in
saying" that Dan "could have done nothing else but to move
out as he did" and "if he had not done so there would have
been no third day at Gettysburg, and General Meade would
have been forced off his position on his left flank and would
have had to withdraw the Army."[8] Longstreet defended his
old enemy as well, saying that Dan's aggressiveness "saved
the battlefield to the Union cause." Longstreet, who later became fast friends with Dan, wrote him forty years after the
battle, "On that field you made your mark that will place you
prominently before the world as one of the leading figures of
the most important battles of the Civil War. As a Northern

veteran once remarked to me, 'General Sickles can well afford to leave a leg on that field.'"[9] Even George Templeton Strong grudgingly admitted at the time, "I suppose Sickles, with his one leg, among our best volunteer officers. His recuperative powers are certainly wonderful. Four years ago he was a ruined man in every sense, a pariah whom to know was discreditable."[10]

Dan had the leg saved, and for many years after the war the splintered bone was displayed at the Army Medical Museum in Washington. Traditionally, on the anniversary of the battle, Dan would visit the exhibit there. Later, the leg was put on permanent display at the Smithsonian Institution.[11]

After the battle, Dan returned on crutches, his pants leg pinned up, to New York, where a celebration in his honor was held. But Teresa was not there to join in his homecoming, and over the Christmas-New Year's holiday period that year Dan took a suite, alone, at a hotel on lower Fifth Avenue instead of being at home.[12] Officially, he gave his business address as 79 Nassau Street, where he had maintained a law office with his father, and his home address either as Bloomingdale, or "foot of West 91st Street," though in truth he was not living at home and apparently rarely, if ever, spent time with Teresa.[13]

Then, in 1865, while the war was still on, Dan was sent on a confidential mission to Colombia. He sailed in January 1865 without Teresa. She, Laura, and Henry Wikoff were at the dock to see him off. Wikoff wrote him afterwards that "Terese was wonderfully affected by your departure—the tears were streaming down her face the whole time she remained on the Pier. She was full of sad presentiments. Her habit is to conceal her feelings & they must be deeply tried to escape in tears. Laura, too, was crying, the first time I have ever known her to do so."[14]

Dan's recuperation from the amputation of his leg was so complete that immediately after the war ended he was appointed by President Andrew Johnson to be military governor of the Carolinas in Charleston. Teresa did not accompany him. The appointment led to yet another controversy. The Reconstruction Acts had made him, Dan acknowledged, "a sort of Sultan, a sort of Roman Consul. I was not only the military commander, I was the Governor of those states; I was the legislature of those two states; I was the Court of Chancery of those two states; I was the Supreme Court of those two states. I was a sort of Poobah."[15] Johnson thought Dan exercised his authority too strenuously and relieved him in 1867. This time, an old friend, onetime House Speaker James Orr, a neighbor from Lafayette Square, defended him. Orr, who had been one of three secession commissioners sent to Washington to demand the surrender of Forts Moultrie and Sumter and had served as a Confederate States senator, was elected governor of South Carolina after the war. He praised Dan for "the wisdom and success" of his administration. His "almost unlimited powers," Orr said, "have been exercised with moderation and forbearance."[16]

◎   ◎   ◎

By then, Teresa was dead. "A recent cold, slightly increased from time to time," the New York *Herald* reported, "took deep root in her constitution, and resulted in the melancholy catastrophe of her premature death." Teresa died on February 5, 1867. She was thirty-one years old. Her funeral was held four days later at St. Joseph's Church in Greenwich Village. Her body was in a "handsome rosewood coffin, literally covered with flowers of rare beauty and exquisite fragrance." On it, as was on Barton Key's casket eight years earlier, was a silver plaque giving her name, age, and the date of her death. The casket was borne up the central aisle of the church attended by ten pallbearers, among them, Charles Graham, the surveyor who had gone on to become a brigadier general, and one of Dan's lawyers from the murder trial, James Brady. The coffin was placed on a catafalque in front of the high altar and surrounded by burning tapers.

Dan returned from Charleston for Teresa's funeral, and, interestingly, the service turned into more of a tribute to him than a testimonial to her. No word was spoken—not in the church, nor in newspaper reports—of Teresa's involvement with Philip Barton Key and Barton's murder. Dan, Laura, his parents—"now advanced in years"—and Teresa's mother and father sat near the altar during the ceremony. The church was full, "crowded to its utmost capacity by multitudes who had come to do honor to the departed and to express their sympathy and respect for General Sickles in the hour of his heavy sorrow." An anthem, "Pray for Me," was "rendered with touching sweetness and profound effect." At the close of the religious service, the pastor of the church, the Rev. Thomas Farrell, delivered a "most earnest and impressive" eulogy, speaking "in words of touching tenderness" and "warm sympathy" about Teresa and the "irreparable loss sustained by the sorrowing parents and bereaved husband. A faithful soldier of the republic, he had been called upon to make many sacrifices. He had given up all to go to the aid of his beloved country in the hour of her need. He had cheerfully undergone the hardships and exposures attendant upon her defence on the field of battle. His sword had helped to perpetuate her national unity and glory. He had suffered in the cause of freedom with a ready alacrity. Now he was called upon to render unto Him who gave her, the chieftest [sic] treasure which had blest his life. It became him as a man to bow in Christian submission to the decree of Divine Wisdom, and to look for support under this severe trial to the Hand which had sustained him hitherto."

With Laura at his side, Dan rose and followed the casket as it was borne from the church. His step was "infirm and tottering" and "the feelings which the solemnity of the occasion had hitherto restrained broke forth, and the immense congregation rushed tumultuously from the building after him, testifying in various ways the hold he had upon their hearts, and the extent to which they shared his affliction."[17]

Until a permanent site could be arranged, Teresa's remains were interred temporarily in the same Catholic cemetery on Second Avenue where old Lorenzo Da Ponte had been buried in an unmarked plot. It is not known where she was finally interred, except that it was not next to Dan.

◎   ◎   ◎

Dan returned to Charleston with Laura. The teenager—she was about thirteen now—was moody, rebellious, "high-strung."[18] Apparently because of her attitude, Dan could not get her into a young ladies' academy there and had to arrange for a tutor to handle her education. Dan took Laura with him when, in July 1869, President Ulysses S. Grant appointed him American minister to Spain. Much to Dan's consternation, a year later, when she was sixteen, Laura had an affair with a Spanish officer. Her behavior continued to be a constant source of friction, and the relationship between father and daughter worsened when, in November 1871, Dan remarried. His second wife was wealthy Señorita Carolina Creagh, "a reigning belle at the court of Queen Isabella of Spain,"[19] whom Dan met while serving in Madrid. He fathered two children with Carolina—George Stanton Sickles and Edith (known as Eda or Ida) Sickles.

Eventually, when she was twenty, Laura bolted from her father, married a butcher, and eventually returned home to New York. She was, according to the researcher for one of Dan's biographers, "wild," "man-crazy," and "addicted to liquor."[20] Laura was reported living with her grandmother, Maria Bagioli, in Brooklyn in 1879. Her grandfather, Antonio Bagioli, had died in 1871 at the age of seventy-six. Laura herself died on December 10, 1891, in a rented room in Brooklyn, when she was about thirty-eight years old. Dan did not attend her funeral. He also never referred to the Bagioli family, but he apparently did support Maria Bagioli, who lived until well into the twentieth century.[21]

Dan's haughty handling of diplomatic matters in Madrid earned him the sarcastic sobriquet "the Yankee King of Spain." He resigned under pressure in 1873 and lived abroad for the next seven years. His mother, who had accompanied him and Laura to Spain after a domestic quarrel with Dan's father, died in a Paris sanitarium in 1874. Seven years later, his father—now living in New Rochelle and "the richest man in town"—married at the age of eighty-four a widow with whom he had been living with for a number of years and who had borne him three children out of wedlock.[22] George Sickles died six years later, in 1887, leaving an estate that included a sixty-acre farm and ten rowhouses in New Rochelle,[23] seventeen parcels of property in Manhattan worth nearly half a million dollars,[24] and three half-sisters—Roma, Pirie and Alta—to contend with Dan for his fortune.

By then, Dan was reestablished in New York, but lived estranged from Carolina and their two young children because she refused to return to America with him. They lived apart and were not reconciled for nearly thirty years. Even when Dan visited Europe, he avoided visiting either her or the children. There is something pathetic about the few surviving letters that his son, George Stanton Sickles, wrote during the first years of their separation. They were written in French in the early 1880s, when the boy was about ten years old. In a few simple paragraphs in a child's handwriting they tell, for example, that Eda has hurt her leg and had to see a doctor, about a church the lad has visited, or a trip his mother is planning to take him on. "Mon cher papá," they begin; "Adieu ton fils qui t'aime tendrement," they end.[25]

Dan and his daughter Eda, who married British diplomat Dayrell Crackanthorpe, were reunited when she returned to New York in 1897, when she was in her twenties. They had not seen each other for seventeen years. Eda died of pneumonia in 1915 while caring for wounded soldiers in France during World War I.[26] Meanwhile, his son, George, grew up to become a member of the American diplomatic corps. He married Ysabel Brocheton, the daughter of a French banker and had one child, Daniel Edgar Stanton Sickles.[27] George served as charge d'affaires in Madrid during the Spanish-American War.

As for Dan, he involved himself in railroad speculations, served another term in Congress in 1893, and continued to get embroiled in financial difficulties. Scandal followed him to his grave. He was made chairman of the New York State Monuments Commission in 1886, but was accused of mishandling its funds—more than $28,000 could not be accounted for—and was relieved of his post in 1912. By then, he was living modestly at 23 Fifth Avenue in Greenwich Village, and though in his nineties, he was still something of a rake. A friend saw "in the General's chamber-dresser, a whole drawer full of ladies' black stockings, and another full of ladies' gloves."[28] Dan was then being attended by a black valet and a housekeeper, Eleanora Earle Wilmerding, an attractive spinster whose attentions prompted malicious gossip. Their relationship prevented his reconciliation with his wife Carolina, who—at the urging of their son George—finally came to New York to try to reunite with him. Carolina, who was pawning her jewels so that Dan would not have to sell any of his art objects or rare editions to pay off his debts, lived nearby with George in a hotel on Eleventh Street. A few months after Miss Wilmerding died in February 1914, Dan and Carolina were finally reunited on April 24 when he suffered a cerebral hemorrhage. He died shortly thereafter, on May 3, 1914, at the age of ninety-four. Despite their reconciliation, Dan ignored both his wife and his son in his will, saying "she had means in her own right."[29] Carolina subsequently returned to Spain, married a man named Amador, and died in Madrid in 1919. George died there in 1939.

◎   ◎   ◎

For many years, Dan had been a regular figure at anniversary celebrations of the Battle of Gettysburg. He liked to dress proudly in the gold-braided, epauletted uniform of a major general and talk about the battle—but, ever the Tammany man, also got a plug in for his political affiliation. "Who fought it?" he would ask. "On the right wing was General Slocum commanding an army corps, a Democrat; on the left was General Reynolds, till he was killed, a Democrat . . . in the Devil's Den was a man named Sickles, a Democrat."[30] Al-

Dan, at the age of eighty-three, at the 1903 Gettysburg reunion. He loved to don his uniform and made a point of attending and speaking at Civil War get-togethers. He would be buried at his death in 1914, when he was ninety-four, in Arlington Cemetery. *Courtesy Library of Congress.*

though he had long before been fitted with an artificial leg, he rarely wore it, and never at reunions. When he could no longer walk with ease with the aid of a cane, he was pushed about in a wheelchair.

Five days after his death, Dan's body was put aboard a train to Washington and that night it lay in state at Union Station. From there it was carried "in solemn procession" across the

Potomac River to Arlington National Cemetery, accompanied by an escort of cavalry and field artillery and followed by a "large number" of Civil War veterans. A riderless horse followed the caisson carrying his body. As the coffin was lowered into the grave, three salvoes of rifle shots rang out and a general's artillery salute echoed through the peaceful countryside.[31]

⊙   ⊙   ⊙

Years before Dan's death, an odd coincidence occurred. It was witnessed by an old Tammany friend of his, Stephen Fiske. One night, Fiske was at the opening of a play in New York when he saw Dan in the theater "sitting composedly in a private box."[32] Fiske had known Dan for years and thought he understood what motivated him: "Under his cool, placid, polished demeanor, he hides a restless and unsatisfied ambition, and has become so used to the pride and power of office that he can never be truly contented." Dan's attention, Fiske noticed, was fixed on the audience below. He was, Fiske suddenly realized, "looking down upon the son of Philip Barton Key in the stalls." James Key looked back. "They recognized each other, undoubtedly," Fiske said, "but neither gave any sign of the recognition."

"It was a strange meeting."

Notes
Bibliography
Index

Notes

Fidelity, in this our catalogue.
Exceptis excipiendis, *as they say . . .*

A WORD OF CAUTION about dates related to Daniel E. Sickles's early years as well as about the accuracy of dates associated with his wife, both his and her families and Philip Barton Key. There are a great many discrepancies with regard to these dates in published accounts—contemporary newspapers and magazines as well as books and articles written afterwards. Not the least of which is the birth date of Sickles himself. Everyone agrees that he was born on October 20, but the year is disputed. For example, the *Dictionary of American Biography* gives the year as 1825, but *Harper's Encyclopaedia of the United States* says it was 1822 and *Appletons' Cyclopaedia* says the year was 1823. One biographer, Edgcumb Pinchon, gives the date as October 20, 1819, contending that the year 1819 "is sustained by the family archives, and is indubitably correct." He also says that "in his last days Dan Sickles gave the year 1825 as the date of his birth. Whether in vanity or as a result of failing memory, he thus lopped six years from his actual age." Although Pinchon is consistently inaccurate about so many facts in his fanciful biography that one can only wonder if he is correct here, his assessment is apparently accurate. It is substantiated by two sources who knew Sickles. One is John W. Forney, who, writing about his recommendation that Sickles be appointed secretary of the American Legation in London in 1853, notes that he "was in his thirty-fourth year," which would conform with a birth year of 1819. The other is the Rev. C.H.A. Bulkley, forty years old in 1859, who knew Sickles when he was a university student and identifies him as being about the same age. The year 1819 is also given in the *Dictionary of American Diplomatic History*. In addition, a number of contemporary newspaper accounts say that Sickles was thirty-two years old at the time of his marriage to Teresa Bagioli, apparently referring to the civil ceremony held a month before his thirty-third birthday in 1852. Accordingly, I have used the year 1819 as the correct one.

Nevertheless, a problem continues to exist about other dates connected with Sickles's early years because of the lack of original materials. In his bibliography, Pinchon cites as sources "Diary and Archives of Daniel E. Sickles—PRIVATE SOURCE" but fails in the text to cite specifically any data regarding him or his family; indeed, much of Pinchon's work seems contrived. A later biographer, W.A. Swanberg (who, by the way, acknowledged making up some of the quoted conversations he uses), makes no mention of either a diary or archives. I have been unable to trace Pinchon's sources, or to find any descendants of the Sickles family who might know about the materials he mentions. Certainly, no known repository of research documents contains them. Interestingly, the Sickles Papers at the Library of Congress are almost totally devoid of any documents relating directly to him before the Civil War. An exception is Sickles's story about the part he played in creating Central Park in New York City, which he wrote after the turn of the century. It is as though Sickles—proud as he was about his role in the creation of Central Park and his service later in the Civil War—wanted to erase everything connected with his early life, especially anything having to do with his marriage to Teresa Bagioli.

◎   ◎   ◎

The following abbreviations are used on second reference to citations in the notes:

Ames   Mary Clemmer Ames, *Ten Years in Washington: Life and Scenes in the National Capital, as a Woman Sees Them*. Hartford, Conn.: A. D. Worthington & Co., 1874.

Boyd   *Boyd's Washington and Georgetown Directory*. New York: William H. Boyd: 1858–65.

Buchanan   John B. Moore, ed., *The Works of James Buchanan*. 12 vols. New York: Antiquarian Press, 1960.

Clay   Ada Sterling, *A Belle of the Fifties: Memoirs of Mrs. Clay, of Alabama, covering Social and Political Life in Washington and the South, 1853–1866*. New York: Doubleday, Page & Company, 1905.

Ellis   John B. Ellis, *The Sights and Secrets of the National Capital*. New York: United States Publishing Company, 1869.

Kelly   Joseph T. Kelly, "Memories of a Lifetime in Washing-
                   ton," *Records of the Columbia Historical Society*, 31–32
                   (1930): 117–49.

NYHS   Manuscripts Room, New-York Historical Society.

NYPL   Manuscripts Division, New York Public Library.

Perley   Ben: Perley Poore, *Perley's Reminiscences of Sixty Years
                   in the National Metropolis*. Philadelphia, Chicago, Kan-
                   sas City: Hubbard Brothers, 1886.

Philp   *Philp's Washington Described*. New York: Rudd &
                   Carleton, 1861.

Pryor   Mrs. Roger A. (Sara Agnes) Pryor, *Reminiscences of
                   Peace and War*. First published 1908. Revised and en-
                   larged, 1970. Freeport, N.Y.: Books for Libraries
                   Press, 1970.

Strong   *Diary of George Templeton Strong*, Allan Nevins and
                   Milton Halsey Thomas, eds. 4 vols. New York: Mac-
                   millan Company, 1952.

Swanberg   W. A. Swanberg, *Sickles the Incredible*. New York:
                   Charles Scribner's Sons, 1956.

Trial   *Trial of the Hon. Daniel E. Sickles for Shooting Philip
                   Barton Key, Esq., U.S. District Attorney, of Washington,
                   D.C.* New York: R. M. De Witt, 1859.

Trow   *Trow's New York City Directory*. New York: John F.
                   Trow, 1852–69.

Wentworth   *Trial of Hon. Daniel E. Sickles*. Washington, D.C.:
                   Wentworth and Stanley, 1859.

Witness   Donald B. Cole and John J. McDonough, eds., *Witness
                   to the Young Republic: A Yankee's Journal, 1828–1870*.
                   Hanover, N.H.: Univ. Press of New England, 1989.

Book Epigraph

1. The description of the room, at 383 Fifteenth Street, is from testimony given at the trial of Daniel E. Sickles by Police Officer Charles Mann
and Defense attorney Daniel Ratcliffe: *Trial of the Hon. Daniel E. Sickles for
Shooting Philip Barton Key, Esq., U.S. District Attorney, of Washington, D.C.*

(New York: R. M. De Witt, 1859) 67 and 68, respectively. The items of clothing that Teresa Sickles wore are given by her in her confession, Trial, 42. Philip Barton Key's remark about "French intrigue" is from the New York *Daily Tribune* of March 3, 1859. His boast is taken from a letter from George B. Wooldridge to Key on March 26, 1858, quoted in the Trial, 37. Teresa's comment about "a wicked woman" is also from her confession, Trial, 42.

Preface

1. Undated newspaper clipping of article copyrighted 1900 by Champ Clark, Papers of Daniel E. Sickles, Manuscripts Division, New York Public Library.
2. *New York World,* June 30, 1869.

Chapter Epigraphs

1. Major John De Haviland, "A Metrical Glance at the Fancy Ball," *The Magazine of History,* Extra Nos. 21–24, VI (1913): 353–70. The poem was written by Haviland to commemorate the masquerade ball given by Senator William McKendree Gwin of California and his wife, Mary, on April 8, 1858. Haviland, who went to the ball as a knight in armor, according to the *Washington Union* of April 10, 1858, delighted in masking the identification of the various partygoers in symbol and allusion. His poem was printed in the *Washington Star* and copied for years afterward. (Lately Thomas, in his biography of Gwin—*Between Two Empires* . . . —identifies Haviland on page 159 as "a former army major, John von Sonntag Haviland.") The quoted edition here contains footnotes identifying by name most of the various participants. Philip Barton Key was one of three English Hunters, Teresa Sickles one of two Riding Hoods. Daniel E. Sickles did not attend the ball. Subsequent quotations preceding each chapter are from this poem.

One. New Year's Day, 1859

1. *National Intelligencer,* January 3, 1859. The description of the president's reception that follows is taken from this newspaper, the *Evening Star* of January 1, 1859, and Singleton, Esther, *The Story of the White House,* 2 vols. (1907; reprint; New York: Benjamin Blom, 1969), 1: 52.
2. Trial, 92.
3. Logan, Mrs. John A., *Thirty Years in Washington, or Life and Scenes in*

Our National Capital (Hartford, Conn.: A. D. Worthington & Co., 1901), 671.

4. Ada Sterling, *A Belle of the Fifties: Memoirs of Mrs. Clay, of Alabama, covering Social and Political Life in Washington and the South, 1853–1866* (New York: Doubleday, Page & Company, 1905), 86. Citations from this work are hereafter designated by the abbreviation Clay.

5. Clay, 59.

6. Ibid., 86.

7. Ibid., 29

8. Mrs. Roger A. (Susan Agnes) Pryor, *Reminiscences of Peace and War* (1908; revised and enlarged; Freeport, N.Y.: Books for Libraries Press, 1970), 49.

9. Clay, 86.

10. The quoted descriptions are from: Ben: Perley Poore, *Perley's Reminiscences of Sixty Years in the National Metropolis* (Philadelphia: Hubbard Brothers, 1886), 24; L. A. Gobright, *Recollection of Men and Things at Washington During the Third of a Century* (Philadelphia: Claxton, Remsen & Haffelfinger, 1869), 145; *In Memoriam: Benjamin Ogle Tayloe,* also known as *Anecdotes and Reminiscences* (Washington, D.C.: private printing, 1872. Rare Book Division, Library of Congress), 183.

11. *In Memoriam . . . Tayloe,* 183.

12. Donald B. Cole and John J. McDonough, eds., *Witness to the Young Republic: A Yankee's Journal, 1828–1870* (Hanover, N.H., Univ. Press of New England, 1989), 288–89.

13. *Witness,* 338.

14. Mary Clemmer Ames, *Ten Years in Washington: Life and Scenes in the National Capital, as a Woman Sees Them* (Hartford, Conn.: A. D. Worthington & Co., 1874), 67.

15. *National Intelligencer,* December 1, 1857.

16. Constance McLaughlin Green, *Washington: Village and Capital, 1800–1878,* 2 vols. (Princeton: Princeton Univ. Press, 1962), 1:187.

17. Green, *Washington,* 1:183.

18. *Boyd's Washington and Georgetown Directory* (New York: William H. Boyd, 1860).

19. Boyd, 1865.

20. Green, *Washington,* 1:186.

21. Henry Watterson, *"Marse Henry": An Autobiography,* 2 vols. (New York: George H. Doran, 1919), 61.

22. Watterson, *"Marse Henry",* 60.

23. *New-York Times,* February 19, 1859.

24. *Evening Star,* January 2, 1858.

25. Jacob R. Shipherd, *History of the Oberlin-Wellington Rescue* (1859; reprint; New York: Da Capo Press, 1972), 218.

26. Mary Cable, *American Manners and Morals* (New York: American Heritage, 1969), 173.

27. Ames, 55.

28. Gerald Carson and Bernard A. Weisberger, "The Great Countdown," *American Heritage* (November, 1989, special supplement), 11.

29. *National Intelligencer,* January 3, 1859.

30. Singleton, *Story of the White House,* 1:31.

31. *Evening Star,* January 1, 1859.

32. John B. Ellis, *The Sights and Secrets of the National Capital* (New York: United States Publishing Company, 1869), 241.

Two. Barton, Dan and Teresa

1. Hoover's home was between Fourteenth and Fifteenth streets.

2. Boyd, 1858.

3. Trial, 39.

4. Ibid., 38.

5. Clay, 98.

6. Now Carroll County.

7. Scottie Fitzgerald Smith, "The Colonial Ancestors of Francis Scott Key Fitzgerald," *Maryland Historical Magazine,* 76 (Dec., 1981): 363.

8. T. J. C. Williams, *History of Frederick County Maryland* (2 vols. Baltimore: L. R. Titsworth & Co., 1910): 313.

9. Williams, *Frederick County,* 303.

10. *Harper's Weekly Magazine,* March 12, 1859.

11. *New-York Times,* February 28, 1859.

12. Hester Dorsey Richardson, *Side-Lights on Maryland History* (Cambridge, Md.: Tidewater, 1967), 153. The Keys were married on November 18, 1845.

13. The exact date of Ellen Key's death is unknown. However, because her youngest surviving child was four years old in February, 1859, she might have died in childbirth or shortly afterwards. Her four children— Lizzie, Mary, James, and Alice—were aged four to twelve years as of that date.

14. *New-York Times,* February 28, 1859.

15. *New-York Daily Tribune,* March 3, 1859.

16. Ibid.

17. Trial, 5.

18. Ibid., 22. According to Dr. Richard H. Coolidge, the autopsy uncovered a "somewhat unusual amount of fatty deposit on the left side of it [Key's heart], but the structure of the heart itself was healthy."

19. *New-York Daily Tribune,* March 3, 1859.

20. *Catalogue of the Library of the late Philip Barton Key, to be sold at Public Sale* (Washington, D.C.: Robert A. Waters, 1859).

21. *Harper's*, March 12,1859.

22. Clay, 97.

23. *New-York Times*, February 28, 1859.

24. *New-York Daily Tribune*, March 3, 1859.

25. *New-York Times*, February 28, 1859.

26. Perley, 26. The colors are given as blue and gold in W. A. Swanberg, *Sickles the Incredible* (New York: Charles Scribner's Sons, 1956), 3.

27. *New-York Daily Tribune*, March 3, 1859.

28. *Frank Leslie's Illustrated Newspaper*, March 26, 1859.

29. *Harper's*, March 12, 1859.

30. *Frank Leslie's*, March 26, 1859.

31. Perley, 26.

32. Trial, 38.

33. See explanatory introduction to Notes section.

34. *Harper's*, April 9, 1859.

35. *New-York Times*, February 12, 1871.

36. Arthur Livingston, ed., *Memoirs of Lorenzo Da Ponte* (Philadelphia: J. B. Lippincott Company, 1929), 491n. The graveyard is referred to as the Old Catholic Cemetery of St. Patrick's Old Cathedral.

37. Ibid, 430n.

38. Trial, 54–55.

39. Boyd, 1841. Swanberg, 81, gives 1843 as the year Sickles was admitted to the bar, but he does not cite the source of that date.

40. Deposition given by George G. Sickles, dated September 15, 1845, Sickles Papers, Manuscript Division, Library of Congress. George Sickles' deposition is attached to a certificate dated November 19, 1845, admitting him to practice before the Court of Common Pleas for the City and County of New York. In it, he wrote that "on or about the ninth day of September 1842, he entered the law office of Daniel E. Sickles, Esq. of said City, as a student at law; that he was in actual attendance in said office as a student until the tenth day of September, 1844, or about that time; that during same herein he studied from seven to eight hours a day, without, as he verily believes, during said time, a vacation exceeding two weeks."

41. *New York Times*, October 9, 1895.

42. Swanberg, 81.

43. *Diary of George Templeton Strong*, Allan Nevins and Milton Halsey Thomas, eds., 4 vols. (New York: Macmillan Company, 1952), 4:449. The entry was written April 20, 1872.

44. Joseph B. Doyle, *In Memoriam: Edwin McMasters Stanton* (Steubenville, Ohio: Herald Printing Company, 1911), 374.

45. Stephen Fiske, *Off-hand Portraits of Prominent New Yorkers* (New York: Geo. R. Lockwood & Son, 1884), 284.

46. Ibid.

47. Swanberg, 34.

48. *Dictionary of American Biography*, 20 vols. (New York: Charles Scribner's Sons, 1928-36), 10:197.

49. John W. Forney, *Anecdotes of Public Men*, 2 vols. (New York: Harper & Brothers, 1873, 1881), 1:58.

50. *New York Panorama* (Federal Writers' Project, Works Progress Administration, American Guide Series. New York: Random House, 1938), 60.

51. Dickens, *American Notes*, 49 and 45.

52. *Panorama*, 60.

53. Iver Bernstein, *The New York City Draft Riots: Their Significance for American Society and Politics in the Age of the Civil War* (New York: Oxford Univ. Press, 1990), 144.

54. Edward R. Ellis, *The Epic of New York City* (New York: Coward-McCann, 1966), 287.

55. Ibid.

56. Dickens, *American Notes*, 45.

57. James D. McCabe, Jr., *Lights and Shadows of New York Life; or, the Sights and Sensations of the Great City* (Philadelphia: National Publishing Company, 1872), 816.

58. Fiske, *Off-hand Portraits*, 284.

59. *Harper's*, April 9, 1859.

60. Swanberg, 83.

61. *New-York Times*, March 15, 1859.

62. Perley, 25, and *Convent of the Sacred Heart, New York City: 1881-1981* (New York: Alumni Association of the Convent of the Sacred Heart, 1981), 47. The school was on a site between the villages of Harlem and Manhattanville.

63. William Hobart Royce to Edgcumb Pinchon, August 31, 1942. Papers of William Hobart Royce, NYPL. Royce was Pinchon's researcher for his biography of Sickles.

64. Trial, 5.

65. *Evening Star*, February 28, 1859.

66. *Frank Leslie's*, March 26, 1859.

67. *Trial of Hon. Daniel E. Sickles* (Washington, D.C.: Wentworth and Stanley, 1859), 4.

68. *New-York Times*, March 15, 1853.

69. Marriage Record Book, October 20, 1838–December 30, 1867, St. Patrick's Old Cathedral, Mulberry Street, New York City. The names of the bride and groom are recorded incorrectly as Therese Bajioli and Daniel Egbert Sickles. Two friends of Dan's, both lawyers, signed the marriage certificate as witnesses–Edward Cleto West and Robert James Dillon.

70. *Trow's New York City Directory* (New York: John F. Trow, 1853).

71. Irving Katz, *August Belmont: A Political Biography* (New York, London: Columbia Univ. Press, 1968), 28.

72. Forney, *Anecdotes*, 1:318.

73. Ibid.

74. James Buchanan to Franklin Pierce, July 29, 1853, in John B. Moore, ed., *The Works of James Buchanan*, 12 vols. (New York: Antiquarian Press, 1960), IX:31.

75. Forney, *Anecdotes*, 318.

76. Speech of General Daniel E. Sickles, delivered at annual dinner of Veteran [*sic*] Association of the Department of the South and Atlantic Blockading Squadrons State of New York, Tuesday, April 18, 1911, at St. Denis Hotel, New York City, 8. Papers of Daniel E. Sickles, Manuscripts Room, New-York Historical Society.

77. *New-York Times,* July 22, 1859.

78. James Buchanan to Harriet Lane, August 6 postscript in letter of August 4, 1853, in Buchanan, IX:32.

79. James Buchanan to Harriet Lane, September 30, 1853, in Buchanan, IX:62. But evidently Buchanan was not keen about having the Sickleses's infant child underfoot. He wrote: "I am entirely willing;—though not that they should live in the house with me."

80. James Buchanan to Daniel E. Sickles, December 22, 1854, in Buchanan, IX:291. Buchanan gave an indication that Teresa's mother came to London with her when he wrote after the family had left, "Please to remember me, in the very kindest terms, to Mrs. Sickles & Mad. Bagioli."

81. Edgcumb Pinchon, *Dan Sickles: Hero of Gettysburg and "Yankee King of Spain,"* (Garden City, N.Y.: Doubleday, Doran and Company, 1945), 51. Pinchon's biography, the first to be written about Sickles, is replete with errors and cannot be trusted unless confirmed by other sources. He manufactured facts or relied too greatly on his researcher, William Hobart Royce, who repeated to him every rumor he ran across without substantiating whether it was true. A typical mistake was Pinchon's location of the Sickleses's home in Bloomingdale as being in New Jersey. I have tried to avoid any reliance on Pinchon's work, although he supposedly had access to a diary and journal that no one else had ever—or has ever—seen, and was in contact with Sickleses's grandson, Capt. Daniel E. S. Sickles. The Pinchon work is obviously an "authorized" biography.

82. Perley, 443–44.

83. James Buchanan to John W. Forney, December 14, 1854, in Buchanan, IX:283.

84. Swanberg, 95–96.

85. James Buchanan to Daniel E. Sickles, December 22, 1854, in Buchanan, IX:290.

86. James Buchanan to William L. Marcy, December 15, 1854, in Buchanan, IX:285. There is evidence that Sickles was considering returning to London. On December 22 (IX:290), Buchanan wrote him that he heard he planned to be back in London "early in January." Buchanan said, "The idea of a visit in August & another in December would expose us to just censure." It is not clear what Buchanan meant, but he had already informed Washington of his need to replace Sickles, and perhaps felt that Sickles's return would place him in an embarrassing position.

87. The Bagioli residence was at 84 East Fifteenth Street.

88. "The Founder of Central Park in New York." Sickles Papers, Manuscript Division, Library of Congress. Sickles wrote this detailed explanation of his role after the turn of the century.

89. McCabe, *Lights and Shadows,* 570. Trinity Church's assets in 1872 totaled between $60 and $100 million.

90. *Argument of the Hon. Daniel E. Sickles, in the Senate of the State of New York, April,* 1857, on the Trinity Church Bill (New York: J. Munsell, 1857), 3.

91. Teresa Sickles to "My own dear sister Florence," May 5, 1856. Papers of Daniel E. Sickles, NYHS. Teresa Sickles's friend Florence is never otherwise identified. Her surname is unknown.

92. *United States Congressional Districts and Data,* 1843–1883 (New York: 1986), 74–75. The population of the district was 43.7 percent foreign-born; 7.3 percent German, 24.1 percent Irish.

93. *Carroll's New York City Directory* (New York: Carroll & Company, 1859), 127.

94. Teresa Sickles to Florence, 1856. Papers of Daniel E. Sickles, NYHS. The month in which the letter was written is illegible. However, the handwriting is clear that the date is a Thursday, the twenty-seventh day of the month. In 1856, there were two Thursdays that fell on the twenty-seventh day of the month—in March and in November. The letter was clearly written after the Sickleses had moved to Bloomingdate.

95. Trial, 5.

96. *New York Evening Post,* February 28, 1859.

97. *New York Evening Post,* March 1, 1859.

98. Strong, 2:77–78. The entry is dated December 20, 1851.

99. Wentworth, 3.

100. *Evening Star,* March 1, 1859.

Three. "The City of Magnificent Intentions"

1. Margaret O. W. Oliphant, *Memoir of the Life of Laurence Oliphant and also of Alice Oliphant, His Wife,* 2 vols. (London: William Blackwood and Sons, 1891), 113.

2. Ellis, 183.

3. Paul Herron, *The Story of Capitol Hill* (New York: Coward-McCann, 1963), 19.

4. Boyd, 1865.

5. Dickens, *American Notes*, 57.

6. Logan, *Thirty Years in Washington*, 518.

7. Joseph T. Kelly, "Memories of a Lifetime in Washington," *Records of the Columbia Historical Society*, 31–32 (1930):118.

8. Ibid., 125.

9. Ibid., 124.

10. Ibid., 123.

11. Ames, 67.

12. Dickens, *American Notes*, 57.

13. Frank Graham, Jr., *Potomac: The Nation's River* (Philadelphia, New York: J. B. Lippincott, 1976), 42.

14. Kelly, 119.

15. Ibid., 127.

16. *New-York Times*, April 19, 1859.

17. Graham, *Potomac*, 42.

18. Pryor, 9.

19. Clay, 28.

20. *Harper's*, April 16, 1859.

21. Oliphant, *Memoir*, 115.

22. *Philp's Washington Described* (New York: Rudd & Carleton, 1861), 39.

23. Kelly, 125.

24. Ames, 68.

25. Graham, *Potomac*, 42.

26. Kelly, 124.

27. Ibid., 142.

28. Ames, 153–54.

29. Graham, *Potomac*, 42.

30. Pryor, 4.

31. Clay, 102.

32. Ames, 157.

33. Ibid., 158.

34. *National Intelligencer*, January 3, 1859.

35. Pryor, 5–6.

36. Clay, 92, 94.

37. Ibid., 89.

38. *National Intelligencer*, January 4, 1858.

39. Pryor, 42.

40. James M. Goode, *Capital Losses: A Cultural History of Washington's*

Destroyed Buildings (Washington, D.C.: Smithsonian Institution Press, 1979), 262.

41. Kelly, 128–29.

42. Clay, 28.

43. Trial, 39.

44. Boyd, 1858.

45. Pryor, 101.

46. The House held its first session in its new chamber on December 16, 1857; the Senate held its first session in its new chamber on January 4, 1859.

Four. "Armed to the Teeth"

1. Ellis, 48.

2. *Evening Star,* February 23, 1859.

3. Ellis, 48.

4. Philip, 40–41.

5. Ellis, 459.

6. Ibid., 188.

7. J. Fairfax McLaughlin, *The Life and Times of John Kelly, Tribune of the People* (New York: American News Company, 1885),194.

8. Ibid, 195.

9. Ellis, 452–53.

10. Green, *Washington,* 1:215.

11. Oliphant, *Memoir,* 113.

12. Stephen VanRensselaer, *American Firearms* (Watkins Glen, N.Y.: Century House, 1947), 67–70. Named after Henry Deringer. Foreign imitations of his guns were spelled with two r's—Derringers—and became the accepted spelling for the weapons.

13. Green, *Washington,* 1:183.

14. Ellis, 457.

15. *Evening Star,* January 3, 1859.

16. Philps, 297.

17. Watterson, *"Marse Henry,"* 63.

18. Ellis, 503.

19. *New-York Times,* May 7, 1857.

20. *New-York Daily Tribune,* March 3, 1859.

21. *New-York Times,* February 19, 1859.

Five. "The Domestic Sphere"

1. Ellis, 431.

2. Clay, 101.

3. *Harper's,* January 29, 1859.

4. Teresa Sickles to Florence, undated, Papers of Daniel E. Sickles, NYHS. Although undated, the letter was obviously written after the fall of 1857, when the Sickleses settled into their home on Lafayette Square for the first session of the Thirty-fifth Congress.

5. Pryor, 101–2.

6. Ibid., 91.

7. Ibid., 90.

8. Ibid., 91.

9. *New-York Times,* February 19, 1859.

10. Mary Cable, *American Manners and Morals* (New York: American Heritage, 1969), 173.

11. Oliphant, *Memoir,* 126–27.

12. Ellis, 423–24.

13. *New-York Times,* February 19, 1859.

14. Pryor, 81.

15. Isaac F. Marcosson, *"Marse Henry": A Biography of Henry Watterson* (New York: Dodd, Mead, 1951), 40.

16. *National Intelligencer,* January 4, 1858.

17. Kelly, 124.

18. Ames, 160–61.

19. Ibid., 160.

20. Major Gist Blair, "Lafayette Square," *Records of the Columbia Historical Society,* 19:3–4 (July–December, 1967): 146–47.

21. It is not clear when Lafayette Square officially got its name, nor when the streets were renamed. *Boyd's Washington and Georgetown Directory* for 1860 still referred to Madison Place as running "from H north to Penn ave., both sides of Lafayette Square," although the west side of the square was already known as Jackson Place.

22. *New-York Times,* March 15, 1859, says the baptism was supposed to have taken place as Sunday, March 14, 1858.

23. Trial, 75.

24. Both the *New-York Daily Tribune* of February 28, 1859, and the *New York Herald* of March 1, 1859, give the address as 7 President's square [*sic*]. Ellis, 436, says "7 Lafayette Square, 16 1/2 Street." The address is given as 14 Jackson Place in Hal H. Smith, "Historic Washington Homes," *Records of the Columbia Historical Society,* II (1908): 251.

25. *New-York Daily Tribune,* March 3, 1859.

26. *In Memoriam* (a.k.a. *Anecdotes and Reminiscences*), 23.

27. Perley. The quotes are a combination of quotes from pages 25 and 444.

28. *Harper's,* January 29, 1859.

29. *New York Herald,* March 1, 1859.

30. *Harper's,* March 12, 1859.

31. Israel Kugler, *From Ladies to Women: The Organized Struggle for Woman's Rights in the Reconstruction Era* (Westport, Conn.: Greenwood Press, 1987), 22.

32. Arthur B. Fuller, ed., *Woman in the Nineteenth Century . . . by Margaret Fuller Ossoli* (1874; reprint; Westport Conn.: Greenwood Press, 1977), 218.

Six. First Encounters

1. Trial, 70.
2. Pinchon, *Dan Sickles*, 136.
3. Teresa Sickles to Florence, May 5, 1856. Papers of Daniel E. Sickles, NYHS.
4. Pinchon, *Dan Sickles*, 136.
5. Teresa Sickles to Florence, 1856. Papers of Daniel E. Sickles, NYHS. This is the letter whose dateline is illegible except for the day of the month, the twenty-seventh.
6. Watterson, *"Marse Henry,"* 62–63.
7. *Catalogue of the Library of the late Philip Barton Key*, 7.
8. *New-York Daily Tribune*, March 3, 1859.
9. Forney, *Anecdotes*, 366–67.
10. *Frank Leslie's*, March 26, 1859. The story that follows, Beekman's rendition, is from this source except as noted.
11. Trial, 37.
12. Ibid., 34.
13. Ibid., 36–37. There was a misprint in the date of the letter from Bacon to Key. It is dated March 29 in the trial report, but that cannot be correct because Beekman responded to it on March 26.
14. *Frank Leslie's*, March 26, 1859.
15. Trial, 39.
16. Ibid., 40.
17. Ibid.
18. Ibid., 70.
19. Ibid.
20. *Washington Union*, April 10, 1858.
21. *Harper's*, April 24, 1858.
22. Clay, 132.
23. Ibid., 126.
24. Major John De Haviland.
25. Clay, 133–34.
26. Ibid., 130, 133. According to Richardson, *Side-Lights*, 153, Alice's full name was Mary Alicia Lloyd Nevins. She was born November 20, 1823.

27. Trial, 72.
28. Ibid., 40.
29. Ibid., 42.
30. Ibid., 71.

Seven. "Disgrace" and "Disgust"

1. Trial, 35.
2. Ibid., 70–72.
3. Ibid., 76.
4. Nat Brandt, *The Man Who Tried to Burn New York* (Syracuse: Syracuse Univ. Press, 1986), 98.
5. Trial, 39.
6. *Evening Star,* March 5, 1859.

Eight. The Anonymous Letters

1. Trial, 42.
2. Ibid., 69.
3. Ibid., 67.
4. Ibid., 66–67. Unless otherwise noted, Nancy Brown's involvement in the story is from these pages, representing her testimony at the trial of Daniel E. Sickles. It is interesting to note that Pinchon in his biography of Sickles says that Mrs. Brown was black, although the listing in Boyd's directory for her husband, Thomas Brown, the president's gardener, does not have "col." for colored attached to his name as was customary when blacks were listed. I have not taken the liberty of describing her as black.
5. *Frank Leslie's,* March 19, 1859, says Key told Mrs. Brown that he was renting the house for a Mr. Wright of Massachusetts. There was no such member of the Massachusetts congressional delegation.
6. Trial, 47.
7. Ibid., 51–52.
8. Ibid., 69–70.
9. Ibid. Here again Pinchon identifies Seeley as black, but he is not listed as such in the city directory. Moreover, on page 70 of the trial record, his daughter Matilda is described as being fair-haired.
10. Trial, 72.
11. *Frank Leslie's,* March 26, 1859.
12. Trial, 48, 85.
13. *Harper's,* May 14, 1859.
14. Trial, 37–38.
15. Ibid., 38.

16. *New-York Times,* February 28, 1859.

17. Trial, 52.

18. Ibid., 69.

19. Witness, 309. The other midshipman is identified as John H. Sherburne of New Hampshire. Philp, 228, gives the year of the duel as 1833, and the name of Key's opponent as Sherborn. Richardson, *Side-Lights,* 153, gives dates of Daniel Murray Key as June 9, 1816, to June 26, 1836.

20. Trial, 76.

21. *New-York Times,* February 19, 1859.

22. Clay, 118. There is obviously a typographical error here. Clay says young Bennett danced with his mother and Daniel E. Sickles, when Clay evidently meant that the young man danced with *Mrs.* Daniel E. Sickles.

23. Trial, 51.

24. Singleton, *Story of the White House,* 53.

25. Trial, 52.

26. Trial, 68.

27. *Washington Union,* February 21, 1859.

28. Philip Lynch.

29. Trial, 55.

30. *New-York Times,* February 28, 1859.

31. Clay, 97–98.

32. Trial, 52.

33. Ibid., 39.

34. Ibid., 66.

35. Ibid., 69.

36. *Harper's,* March 12, 1859. Curiously, *Harper's* of May 14, 1859, says the cipher letter was actually written by Teresa Sickles. It said it "contained declarations of love from Mrs. Sickles."

37. Trial, 39.

38. At Fifteenth Street and New York Avenue.

39. *New-York Times,* February 28, 1859.

40. Trial, 72.

41. Ibid., 53.

42. Ibid., 52. Rapley's name is given in the trial report as Ratley, but there was no Ratley listed in the city directory and I have assumed this is a typographical error. Several other such errors occur in the trial report. For example, the surname of Jonah Hoover is first given in the trial record as Doover.

43. Ibid., 53.

44. Ishbel Ross, *Rebel Rose: Life of Rose O'Neal Greenhow* (New York: Harper & Brothers, 1954), 49.

45. Ibid., 78.

46. Ibid., 38.

47. Ibid., 34.

48. R. P. G. to Hon. Daniel Sickles, February 24, 1859. Papers of Daniel E. Sickles, NYHS.

49. Wentworth, 6.

50. Trial, 46.

Nine. The Cuckold

1. Wentworth, 18–19.

2. *Harper's,* April 16, 1859.

3. *Evening Star,* February 26, 1859.

4. The scenes involving Wooldridge that follow are an amalgam of John Graham's opening argument and Wooldridge's testimony, Trial, 34, 48, 72–75.

5. Witness, 308.

6. Trial, 39.

7. Wooldridge's quarters were between C and D streets.

8. Trial, 41–42. Mohun incorrectly testified that this scene took place on Sunday, not Saturday. It could not have occurred on Sunday.

9. Trial, 40.

10. The following scene is an amalgam of the testimony of Bridget Duffy and Octavia Ridgeley, Trial, 42, 46–47.

11. Ibid., 42–43.

Ten. A Matter of Honor

1. Trial, 46.

2. Ibid., 42.

3. Ibid., 75.

4. Ibid., 48.

5. *Evening Star,* February 28, 1859.

6. Trial, 20.

7. Ibid., 21.

8. Ibid., 52.

9. Ibid., 46.

10. Ibid., 47.

11. Ibid., 49.

12. Ibid., 52. The parishioner was Jeremiah Boyd.

13. Ibid., 52 and 55. The architect was A. B. Young. His friend was Jesse Haw.

14. Ibid., 47.

15. *New-York Times,* March 3, 1859.

16. Trial, 72 and 78. The coachman was John Cooney, the footman John McDonald.

17. Ibid., 52.

18. Ibid., 55.

19. Ibid., 47–48. The lawyer was William W. Mann.

20. Perley, 26.

21. Trial, 46–47.

22. Ibid., 49.

23. Ibid.

24. New-York Times, March 2, 1859.

25. Trial, 74.

26. New-York Times, March 2, 1859.

27. Trial, 74–75.

28. New-York Times, March 2, 1859.

29. The scenes that follow, except as otherwise noted, are an amalgam of the trial testimony of eleven of the witnesses—the page, Bonitz, never testified—Trial, 16–23, and Samuel Butterworth's statement in The New-York Times, March 2, 1859. Some of the eyewitnesses can be identified: Reed was a wood-and-charcoal dealer; Dudrow a flour-and-feed merchant; Pendleton was from Virginia; Downer was a carpenter; Van Wyck was a clerk in the Treasury Department; Tidball also worked as a clerk in the Treasury Department; Doyle was a clerk in the First Auditor's Office; Upshur was a Navy Department clerk.

30. Trial, 82. The clerk was De Wilton Snowden.

31. Ibid., 48. The physician was Dr. Thomas Miller.

32. Ibid., 23.

33. New York Evening Post, February 28, 1859.

34. Washington Union, March 1, 1859.

35. Swanberg, 55.

Eleven. "The Washington Tragedy"

1. Clay, 97.

2. Trial, 77.

3. Ibid., 87.

4. Ibid., 77.

5. Ibid., 49.

6. Ibid., 77.

7. Ibid., 75.

8. Ibid., 83.

9. The following scene, involving Walker and Butterworth, is an amalgam of Trial, 40–41, and Butterworth's statement in The New-York Times, March 2, 1859.

10. Trial, 40.
11. Ibid., 83. The officers were William Daw and James H. Suit.
12. *New-York Daily Tribune,* March 1, 1859.
13. Trial, 84.
14. Ibid. 83
15. Ibid.
16. Perley, 531.
17. Philp, 206.
18. Goode, *Capital Losses,* 304–5.
19. *Harper's,* March 19, 1859.
20. Wentworth, 11.
21. *Frank Leslie's,* April 30, 1859.
22. Ibid., March 19, 1859.
23. *Evening Star,* April 27, 1859.
24. *New-York Daily Tribune,* March 1, 1859.
25. *Frank Leslie's,* March 19, 1859.
26. Strong, 2:447. The entry is dated April 19, 1859.
27. Clay, 97.
28. *Harper's,* March 12, 1859.
29. *New-York Times,* March 15, 1859.
30. *New-York Daily Tribune,* March 2, 1859.
31. Ibid., March 1, 1859.
32. *Harper's,* March 12, 1859.
33. *Evening Star,* March 5, 1859.
34. *Evening Star,* March 7, 1859.
35. Journal, Papers of Samuel Rush, American Philosophical Society, 9–11.
36. Strong, 2:448. The entry is dated April 22, 1859.
37. Swanberg, 57.
38. *Evening Star,* March 5, 1859.
39. *Frank Leslie's,* March 19, 1859.
40. *New-York Times,* February 28, 1859.
41. *Harper's,* March 12, 1859.
42. Ibid., March 26, 1859.
43. *Evening Star,* March 7, 1859.
44. Ibid., March 2, 1859.
45. *New York Evening Post,* March 1, 1859.
46. Ibid.
47. *Evening Star,* March 8, 1859.
48. Ibid., March 5, 1859.
49. *New York Herald,* March 1, 1859.
50. *Harper's,* March 26, 1859.
51. Strong, 2:438. The entry is dated February 28, 1859.

52. *Evening Star,* March 8, 1859.
53. Ibid., March 5, 1859.
54. *Harper's,* March 12, 1859.
55. Joseph Drayton to Daniel E. Sickles, April 6, 1859. Papers of Daniel E. Sickles, NYHS.
56. *New-York Times,* March 15, 1859.
57. Poem, Miscellaneous papers, Daniel E. Sickles, Widener Library, Harvard University. The poem is in the nature of a clipping. There is no indication of its author or source.
58. *New York Herald,* March 1, 1859.
59. *Frank Leslie's,* March 12, 1859.
60. Witness, 308–9.
61. *In Memoriam: Benjamin Ogle Tayloe* (Philadelphia: Sherman & Co., 1872), 52–53.
62. *New-York Daily Tribune,* April 4, 1859.
63. *Evening Star,* March 2, 1859.
64. *New York Herald,* March 1, 1859.
65. *Evening Star,* March 2, 1859.
66. Ibid., March 7, 1859.
67. Strong, 2:438. The entry is dated February 28, 1859.
68. *Harper's,* March 26, 1859.
69. *New York Herald,* March 1, 1859.

Twelve. Incarcerated

1. Trial, 22.
2. The description of the funeral is from the *New-York Daily Tribune,* March 3, 1859.
3. The plaque, according to the *Evening Star,* March 1, 1859, gave Key's age as thirty-nine. However, I have used the birth date given by Richardson, *Side-Lights,* 153, which would make him forty years old. It is possible Richardson is wrong. It is also possible that Key's family made a mistake about his age.
4. *Frank Leslie's,* April 16, 1859.
5. *New York Evening Post,* March 3, 1859.
6. *Harper's,* March 19, 1859.
7. *New-York Times,* April 6, 1859.
8. *New York Evening Post,* March 3, 1859.
9. Witness, 312.
10. *Evening Star,* April 4, 1859.
11. *New-York Times,* March 15, 1859.
12. *Harper's,* March 19, 1859.
13. *New-York Times,* April 6, 1859.

14. *Evening Star,* March 1, 1859.

15. *New York Herald,* March 2, 1859.

16. Blair, "Lafayette Square," 164.

17. *Harper's,* March 19, 1859.

18. *New-York Times,* March 3, 1859.

19. Trial, 5.

20. L. A. Gobright, *Recollection of Men and Things at Washington during the Third of a Century* (Philadelphia: Claxton, Remsen & Haffelfinger, 1869), 192–93.

21. Reel 2, Cranch Vol. 5–6; Haywood & Hazelton, Vol. 1–2:319–320. Criminal Court Records, District of Columbia. School of Law Library, New York University.

22. The description of the search of 383 Fifteenth Street is from the testimony of Daniel Ratcliffe and Charles W. Mann, Trial 67–68.

23. *Harper's,* March 12, 1859.

24. *New-York Times,* March 2, 1859.

25. Strong, 2:448. The entry is dated April 24, 1859.

26. Trial, 99.

27. Forney, *Anecdotes,* 71.

28. *Harper's,* April 16, 1859.

29. Perley, 29.

30. *Harper's,* April 16, 1859.

31. Scrapbook, 1847–61. Papers of John Lorimer Graham, NYHS.

32. Perley, 29.

33. Strong, 2:453. The entry is dated May 26, 1859.

34. *Harper's,* April 16, 1859.

35. Ibid.

36. Ibid. Ratcliffe is often described in contemporary newspapers and magazines as a partner of Magruder and Chilton, but he was not. He maintained separate law offices.

37. Ibid.

38. Pendleton and Jones's search of 383 Fifteenth Street is described by Pendleton, locksmith Jacob Wagner, John Seeley and his friend Louis Poole, Trial, 53–54, 80.

39. Perley, 27.

40. *Harper's,* April 16, 1859.

41. Ibid.

42. Wentworth, 29.

43. Joseph H. Bradley.

44. *New York Herald,* April 4, 1859.

45. *Harper's,* March 19, 1859.

46. Pinchon, *Dan Sickles,* 134–35.

47. Ibid, 136.

48. *Harper's*, April 16, 1859.
49. *New York Herald*, April 4, 1859.
50. Ibid., April 5, 1859.

Thirteen. The Trial

1. Philp, 205.
2. Unless otherwise noted, the description of the courtroom that follows is an amalgam of the *New-York Times*, April 5 and April 7, 1859; the *New York Herald*, April 5, 1859; *Harper's*, April 16, 1859.
3. *Evening Star*, April 23, 1859.
4. Trial, 48.
5. Ibid., 53.
6. Ibid., 8.
7. The description of the judge that follows is an amalgam of the *Evening Star*, March 7, 1859; *New York Herald*, April 5, 1859; *Frank Leslie's*, April 16, 1859; Perley, 27; and Wentworth, 29.
8. *New-York Times*, April 4, 1859.
9. The scene on the day the trial opened is from the April 5, 1859, editions of the *New York Herald*, *Evening Star*, and *New-York Times*.
10. *New-York Times*, April 6, 1859.
11. *Evening Star*, April 6, 1859.
12. *New York Herald*, April 6, 1859. The couple were wed on April 5. The New York contingent of Sickles's friends included Isaac Bell of the Board of Supervisors; Capt. William L. Wiley, deputy surveyor, under Manny Hart, of the Port of New York; former Congressman John Kelly, now sheriff of New York City; Charles Graham, surveyor of the Brooklyn Navy Yard; Robert J. Dillon, a longtime friend and a Central Park commissioner; Alderman John Clancy; County Register William Miner; Superintendent of Land and Places Thomas Byrnes; Benson McGowan Jr. of the City Bureau of Repairs and Supplies, and John Cisco, now treasurer of the U.S. Assay Office on Wall Street.
13. Kelly, 135.
14. The description of Sickles in this paragraph is an amalgam of the *Washington Union*, April 5, 1859; *Evening Star*, Apr. 4, 1859, and *New-York Times*, April 6, 1859.
15. The description of the dock is an amalgam of Perley, 29; *Harper's*, April 16, 1859; and Wentworth, 22.
16. *New-York Times*, April 4, 1859.
17. Fifty-two of the jurors.
18. Trial, 8. The talesman was George C. Kirk.
19. Ibid., 12. The talesman was Elijah Admonston.
20. Ibid., 15. The juror was William L. Moore.

21. Ibid., 12. The talesman was Charles H. Kiltberger.

22. *Frank Leslie's,* April 16, 1859.

23. Trial, 15.

24. Ibid., 15–16.

25. Ibid., 23.

26. Ibid., 23–24.

27. The excerpts of Graham's opening speech are taken from *Opening Speech of John Graham, Esq., to the Jury, on the Part of the Defence, on the Trial of Daniel E. Sickles* (New York: W. A. Townsend & Co., n.d.).

28. Henry Weihofen, *Mental Disorder as a Criminal Defense* (Buffalo: Dennis & Co., 1954), 137. "Impulse" is incorrectly spelled "impluse," but I refrained from repeating the error so as not to confuse the reader.

29. Trial, 55.

30. Ibid., 56.

31. Ibid., 58.

32. Ibid., 59.

33. Ibid., 61.

34. Ibid., 62.

35. Ibid., 63.

36. Ibid., 66.

37. Ibid., 67. The incident occurred on the thirteenth day of the trial, April 18, 1859.

38. Ibid., 70. The incident occurred on the fourteenth day of the trial, April 19, 1859.

39. Ibid., 100. This is Thomas Meagher's description of the incident, which occurred on the eighth day of the trial, April 12, 1859.

40. Ibid., 41, and *Harper's,* April 23, 1859.

41. Trial, 41.

42. Ibid., 46.

43. *New York Herald,* July 19, 1859.

44. *Harper's,* May 14, 1859.

45. Trial, 83.

46. Ibid., 80. The letter was sent to juror Jesse B. Wilson.

47. Ibid.

48. *New-York Times,* April 27, 1859.

49. Ibid.

50. Trial, 84. Easter Sunday that year was celebrated on the latest day in the year since April 24, 1791, and will not occur so late again until April 24, 2011.

51. *Evening Star,* April 25, 1859.

52. The excerpts of Stanton's remarks are from Trial, 91–93.

53. The excerpts from Brady's argument are from Trial, 95–100.

54. Trial, 100.

55. Ibid., 103.

56. Wentworth, 60.

57. *New York Herald,* April 27, 1859.

58. Trial, 105–6.

59. Weihofen, *Mental Disorder,* 246.

60. *New York Herald,* April 27, 1859. Unless otherwise noted, as in the case of this note, the description of the courtroom scene both before and after the verdict as well as the celebration party given by Brady that follows is from *The New-York Times,* April 27, 1859. *The Times* not only ran the story in its regular edition but also published a special supplement that day.

61. Strong, 2:447. The entry is dated April 22, 1859.

62. *New York Herald,* April 27, 1859.

63. *Evening Star,* April 26, 1859.

64. Mary B. Chesnut, *A Diary from Dixie* (Ben Ames Williams, ed. Cambridge, Mass.: Harvard Univ. Press, 1980), 132. Both Virginia Tunstall Clay, in her memoirs, and the *Biographical Directory of the American Congress, 1774–1961* (U.S. Government Printing Office, 1961) incorrectly spell Chesnut's name as Chestnut.

65. *Evening Star,* April 26, 1859.

66. Wentworth, 60.

67. *Evening Star,* April 26, 1859.

68. The orange vendor was John Scott.

69. *Evening Star,* April 27, 1859.

70. Ibid., April 30, 1859.

71. Ibid.

72. *New-York Daily Tribune,* April 28, 1859.

73. Swanberg, 66.

74. Ibid.

75. Strong, 2:449. The entry is dated April 26, 1859.

76. *New-York Daily Tribune,* April 27, 1859.

77. *Frank Leslie's,* May 7, 1859.

78. Witness, 313.

79. *Evening Star,* April 30, 1859.

80. *Harper's,* May 14, 1859. Swanberg, 67, which cites *Harper's,* turns an indirect quotation into a direct quote—"Of course I intended to kill him. He deserved it"—and says, without citing any source, that the two friends he was with were William Wiley and Henry Wikoff.

Fourteen. "Hail! Matchless Pair"

1. Thomas C. Fields.

2. *New York Herald,* July 12, 1859.

3. Ibid., July 19, 1859.

4. Ibid.

5. *Evening Star,* July 20, 1859.

6. *New York Herald,* July 19, 1859.

7. Ibid.

8. Ibid.

9. Ibid.

10. Ibid.

11. Ibid.

11. Ibid., July 20, 1859.

12. Stephen Gooding to Daniel E. Sickles, July 21, 1859. Papers of Daniel E. Sickles, NYHS. Gooding was a resident of Lockport, New York.

13. Jos. L. Bennett to Daniel E. Sickles, August 1, 1859. Papers of Daniel E. Sickles, NYHS.

14. Strong, 2:456–N57. The entry is dated July 20, 1859.

15. Boyd, 1860.

16. *Harper's,* December 24, 1859.

17. Ross, *Rebel Rose,* 68.

18. Chesnut, *Diary from Dixie,* 246–47.

Fifteen. "A Sort of Poobah"

1. Teresa Sickles to Daniel E. Sickles, April 20, 1861. Papers of Daniel E. Sickles, NYHS.

2. Speech of Daniel E. Sickles, Veteran Association of the Department of the South and the Atlantic Blockading Squadron State of New York, April 18, 1911. Papers of Daniel E. Sickles, NYHS.

3. Swanberg, 114.

4. Teresa Sickles to Daniel E. Sickles, April 20, 1861. Papers of Daniel E. Sickles, NYHS.

5. Teresa Sickles to Florence, July 9, 1861. Papers of Daniel E. Sickles, NYHS.

6. Laura Sickles to Daniel E. Sickles, October 27, 1861. Papers of Daniel E. Sickles, NYHS. The date—"Oct 27th 61."—and place—"91st St. N.Y."—of the letter are in a hand other than Laura's childish writing. They appear to be written in Teresa Sickles's handwriting.

7. Swanberg, 157.

8. Affidavit of L. Edward Jenkins. Papers of Daniel E. Sickles, NYHS.

9. James Longstreet to Daniel E. Sickles, September 19, 1902 (typed copy). Papers of Daniel E. Sickles, NYHS.

10. Strong, 3:351. The entry is dated August 21, 1863.

11. Because of renovations, the exhibit had been temporarily removed and I was not able to see it when in Washington, D.C., on a research trip in December, 1989.

12. Swanberg, 243. The hotel, the Brevoort House, was at 9 Fifth Avenue, at Ninth Street.

13. Trow, 1865–66.

14. Swanberg, 270.

15. Speech of Daniel E. Sickles, Veteran Association of the Department of the South and the Atlantic Blockading Squadron State of New York, April 18, 1911. Papers of Daniel E. Sickles, NYHS.

16. James L. Orr to Daniel E. Sickles, September 7, 1867 (typed copy). Papers of Daniel E. Sickles, NYHS.

17. *New York Herald,* February 10, 1867.

18. Swanberg, 287.

19. *New York Times,* July 19, 1919. The marriage took place on Nov. 28, 1871.

20. William Hobart Royce to Edgcumb Pinchon, October 7, 1942. Papers of William Hobart Royce, NYPL.

21. William Hobart Royce to Edgcumb Pinchon, November 30, 1941. Papers of William Hobart Royce, NYPL.

22. *New York Times,* September 17, 1884.

23. Ibid.

24. Ibid., October 9, 1895.

25. Three letters from George Stanton Sickles to his father are on file with the Sickles Papers, Manuscript Division, Library of Congress. Through they carry the month and day on which they were written, the year is missing. Someone has afterwards added on two of the letters the year they were supposedly written—1881, in one case, and 1882 in the other. The three, in George Stanton Sickles's handwriting, are other-wised datelined: Madrid, 17 Juin [1881]; Alcala de Henares, 28 Avril [1882], and Chiclana, 20 Septembre. About the time they were written, Daniel Sickles was involved in an odd lawsuit against the Manhattan Gas-light Company to prevent it from cutting off gas service to his apartment at 14 Fifth Avenue. According to *The New York Times,* April 12, 1882, the meter in his apartment was alleged to have shown that gas was consumed while Sickles was abroad between January 29, 1881, and May 6, 1882, and his apartment locked up. He was in Europe at the time, but made no effort to see his children.

26. William Hobart Royce to Edgcumb Pinchon, December 16, 1941. Papers of William Hobart Royce, NYPL.

27. Ibid.

28. William Hobart Royce to Edgcumb Pinchon, November 30, 1941. Papers of William Hobart Royce, NYPL. The friend was a Captain Denham.

29. *New York Times,* July 19, 1919.

30. Swanberg, 366.

31. *New York Times,* May 10, 1914.

32. The scene described here is from Fiske, *Off-hand Portraits,* 287–88.

Bibliography

No more digression—let us go right on,
Or e'en this meagre list will ne'er be done . . .

Manuscript Sources

American Philosophical Society, Philadelphia
   Papers of Samuel Rush
Geography and Map Division, Library of Congress
Library, Historical Society of Washington, D.C.
Manuscript Division, Library of Congress
   Sickles Papers
Manuscripts Division, New York Public Library
   Papers of Anthony J. Griffin
   Papers of William Hobart Royce
   Papers of Daniel E. Sickles
Manuscripts Room, New-York Historical Society
   Papers of John Lorimer Graham
   Papers of Daniel E. Sickles
Rare Book Division, Library of Congress
School of Law Library, New York University
   Criminal Court Records, District of Columbia (Hayward and Hazelton 2, microfilm)
St. Patrick's Old Cathedral, Mulberry Street, New York City
   Marriage Record Book, October 20, 1838–December 30, 1867
Widener Library, Harvard University
   Miscellaneous papers, Daniel E. Sickles

Printed Documents

American Railway Guide for the United States. New York: Dinsmore & Co., 1855.

Argument of the Hon. Daniel E. Sickles, in the Senate of the State of New York, April, 1857, on the Trinity Church Bill. New York: J. Munsell, 1857.

Baltimore City Directory for 1859–60. Baltimore: Sherwood & Co., 1859.

Boyd's Washington and Georgetown Directory. New York: William H. Boyd: 1858–65.

Carroll's New York City Directory. New York: Carroll & Company, 1859.

Catalogue of the Library of the late Philip Barton Key, to be sold at Public Sale. Washington, D.C., Robert A. Waters, 1859.

Congress of the United States and Congressional Cemetery. Washington, D.C.: Association for the Preservation of Historic Congressional Cemetery, n.d.

Convent of the Sacred Heart, New York City: 1881–1981. New York: Alumnae Association of the Convent of the Sacred Heart, 1981.

Diary of George Templeton Strong, Allan Nevins and Milton Halsey Thomas, eds. 4 vols. New York: Macmillan Company, 1952.

Doggett's New York City Directory volumes for the years 1842–51. New York: John Doggett, Jr. & Co.

Francis's New Guide to the Cities of New-York and Brooklyn, and the Vicinity. New-York: C. S. Francis & Co., 1859.

Historical Statistics of the United States: Colonial Times to 1970. Part 1. Washington, D.C.: Government Printing Office, 1975.

Historical Survey of Lafayette Square. Washington, D.C.: John Carl Warnecke and Associates, 1963.

In Memoriam: Benjamin Ogle Tayloe [a.k.a. *Anecdotes and Reminiscences*]. Private printing. Washington, D.C.: 1872.

———. Philadelphia: Sherman & Co., 1872.

In Memoriam. James T. Brady. Report of Proceedings of the New York Bar, February 13, 1869. New York: Baker, Voorhis & Company, 1869.

Longworth's American Almanac, New-York Register, and City Directory. Volumes for the years 1838–43. New York: Thomas Longworth.

New York Almanac and Yearly Record for the Year 1858. New York: Mason Brothers, 1858.

New York City Directory for 1851–52. New York: Doggett & Rode, 1851.

New York City Directory for 1853–54. New York: Charles R. Rode, 1853.

New York Panorama. Federal Writers' Project, Works Progress Administration, American Guide Series. New York: Random House, 1938.

Opening Speech of John Graham, Esq., to the Jury, on the Part of the Defence, on the Trial of Daniel E. Sickles. New York: W. A. Townsend & Co., n.d.

Philp's Washington Described. New York: Rudd & Carleton, 1861.

Trial of Hon. Daniel E. Sickles. Washington, D.C.: Wentworth and Stanley, 1859.

Trial of the Hon. Daniel E. Sickles for Shooting Philip Barton Key, Esq., U.S. District Attorney, of Washington, D.C. New York: R. M. De Witt, 1859.

Trow's New York City Directory. New York: John F. Trow, 1852–69.

United States Congressional Districts and Data, 1843–1883. New York: N.p., 1986.

Washington: City and Capital. Federal Writers' Project, Works Progress Administration, American Guide Series. Washington, D.C.: Government Printing Office, 1937.

Welcome to St. John's. Washington, D.C.: St. John's Episcopal Church, n.d.

Newspapers and Periodicals

The following newspapers and periodicals were used extensively, chiefly to recreate the events surrounding February 27, 1859, and the trial of Daniel E. Sickles, April 5–25, 1859, but as otherwise noted in notes: *Congressional Globe, Daily National Intelligencer* (Washington, D.C.), *Evening Star* (Washington, D.C.), *Frank Leslie's Illustrated Newspaper, Harper's Weekly, New-York Daily Tribune, New York Evening Post, New York Herald, New-York Times, New York World, Washington Union.*

Books

Ames, Mary Clemmer. *Ten Years in Washington: Life and Scenes in the National Capital, as a Woman Sees Them.* Hartford, Conn.: A. D. Worthington & Co.; Chicago: Louis Lloyd & Co.; and San Francisco: F. Dewing & Co., 1874.

Appletons' Cyclopaedia of American Biography. Revised edition, 6 vols. New York: D. Appleton and Company, 1866–99.

Bernstein, Iver. *The New York City Draft Riots: Their Significance for American Society and Politics in the Age of the Civil War.* New York: Oxford Univ. Press, 1990.

Biographical Dictionary of the Confederacy. Westport, Conn.: Greenwood Press, 1977.

Biographical Directory of the American Congress, 1774–1961. U.S. Government Printing Office, 1961.

Blair House Past and Present: An Account of its Life and Times in the City of Washington. U.S. Department of State, 1945.

Bowen, Croswell. *The Elegant Oakey.* New York: Oxford Univ. Press, 1956.

Brandt, Nat. *The Man Who Tried to Burn New York.* Syracuse: Syracuse Univ. Press, 1986.

Cable, Mary. *American Manners and Morals.* New York: American Heritage, 1969.

Caemmerer, H. P., ed. *Washington, The National Capital.* 71st Cong. 3d sess. Doc. 332. Washington, D.C.: Government Printing Office, 1932.

Chesnut, Mary B. *A Diary from Dixie.* Edited by Ben Ames Williams. Cambridge, Mass.: Harvard Univ. Press, 1980.

Chinn, George Morgan, Jr., and Bayless Evans Hardin. *Encyclopedia of American Hand Arms.* Huntington, W. Va.: Standard Printing and Publishing Company, 1942.

Cole, Donald B., and John J. McDonough, eds. *Witness to the Young Republic: A Yankee's Journal, 1828–1870.* Hanover, N.H.: Univ. Press of New England, 1989.

Devens, R. M. *Our First Century.* Springfield, Mass.: C. A. Nichols & Co., 1876.

Dickens, Charles. *American Notes; & Pic-nic Papers.* Philadelphia: T. B. Peterson & Brothers, n.d.

Dictionary of American Biography. 20 vols. New York: Charles Scribner's Sons, 1928–36.

Dictionary of National Biography. Vol. 14. London: Oxford Univ. Press, 1917.

Dix, Morgan. *Memoirs of John Adams Dix.* 2 vols. New York: Harper & Brothers, 1883.

Donaldson, Frances F. *The President's Square.* New York: Vantage Press, 1968.

Doyle, Joseph B. *In Memoriam: Edwin McMasters Stanton.* Steubenville, Ohio: Herald Printing Company, 1911.

Ellis, Edward R. *The Epic of New York City.* New York: Coward-McCann, 1966.

Ellis, John B. *The Sights and Secrets of the National Capital.* New York: United States Publishing Company, 1869.

Fiske, Stephen. *Off-hand Portraits of Prominent New Yorkers.* New York: Geo. R. Lockwood & Son, 1884.

Fitch, Charles E. *Encyclopedia of Biography of New York.* New York: American Historical Society, 1916.

Forney, John W. *Anecdotes of Public Men.* 2 vols. New York: Harper & Brothers, 1873 and 1881.

Frary, Ihna Thayer. *They Built the Capitol.* First published 1940. Reprinted 1969. Freeport, N.Y.: Books for Libraries Press, 1969.

Fuller, Arthur B., ed. *Woman in the Nineteenth Century . . . by Margaret Fuller Ossoli.* Reprint of 1874 edition by Roberts Brothers, Boston. Westport, Conn.: Greenwood Press, 1977.

Gobright, L. A. *Recollection of Men and Things at Washington During the Third of a Century.* Philadelphia: Claxton, Remsen & Haffelfinger, 1869.

Goode, James M. *Capital Losses: A Cultural History of Washington's Destroyed Buildings.* Washington, D.C.: Smithsonian Institution Press, 1979.

Graham, Frank Jr. *Potomac: The Nation's River.* Philadelphia: J. B. Lippincott, 1976.

Green, Constance McLaughlin. *Washington: Village and Capital, 1800–1878.* 2 vols. Princeton: Princeton Univ. Press, 1962.

Guide to American Law: Everyone's Legal Encyclopedia. 12 vols. New York: West Publishing Co., 1983–85.

Gutheim, Frederick. *The Potomac.* New York: Rinehart & Company, 1949.

Harlow, S. R., and Hutchins, S. C. *Life Sketches of the State Officers, Senators, and Members of the Assembly, of the State of New York, in 1868.* Albany: Weed, Parsons & Company, 1868.

Harris, Charles T. *Memories of Manhattan in the Sixties and Seventies.* New York: Derrydale Press, 1928.

Herron, Paul. *The Story of Capitol Hill.* New York: Coward-McCann, 1963.

Hodges, Sheila. *Lorenzo Da Ponte: The Life and Times of Mozart's Librettist.* New York: Universe Books, 1958.

Josephy, Alvin M., Jr. *The Congress of the United States.* New York: American Heritage, 1975.

Katz, Irving. *August Belmont: A Political Biography.* New York: Columbia Univ. Press, 1968.

Kugler, Israel. *From Ladies to Women: The Organized Struggle for Woman's Rights in the Reconstruction Era.* Westport, Conn.: Greenwood Press, 1987.

Lampe, Philip E., editor. *Adultery in the United States: Close Encounters of the Sixth (Or Seventh) Kind.* Buffalo, N.Y.: Prometheus Brooks, n.d.

Livingston, Arthur, ed. *Memoirs of Lorenzo Da Ponte.* Philadelphia: J. B. Lippincott Company, 1929.

Logan, Mrs. John A. *Thirty Years in Washington, or Life and Scenes in Our National Capital.* Hartford, Conn.: A. D. Worthington & Co., 1901.

McCabe, James D., Jr. *Lights and Shadows of New York Life; or, the Sights and Sensations of the Great City.* Philadelphia: National Publishing Company, 1872.

McLaughlin, J. Fairfax. *The Life and Times of John Kelly, Tribune of the People.* New York: American News Company, 1885.

Marcosson, Isaac F. *"Marse Henry": A Biography of Henry Watterson.* New York: Dodd, Mead, 1951.

Marks, Edward B. *They All Had Glamour.* Westport, Conn.: Greenwood Press, 1944.

Martis, Kenneth C. *Historical Atlas of the United States Congressional Districts, 1789–1983.* New York: Free Press, 1982.

Monahan, John, and Henry J. Steadman, eds. *Mentally Disordered Offenders: Perspectives from Law and Social Science.* New York: Plenum Press, 1983.

Moore, Charles. *Washington Past and Present.* New York: Century Co., 1929.

Moore, John B., ed. *The Works of James Buchanan.* 12 vols. New York: Antiquarian Press, 1960.

Morris, Lloyd. *Incredible New York.* New York: Random House, 1951.

Mushkat, Jerome. *Tammany: The Evolution of a Political Machine: 1789–1865.* Syracuse: Syracuse Univ. Press, 1971.

National Cyclopaedia of American Biography. 64 vols. New York: James T. White & Company, 1891–1984.

Nice, Richard W., ed. *Crime and Insanity.* New York: Philosophical Library, 1958.

Oliphant, Margaret O. W. *Memoir of the Life of Laurence Oliphant and also of Alice Oliphant, His Wife.* 2 vols. London: William Blackwood and Sons, 1891.

Olszewski, George J. *History of the Mall.* Washington, D.C.: National Park Service, U.S. Department of the Interior, n.d.

Pinchon, Edgcumb. *Dan Sickles: Hero of Gettysburg and "Yankee King of Spain."* Garden City, N.Y.: Doubleday, Doran and Company, 1945.

Poore, Ben: Perley. *Perley's Reminiscensces of Sixty Years in the National Metropolis.* 2 vols in 1. Philadelphia; Hubbard Brothers, 1886.

Proctor, L. B. *The Bench and Bar of New-York.* New York: Diossy & Company, 1870.

Pryor, Mrs. Roger A. (Sara Agnes) *Reminiscences of Peace and War.* First published 1908. Revised and enlarged, 1970. Freeport, N.Y.: Books for Libraries Press, 1970.

Richardson, Hester Dorsey. *Side-Lights on Maryland History.* Cambridge, Md.: Tidewater, 1967.

Ross, Ishbel. *Rebel Rose: Life of Rose O'Neal Greenhow.* New York: Harper & Brothers, 1954.

Russo, Joseph L. *Lorenzo Da Ponte: Poet and Adventurer.* New York: AMS Press, 1966. Reprint of Columbia Univ. Press edition, 1922.

Sadie, Stanley, ed. *New Grove Dictionary of Music and Musicians.* Vol. 5. New York: Macmillan, 1980.

Schell, Francis. *Memoir of the Hon. Augustus Schell.* New York: privately printed, 1885.

Schwartz, Bernard. *The Law in America.* New York: American Heritage Publishing Co., 1974.

Shipherd, Jacob R. *History of the Oberlin-Wellington Rescue.* Boston: John P. Jewett and Company, 1859. Reprint edition, Da Capo Press, New York, 1972.

Simon, Rita J., and David E. Aaronson, eds. *The Insanity Defense: A Critical Assessment of Law and Policy in the Post-Hinckley Era.* New York: Praeger, 1988.

Singleton, Esther. *The Story of the White House.* 2 vols. Reprint of 1907 edition. New York: Benjamin Blom, 1969.

Sterling, Ada. *A Belle of the Fifties: Memoirs of Mrs. Clay, of Alabama, covering Social and Political Life in Washington and the South, 1853–1866.* New York: Doubleday, Page & Company, 1905.

Stokes, I. N. Phelps. *New York Past and Present: Its History and Landmarks, 1524–1939.* New York: Plantin Press, 1939.

Swanberg, W. A. *Sickles the Incredible.* New York: Charles Scribner's Sons, 1956.

Thomas, Lately. *Between Two Empires: The Life Story of Califonia's First Senator, William McKendree Gwin.* Boston: Houghton Mifflin Company, 1969.

VanRensselaer, Stephen. *American Firearms.* Watkins Glen, N.Y.: Century House, 1947.

Wakelyn, Jon L. *Biographical Dictionary of the Confederacy.* Westport, Conn.: Greenwood Press, 1977.

Watterson, Henry. *"Marse Henry": An Autobiography.* 2 vols. New York: George H. Doran, 1919.

Weihofen, Henry. *Mental Disorder as a Criminal Defense.* Buffalo: Dennis & Co., 1954.

Wharton, Anne Hollingsworth. *Social Life in the Early Republic.* Philadelphia: J. B. Lippincott Company, 1902.

Williams, T. J. C. *History of Frederick County Maryland.* 2 vols. Baltimore: L. R. Titsworth & Co., 1910.

Wilson, James Grant, ed. *The Memorial History of the City of New-York.* 4 vols. New York: New York History Company, 1893.

Wilson, Rufus R. *Washington: The Capital City and Its Part in the History of the Nation.* Philadelphia: J. B. Lippincott Company, 1902.

Articles

Balderson, Thomas. "The Sad, Shattered Life of Teresa Sickles." *American History Illustrated* XVII, No. 5, (September 1982): 41–45.

Blair, Major Gist. "Lafayette Square." *Records of the Columbia Historical Society* 28 (1926): 133–73.

Bullock, Helen Duprey. "A View from the Square." *Historic Preservation* 19, nos. 3–4 (July-December 1967), 53–68.

Carson, Gerald, and Bernard A. Weisberger. "The Great Count-
   down." *American Heritage,* November 1989, special supplement,
   3–23.
De Haviland, Major John. "A Metrical Glance at the Fancy Ball."
   Magazine of History, extra nos. 21–24, Vol. VI (1913): 353–70.
Fleming, Thomas J. "A Husband's Revenge." *American Heritage,*
   April, 1967, 65–75.
Kelly, Joseph T. "Memories of a Lifetime in Washington," *Records
   of the Columbia Historical Society* 31–32 (1930): 117–49.
Longacre, Edward. "Damnable Dan Sickles: He Lusted for Love
   and Battle." *Civil War Times Illustrated* XXIII, no. 3 (May, 1984):
   16–25.
Smith, Hal H. "Historic Washington Homes," *Records of the Colum-
   bia Historical Society* II (1908): 243–76.
Smith, Scottie Fitzgerald. "The Colonial Ancestors of Francis Scott
   Key Fitzgerald," *Maryland Historical Magazine* 76, (December
   1981): 363–75.

Index

Buchanan, James (*cont.*)
  47, 62, 198, 225n.79; social life
  of, 6–7, 79
Bulkley, C. H. A., 20, 172
Burroughs, John, 40, 43
Butler, Benjamin F., 20
Butterworth, Samuel F., 115–16,
  117–19, 143; absence from
  trial, 164, 170–71; after murder, 122–23, 127, 128–29, 130,
  132; as witness, 125–26, 152–
  53

Cagger, Peter, 166
Capitol Building, 40, 47, 51
Capitol Hill, 47
Carlisle, James M., 157, 174, 177,
  185
Carolinas, 206–7
Carroll Row, 58
Cass, Lewis, 4, 7
Central Park, 32
Centre Market, 45–46
Chancellorsville, 204
Chesapeake and Ohio Canal, 47
Chesnut, James, Jr., 198
Chesnut, Mary Miller, 198
Chilton, Samuel, 155, 170, 183,
  184, 187
Cisco, John J., 32
City Hall, 162–64
City Hotel. *See* Willard's Hotel
Civil War, 65, 200, 201–6
Clay, Clement C., Jr., 2, 128, 134
Clay, Henry, 59, 64
Clay, Virginia Tunstall, 2, 42, 44,
  46, 55, 58, 128, 134; on Teresa,
  93, 95–96
Clubhouse, The. *See* Washington
  Club
Cobb, Howell, 3, 4, 148
Compromise of 1850, 4–5

Confederacy, 4
Congress, 2, 6; behavior of, 50–
  53; sessions of, 49–50, 70, 105,
  106, 160; Sickles in, 34–35,
  197–99, 210
Congressional Cemetery, 47–48,
  78, 81
Cooke, Maria. *See* Bagioli, Maria
  Cooke
Coolidge, Richard H., 124, 145,
  170, 222n.18
Cooney, John, 90, 99, 100
Corcoran, Louisa. *See* Eustis,
  Louisa Corcoran
Corcoran, W. W., 61, 65–67
County Jail. *See* Washington Jail
Courier (newspaper), 138
Crackanthorpe, Dayrell, 210
Crackanthorpe, Edith Sickles,
  209, 210
Crawford, Thomas Hartley, 164,
  174, 175; trial procedure of,
  166–67, 177, 181–82, 184
Creagh, Carolina. *See* Sickles,
  Carolina Creagh
Crime, 51–52
Cuba, 7, 31, 106
Curiosity seekers, 149
Cutts, Richard, 65
Cuyler, John, 93

Daily News (newspaper), 142–43
Daily States (newspaper), 103–4
Daily Tribune (newspaper), 187–
  88
Da Ponte, Lorenzo (father), 18–19
Da Ponte, Lorenzo L., 17–18, 19–
  20, 127, 172
Davis, Jefferson, 4
Decatur, Stephen, 62
Decatur House, 5, 62–63

THE CONGRESSMAN WHO GOT AWAY WITH MURDER
was composed in 11½ on 13½ Bembo on a Mergenthaler Linotron,
with display type in Chisel, by Eastern Graphics;
printed by sheet-fed offset on 50-pound, acid-free Glatfelter Natural Hi Bulk
and Smyth-sewn and bound over binder's boards in Holliston Roxite B
with dust jackets printed in 4 colors
by Braun–Brumfield, Inc.;
and published by
SYRACUSE UNIVERSITY PRESS
Syracuse, New York 13244-5160